D1648603

MEMORIES OF EDEN

Memories of
EDEN

A JOURNEY THROUGH JEWISH BAGHDAD

Violette Shamash

EDITED BY *Mira and Tony Rocca*

NORTHWESTERN UNIVERSITY PRESS

EVANSTON, ILLINOIS

Northwestern University Press
www.nupress.northwestern.edu

Copyright © 2010 by Mira and Tony Rocca. Published 2010 by Northwestern University Press. Originally published by Forum Books Ltd., copyright © 2008 by Mira and Tony Rocca. All rights reserved.

Printed in the United States of America

10 9 8 7 6 5 4 3 2 1

Library of Congress Cataloging-in-Publication Data

Shamash, Violette, 1912–2006.
    Memories of Eden : a journey through Jewish Baghdad / Violette Shamash ; edited by Mira and Tony Rocca.
        p. cm.
    Originally published: London : Forum Books, 2008.
    Includes bibliographical references and index.
    ISBN 978-0-8101-2634-3 (trade cloth : alk. paper)
    1. Shamash, Violette, 1912–2006. 2. Jews—Iraq—Baghdad—Biography.
3. Jews—Iraq—History—20th century. 4. Baghdad (Iraq)—Social life and customs—20th century. 5. Iraq—History—1921– I. Rocca, Mira, 1941– II. Rocca, Tony. III. Title.
DS135.I713S39657 2009
305.892'4056747092—dc22
    [B] 956.747
        (Shamash)   2009043816

♾ The paper used in this publication meets the minimum requirements of the American National Standard for Information Sciences—Permanence of Paper for Printed Library Materials, ANSI Z39.48-1992.

To my dear children—Lena, Mira, and Simon

To my dear grandchildren—Robin, Sarah, Samantha, and David

And to their dear children, present and future

CONTENTS

ILLUSTRATIONS

FOREWORD

Memoirs generally have one aim: a reckoning with the past, usually a bittersweet story steeped in the nostalgia of childhood and based on emotions and memories stirred by historical events.

So far, memoirs about the Jewish community of Iraq have been about the downturn in our fortunes following World War II, and they have been written chiefly by men. They waver between feelings that are sentimental and embittered, especially toward the community's past in Iraq and their plight in the *ma'abarot* (temporary tent camps) in which they found themselves unceremoniously dumped upon arrival in Israel. Now comes Violette Shamash's contribution—a refreshing rarity. This fascinating and evocative story is about a forgotten, earlier era, written with a young person's hand and a sense of wonderment that draws the reader effortlessly into the City of Caliphs and the days of imperial Ottoman and British rule.

These memoirs have only one motive: to leave for posterity a record of the daily lives of our ancestors. In this they succeed brilliantly, for these memoirs are a real testament to a vanished way of life and a language that is also sadly disappearing. We have a first-hand witness to the development of life in Baghdad during the nineteenth century, when people were still living in near-biblical conditions, and to the gradual impact of Western civilization in the early twentieth century. The country's customs and ways of life changed, but ancient traditions were kept and respected, religious conventions maintained, and life with the Muslims conducted in harmony. As Violette says: "We always shared [Baghdad's] moments of sadness and happiness and we took part, a great part, in pushing it to advance into civilisation, bringing a better life and comfort to the benefit of all."

Violette's story concentrates on the decisive period between her birth in Baghdad in 1912 and the rise of pro-Nazi elements and anti-British sentiment that culminated in tragedy for the Jews of Baghdad with the Farhud (pogrom) of 1941. She was born into a venerable and prosperous Jewish family that was able to build the first *qasr* (palace) in the Karrada district on the banks of the Tigris—then a wilderness, but in 2008, directly facing the brand-new U.S. Embassy. This moving saga is based on recollections, originally intended simply as a record for the family, which were written over a period of twenty years. So different from any academic work, they are told in humorous style with jokes and anecdotes that add up to an attractive narration of daily and festive religious life. The story is full of detail: the heat, the holy days, the rituals, the food; the smells and sounds of the souq; the river, its water and fish; the costumes and clothes people wore; school days and rides on donkeyback before motorized transport became available.

The Eden-like life began to darken with the evil clouds of nationalist extremism, when Fascist and Nazi ideologies propounded by pro-Axis officials and Palestinians, indoctrinated by the Templars' pro-Nazi ideology in the Holy Land, who sought sanctuary in Iraq (1936–41) stirred hatred and incitement against the Jews. This led, ultimately, to the seizure of power by Rashid Ali al-Gaylani, the dispatch of a British force to secure his overthrow, and the massacre of the Jews of Baghdad during the tragic Shavuot of June 1941.

This crucial period is well chronicled by Violette's son-in-law Tony Rocca, a former London *Sunday Times* journalist, in his afterword, which gives historical depth to Violette's first-person narrative. For the first time, we have a full account of the British stand during the Farhud and an explanation of why British soldiers, who could have stepped in to stop the bloodletting, were ordered to hold back. In an epilogue to Violette's story, Tony brings the reader up to date with reminders of the momentous events that shaped the world around his mother-in-law—a perspective understandably missing from the viewpoint of a very young girl growing up in a fast-developing country, created out of pure expedience and doomed to eventual disaster.

Historians, scholars, sociologists, and those simply interested in a fascinating autobiography will find in this enjoyable book a treasure trove of information that will enable them to understand what life in Iraq was like until extreme nationalism and religious fanaticism destroyed it. On behalf of the Association of Jewish Academics from Iraq and the Babylonian Jewry Heritage Center, I would like to thank Violette, and her editors, for this fascinating work. My congratulations on a great achievement and service that you have rendered the Jewish community from Iraq. It is a real chronicle, not only of your family history but also of the modern history of the oldest Jewish community in the world, the Jewish community of Iraq.

Professor Shmuel Moreh

Israel Prize Laureate

Institute of Asian and African Studies,
The Hebrew University, Jerusalem

Chair, Association of Jewish
Academics from Iraq in Israel

On April 9, 2003, along with millions of others around the world, I watched as the huge statue of Saddam Hussein was toppled in Baghdad and Iraqis danced and waved flags in celebration of the demise of his hated regime. The crowds were joyous, dragging the head of the tyrant through the streets I remembered so well but could no longer recognise.

My grandson Robin had given me the television set. My daughter Mira had put in the satellite connection. My son-in-law Tony had brought me the sheaves of documents that lay scattered around my desk, containing the history of my country and the background to my life story. The events and dramas I was unaware of in my early years were coming alive with hindsight, and my eyes were misty with the images of the past.

As American tanks rumbled past the TV cameras and Baghdadis threw shoes at Saddam's portrait—the gravest of all Arab insults—my mind turned to another era. For I was born a quarter of a century before Saddam, before the creation of Iraq, before another foreign army, British that time, marched victoriously into the city in the name of bringing democracy to the people.

I saw my country emerge from a primitive past into what promised to be a brilliant future. It was *my* Baghdad, *my* native land where I grew up, happy and privileged, in a Jewish community living harmoniously with our Muslim neighbours. My Baghdad was beautiful, civilised, full of cherished memories. Now it has been replaced altogether, erased like chalk on a blackboard, and a new story is being written.

Saddam's regime developed from the ashes of events we had endured sixty-five years before, when a previous tyrant unleashed an earthquake that split asunder the oldest community in the Diaspora. I still shudder every time I think of the gravity of the situation we were in. Then I count my blessings to be among the fortunate survivors.

I feel as if I were telling you a dream and that it will be very hard for you to join the pieces together.

V. S.
London, January 2006

Just as there are hardly any Jews left in Iraq today, very few people outside a diminishing band of elderly members of the old community, scattered around the world, communicate in Judeo-Arabic. It is a dying language that the younger generations in their new countries have lost entirely. For this reason, we have kept so many of the words and expressions Violette used, and we have added a special glossary at the end of the book. We have also kept the British spellings in the text of the memoir.

Arabic words and names, when Westernized, can be spelled in various ways. We have tried to conform to accepted academic standards, with pronunciation of vowels and consonants as follows:

aa = long vowel (*alif,* a letter in Arabic), as in the word *harder*
ii = long vowel (Arabic *yaa'*), as in *teeth*
oo = long vowel (Arabic *waaw*), as in *wood*
dh = as the "th" in the English word *the*
gh = the letter *r* in Judeo-Arabic, in the throat—like gargling

The closing single quotation mark (') represents *hamza* in the Arabic alphabet or the letter *'ayin* in Hebrew, indicating a guttural sound, a glottal stop.

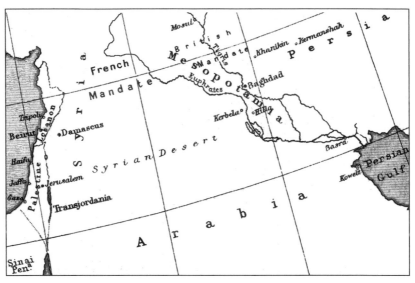

The Middle East in perspective, from a British school atlas, 1921

MEMORIES OF EDEN

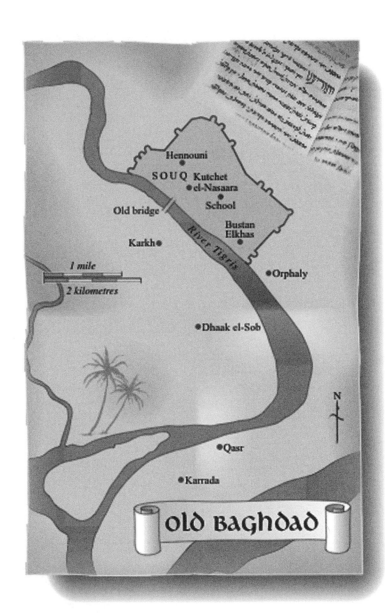

The Palace

THE LAST CENTURY was not even in its teens when I arrived in this fascinating world one winter's night in the centre of Baghdad. It was Hanukka, but there was no cause for celebration in our house in that warren of narrow alleyways that was the old Jewish quarter. Quite the opposite: my delivery was an unmitigated disaster for my dear parents, bless their souls. I, their fifth child, was their fourth daughter, as much a calamity as the recent news of the sinking of the *Titanic.*

In our community, the birth of a daughter was perceived as a blemish and a burden. It mattered little how pretty or how healthy the newborn was; the fact was that a daughter was a liability. A girl cost about as much as a boy to bring up, educate, and feed, and at the end of it, not only did she leave home to enter another family but a costly dowry had to go with her, depending on her father's means. There was no way out: like income tax, it was a total loss. In Jewish families, the birth of a daughter caused depression and sadness instead of joy. The greeting "mazal tov" would always be accompanied by a consolation: "Thank God for the health of the mother!" or "May she be followed by sons!" On the other hand, had I been a son, the greeting would have been "May he be a sign for seven [sons]!" or "May this be an augury!" As a son, I could grow up to help my father in his business and perhaps marry a wealthy girl with a considerable dowry and bring her home to help look after my parents.

Anyway, the loss of the *Titanic* had really shocked Baba, my father, who had been following all the stories about the ship. He was still talking about it as I grew up, living in the home he had built that same year—1912—on the site of a large date-palm orchard to the south of the city. Oh, what a long time ago it all was! Looking at a map of Baghdad today, I see that the Karrada district, which then was nothing but countryside, is now right at the centre of things: what greater accolade could the old place have but that Saddam Hussein chose to build his bunker and command headquarters directly across the Tigris from where we once lived? It is called the Green Zone now.

Our *qasr*—any large, solidly built house overlooking the river was a "palace" in a city of homes built of clay and mud—was practically ready to move into when my mother, Nana, was in the final stages of pregnancy, but it was considered to be so far out of town and isolated that they decided not to rush things. She had been told to expect a boy (hence the big letdown) and superstitiously believed it would help matters if the birth could take place at their old house, where my brother, Salman, had been born four years earlier. My parents made the best possible preparations for my arrival, sending word to family and friends that there would be a baby-boy party: the *brit mila* (circumcision) held a week after the birth. They had to change that hurriedly to a *lailt el-settee,* the baby-girl naming party held five days after the birth.

No expense was spared for the party, as Baba's business was prospering and everyone was in a good mood. As the guests arrived, a *deqqaaqa* (lady musician) sang "mazal tov" and a traditional pottery water jug (*tengaayee*) was smashed for good luck. *Shashsha,* the time-honoured mixture of small sweets, nuts, and popcorn, was scattered for the children to collect excitedly as they sang: "Shashsha beit Abu Violette tabkhou m-hasha"—just a silly rhyme. A modern name—Violette—was chosen for me and added to the biblical name, Simha (happiness), which also happened to be the name of my maternal grandmother. There was saffron rice and chicken grilled on charcoal to eat, then more lavish food, laughter, and jokes—and then one young lady laughed so much she tripped and

COLLECTION OF VIOLETTE SHAMASH

COLLECTION OF VIOLETTE SHAMASH

Baba (Menashe Ishayek) and Nana ("Khatoon")

rolled down the stairs. Amazingly, she was not in the least bit hurt, so this caused renewed merriment. I heard all about it countless times as I grew up, for none of the guests present that night would ever miss an opportunity to retell the story to me.

Coincidentally, in the same month and year that I was born, daughters were also born to two of my uncles: Uncle Joe, who had already moved to London, and Uncle Moshi, who lived near us in the old Jewish quarter of Hennouni. Three disasters on my mother's side. But how could my dear parents guess that there was worse to follow? There were to be two more calamities: my sisters Daisy and, the youngest of us all, Marcelle. And no more sons. But by then my parents were resigned to their fate. Despite their early disappointments at the moments of birth, both Baba and Nana loved each and every one of us seven children and always did their best for us.

Unusually, the marriage between Baba and Nana, who were second cousins, had been a love match, although it had been arranged, as they all were then. But it had also, in a way, been a marriage of convenience, for Nana had come with a substantial dowry. At the time, Baba had been an imposing young twenty-year-old, six feet tall but, with his upright posture, appearing even taller. He was handsome, with unusual grey piercing eyes, and like most men of the time, he sported a heavy moustache *à la turque* and also wore a Turkish fez.

Nana was one or two years his senior and came from a rich and respected family. Being petite, she had been nicknamed Nounou, which means "small" and "dainty" in Arabic. But Baba soon coined his own name for her—Khatoon, which came from the Turkish word for "lady"—which he was to call her until the end of their lives. She was pretty, with long, light-brown hair that she kept in tresses, and she, too, had grey eyes—a family trait.

Baba had followed in the footsteps of his father, Heskel, and was starting a business career as a successful merchant and private banker, or *saghaaf*. It was a path that his mother, Ghalla (Yemma— "Granny"—to us), had planned for him, despite the fact that he had wanted to become a *muallem* (teacher) like his grandfather Hayim, a religious man who taught in the synagogue Beit Zilkha, a rabbinical college founded as long ago as 1839. Like all his colleagues, at least twice a week Hayim would receive from the community a huge platter of cooked rice and four loaves of bread for himself and his family. As a boy, Baba had joined his grandfather at the synagogue, which was for advanced religious learning, and by the time he was twelve, his education had been "completed"—that is, he had learned everything his religious tutor could teach him and he now possessed the same qualifications. He had even transcribed, in his own handwriting with quill and ink, the whole of the Hagada-shel-Pessah, the prayer book that is read at Passover. He would wake up at daybreak every morning and join in the reading, discussions, and teaching. It was just the start of an amazing educational journey that was to open a world to him that few of his generation could have aspired to, and which would bring him respect as a savant and philosopher. At home, through the years, we felt so good that Baba knew everything that we were learning at school; as we grew up, he would often quiz us at dinner and he liked to be quizzed in return.

Many of my early lessons were about the land I was growing up in, Mesopotamia—from the Greek for "between the rivers"—so called because it was squeezed in between the mighty Tigris and Euphrates that carried melted snow from the mountains of Turkey to the warm seas of the Persian Gulf. Baba explained that we were

Mesopotamians, living in the Turkish Ottoman Empire, and had been governed by the Turks for almost four centuries. Our Jewish forefathers had arrived some 2,600 years earlier to begin a long and proud history that had witnessed what he called the flowering of mankind here, in Babylon, our ancestral home.

So Nana was over twenty when she married Baba, which would seem normal today. Just one generation earlier, however, she would have been considered surprisingly mature for a bride. For much of the nineteenth century, daughters were married off when they were extraordinarily young—especially in the case of less-well-to-do families worried about the financial expenses ahead. The typical age for a girl to marry was eight to ten; for a boy, eighteen to twenty. A girl was considered an old maid by fifteen, with no hope of marriage. For instance, Yemma had found herself married off at the tender age of nine to a mature man, a widower twice over who had two sons. She was still playing with dolls at the time of her wedding—and they had to wait until she reached puberty before consummating the marriage. She was only fifteen when she gave birth to Baba and was still in her twenties when he achieved his scholarship, by which time she had had three more sons and two daughters.

To be or have a child bride was then considered normal. The newlyweds usually lived in the home of the groom's parents, where his mother ruled the roost. The bride's life in her mother-in-law's home was not easy and could give rise to family crises (they could be "like a tiger and goat living together," as the saying went). The husband controlled his wife, who also had to obey and honour her mother-in-law and accept her training in domestic duties from the start.

Although she was never literate, Yemma grew up with just such discipline to be a wise and capable lady, managing what, by today's standards, must have been a huge household. Can you imagine? Her youngest daughter was born in the same year as my eldest sister, Regina, so aunt and niece were the same age. My grandmother was a nice-looking, hazel-eyed woman, petite and tidy, firm but kind. She loved Baba dearly—he was the firstborn of altogether eight children. She also loved her two stepchildren. She and my grandfather Heskel (whom we called Seeda, "Grandpa") used to care for me whenever I visited them as a child. He began teaching

*Violette's
grandparents,
"Seeda" Heskel and
"Yemma" Ghalla*

me to read almost before I could talk and later, when he thought
I would be able to understand them, told me stories about the
Garden of Eden, the Tower of Babel, and the Hanging Gardens of
Babylon, all of which were part of our fabulous heritage. And we
were living right there.

During my childhood, our way of life hardly differed from that of
our ancestors. Even our customs and expectations were the same.
The whole family, even Baba's grandfather and grandmother, lived
in the same house in Hennouni, which had ten bedrooms. And
that's where we were living when I was born.

All the houses in the neighbourhood were designed to cope with the climate and provide facilities for extended family life. They were built in on themselves for security and protection, away from prying eyes. The idea was that, if you had no windows on the outside, you would not have any break-ins, so from the streets, which were just wide enough for a cart to pass, all you could see were brick walls. Far from being attractive, these lanes were squalid, infested with rats, cockroaches, and food for stray cats, so Nana was obsessed with cleanliness inside our home.

Like everyone else's front door, ours could only be opened with a massive key almost sixteen inches long, which required two hands to turn it. The door opened onto a *daghboona* (corridor) that led to a central courtyard, open to the skies, where palm trees and flowers grew. A typical house would have several levels above and below ground, and it was often connected—by paths called *maslak* on both the ground floor and the first floor—to adjacent houses, where other members of the family lived. So the houses were all a bit like a honeycomb.

The semi-basements, or *niim*—ventilated by means of a wide duct (*b'khaaree*) running up to the roof to trap the wind—provided cool spaces to keep food fresh. It was here that the family also took refuge on hot summer days for their siesta. There was another level below that called the *sirdaab*, cool and dark, where cheese, jams, vinegar, pickles—our wonderful *torshi*—and the like would be stored in big glazed clay jars. And below the *sirdaab* could be an immersion pool or well called the *biirgh tebiila* (or *mikve* in Hebrew), where all married women had to bathe to purify themselves after their time of the month: down a few steps and then dip three times in the freezing water. In winter, they would take a jug of hot water to rinse with and warm up after the dip.

Above ground were the living and reception rooms. One, the *shanaashiil,* projected over the street on one side like a loge or veranda. Through its *mashrabiyah,* a trellis-style lattice window, we could look out and see passersby without being seen ourselves. (On the Tigris, houses that overlooked the banks of the river were also hidden behind balconies like these.)

For our water, we had the river, just as in biblical times. Every day, men called *saqqa*s used to haul up water in goatskins and fill our *hubb,* a massive earthenware container. Due to Baghdad's dry

TOP AND LEFT.
Life on the riverbank

RIGHT. *A* saqqa
*waterseller, loading
up by the Tigris*

climate, water evaporated through its pores, cooled, and then
dripped gently into a clay receptacle to be filtered through mus-
lin into pitchers and used for drinking and cooking. Another container held water that was to be used for washing. It was quite a
business, with each household appointing its own trusted *saqqa* to
keep the supply coming. There was no water closet—what a concept! Our toilet was a slit in the ground about a metre deep and a
metre long, connected to the septic pit below. The stench hit you
the moment you opened the door.

As you can see, life in what passed as the "city" of Baghdad was
still quite primitive. Take lighting a fire. Matches were unheard of;
people still used a wax-coated cord with a compound on one end
that was ignited by friction. (When matchboxes eventually arrived,
they were an amazing novelty but relatively expensive.) To fuel their
fires, everybody had what they called a fuel room, but it wasn't coal
or logs that were kept there. It was full of sacks of different kinds of
combustible material, some to give a quick fire and some to burn
slowly for use in the oven when baking. Dried sheep dung, bought
by the sackload, was popular because it was smokeless. *Khash khash,*
the red, inedible fruit of the hawthorn, was the most sought after
because it gave off a nice scent.

COURTESY OF THE IMPERIAL WAR MUSEUM (IWM Q24189)

I have seen a map of the city in the seventeenth century and now realise that, in the second decade of the twentieth century, it had hardly changed in size or, I suppose, in character. In the old quarters, there were no street names: you simply referred to a street by the name of the richest family living there—for example, Kutchet Beit Baher, where all the Bahers lived. The alleyways were always filthy, as street cleaners were unheard of, and they formed a labyrinth in which it was easy to get lost. They were lined with sellers, not all of them nice. A barber would squeeze himself into a corner: he might have no shop, but this did not stop him from offering a range of interesting services besides shaves and haircuts—pulling teeth, for example, and lancing boils in full public view. Further down the lane could be a knife sharpener, then you might come across peddlers selling such delicacies as *taaza ya fijil,* fresh radishes with long leaves, or *khastawee ya nabeg,* lotus berries (hackberries) as sweet as dates, weighing them using old-fashioned iron scales, with their produce on one side and rocks, instead of lead weights, on the other. They were always cheating and bargaining.

Passing the unpainted mud-brick houses in the poor quarters, you might see at the top of their doors an old shoe or threadbare slipper nailed there as protection against the evil eye, with Jewish homes adding a *mezuza* with its short prayer to protect the house and those in it. You might come across the milkmaid with her cow, just managing to squeeze through to visit the homes of newborn babies so their mothers could be guaranteed a supply of fresh milk. She would milk the animal on the doorstep, always being watched carefully to make sure she did not dilute the milk with water. And through all this there was the remarkable sight of young country girls arriving from distant villages and heading for the Shorjah, the main market. Piled on their heads were towers of *'elba laban,* wooden yoghurt containers that slotted together. Each load could weigh up to ninety pounds— over six stone!—and were often as tall as the girls.

My earliest memories are of water and heat. Both elements dominated our daily lives, most particularly in summer, which every year was incredibly hot and interminably long. With temperatures of up to 122 degrees Fahrenheit, it was simply impossible to sleep indoors; the only place to be was on the roof to try to catch a whiff of any passing breeze in the sultry nights. A low wall, or *teigha,* divided us from our neighbours, most of whom were related to us, and at

night when preparing our beds, it was inevitable that we children
would jump across to see our playmates, while everyone else would
chatter—in Arabic, naturally, though the adults invented what they
called *lsiin el-tyough,* or "bird language," for when they didn't want
us children to understand. (We saw through that quickly enough:
they were simply adding a *z* to every syllable.) I hear your question:
so what about the newlyweds and how did babies happen? Simple:
the married couple would drape a particular type of canopy, a *kalla,*
around their bed to indicate "do not disturb."

And then it would be morning. We'd awake at cock's crow—
well, you could hardly do otherwise in a place where everyone kept
chickens and a rooster, and everyone's rooster would crow and
crow nonstop at the same time. Contrary to popular belief, cocks
do crow in the night—the first, soon after midnight. So if you said,
"I woke up with the first cock's crow," you really meant you had
hardly slept that night.

We didn't have clocks in those early days. When the first watches
appeared, children would stand on the street corner, waiting to ask
any prosperous-looking passerby if he could tell them what time
it was. It was a constant marvel just to know someone could pull a
piece of metal out of his pocket and get the answer by reading the
dial. And here we were, learning at school that five thousand years
earlier, almost on the same spot, the Sumerians had invented the
idea of the clock with its sixty minutes and twelve hours, along with
the twelve-month calendar.

The idea of building a palace had come to Baba just after what
everyone would come to call the Big Flood, when cholera broke out
in Baghdad. The sanitation was so bad that it was easy to see how
disease could spread down those dirty paths, which were muddy in
winter, too, and so narrow that, if you came across a couple walking
the other way, someone would have to turn sideways so that you
could brush past. *Hygiene* and *sanitation* were not in the vocabulary then. Under Ottoman rule, right until 1917, the supervision
of public services—whatever cleaning and lighting of the streets
there was, as well as the water supply, firefighting, and state of the
markets—was the responsibility of the *qaadi,* or judge.

Each of the city's various quarters had separate police forces for day and night; they were also protected by watchmen and gates. The rich lived in the centre, near the seat of power, or in a district where they had influence—either that, or on the outskirts where the air was fresher and land plentiful. Craftsmen and small traders lived in the populous quarters that spread out along the lines of their trade, and the communities separated along religious lines, clustering around a mosque, synagogue, or church—it was only at the great market, the Shorjah, that people from all religions met. These quarters were the focus of life for their inhabitants, who were united by ceremonies, festivities, births, marriages, and funerals. Over the years, as Baghdad developed and spread, it was remarkable to see how new areas became fashionable and old quarters like Hennouni, which had once enjoyed high status, were downgraded to become the new "poor" areas.

All the communities lived together peaceably, teasing each other good-naturedly and without inhibition about their religion. For instance, jewellery was the speciality of the Jews. A lovely story was told of how a Christian woman ordered a golden cross, encrusted with diamonds, to wear as a pendant for Christmas. When it was ready, she pointed out that one arm was ever so slightly bent and there was no symmetry to the piece.

"As if it wasn't enough that you Jews killed our Jesus, now you've deformed his image!" she complained.

"Look, madame," replied the jeweller Yakoub el Saa-yegh, "if you accuse me of killing your Jesus, I should know how it was done, and I assure you that the cross was not symmetrical. This is the correct way, and to prove it, you will find that it is the best talisman you ever wore." She paid up and was still laughing when she reached home.

Baba was afraid that the cholera outbreak might turn into an epidemic in those cramped, unhygienic conditions, so he and a friend from his school days bought orchard land on what were then the city's outskirts, in the region known as Karrada e'Sharggieh, and divided their plot with the intention of each building a palace. It was a courageous decision and a costly exercise, as all the material and manpower to build the houses had to be transported from the city by *guffa*, a round, black boat shaped like a giant car tyre, made of wicker covered with bitumen, a type of coracle similar to those that had been in use for the previous seven thousand years or so, since Sumerian times, for paddling goods and people up and down the Tigris and Euphrates. There was no place to sit, so everyone on board had to stand. Naturally, this was not good enough for my father's foreman, who had to have a rowing boat all to himself. There was a lot of pilfering to contend with, too, and it wasn't long before Baba's friend pulled out, deciding to leave his half of the orchard to run wild. I know Baba was disappointed, but far from treating it as a setback, we turned it to our advantage: the lack of any immediate neighbours or adjacent building meant that we were not going to be overlooked.

Baba's fear of the old quarter's health risks may have been why his parents soon afterwards decided to leave their house in Hennouni and move further in our direction to Kutchet el-Nasaara—but it would still take us an hour to reach them by 'arabaana, the horse-drawn coach we relied on for everyday transport. There they had a huge house called Beit el Barazali; it had a massive courtyard, and they kept a cow and calf in one of the ground-floor rooms. Yet despite its size, they must have found it inconvenient, what with their seven grown-up children and two married daughters. I can't

A guffa on the Tigris

tell you how many people lived there—it was just so crowded. I loved it—so many rooms to play in and so many people to be pampered by.

Some years later, on one of those Saturday nights when we were all assembled in the dining room at the *qasr*, eating a light supper, the samovar brewing contentedly on the table, we all began shouting in unison: about five yards from where we were sitting a raging fire had appeared. Everybody rushed downstairs shouting and screaming, looking for buckets, saucepans, bowls—anything to put water in, to extinguish the flames. It was centred on the room where the fuel was stored, but we had no idea how it could have started.

We younger children were sent out into the street calling, "Police, police!" But we were isolated. There were no services, no fire brigade, no telephone, no insurance. Then we saw an *'arabaana* approaching, and as it drew closer, to our surprise we could see my grandmother Yemma inside, with my aunt and uncle—an unprecedented visit. Reinforcements! With their help, we managed to control the blaze and put it out before too much damage was done.

Yemma was distressed but couldn't explain what had made her come to our house. She had had a premonition and suddenly asked to be taken immediately to see Baba. Everyone had tried to convince her to wait until the next day, but she had insisted that they go right then.

What a change moving to Karrada brought to our lives. Our *qasr*—a two-storey villa occupying a dominant position on the riverbank—had solid walls painted yellow, with white grouting to catch the eye. It was almost a copy of the old house in Hennouni, but with some modifications that proved misguided. (Baba had engaged an unqualified building engineer, who had forgotten to include the *b'khaaree* ventilator shaft, which we much regretted during the summer.) From the outside, it was massive: metre-thick walls with balconies all around. The windows had iron bars and were reinforced by two strong shutters that locked securely at night. The *shanaashiil* protruding over the Tigris were especially nice, as they made you feel as if you were standing in the middle of the river.

Although Baghdad was a couple of hours' walk to the north, we could see it clearly, and if we looked west down the river, we could see the small island of Jazra. A little way south of us was a police station, also overlooking the river, and the road from there led to an area known as Sab'e Qessoor, or Seven Palaces. Instead of having to press past people in cramped alleyways, it suddenly seemed as if we were flying on a magic carpet alongside the bulbul songbirds that nested there and filled the air with musical notes of incredible beauty, similar to the nightingale's. Everywhere our eyes could see were groves of palm trees, orchards, and vegetable plots. Oh, how those fabulous views gave me a tremendous uplift, a feeling of well-being and joie de vivre. Childhood became even more magical when I was able to absorb and adore the tales of Aladdin, Ali Baba, and Sinbad the Sailor (Sandibaad) as told by Scheherazade to her husband Harun al-Rashid, caliph of Baghdad in the eighth century.

The *qasr* was one of the first stone-and-brick houses to be built in the neighbourhood, which in those days was almost all agricultural land, unfenced plots without any obvious demarcation or concerns about security. I remember the local place-names as if it were yesterday: Bustaan Djassem, Bustaan Mussa, Beit el-Asswad, and Beit el-Naqiib. *Bustaan* means "orchard"; *beit*, "house"; and *asswad*, "black." Such dwellings that existed when Baba decided to build here looked totally lost surrounded by those big orchards, as they were small and made simply from mud bricks. (Now I see that the district is where the Ministry of Transport and Communications is housed, just by an area dominated by the University of Baghdad.)

The only one that stood out, Beit el-Naqiib, belonged to the head of the Sunni community, probably the most important religious leader of the day. It was built on reclaimed land in the river, like a pier, with water on three sides. Next to us was Beit Etwami, where another Muslim lived in a single-storey dwelling. He owned a *na'oor*, a water mill made of perpendicular wheels driven by an ox with a man guiding it to draw water from the river. The water went from one bucket to the next before the load emptied into the man-made channel in his orchard. In the beginning, before Baba set up his own irrigation system, he made an agreement with our neighbour to divert this stream into our garden for part of each day.

Our new home was vast, more than ample for our family, with eight bedrooms and a huge cloister called a *taraar* that we could use

The tarma *balcony, above the* taraar *cloisters and courtyard of a* qasr

COURTESY OF *THE SCRIBE*

as an open-air lounge around the central courtyard. We had a *mikve,* of course, entered via the garden, and when a few people moved to the area, my parents kindly invited the ladies to make use of it. Discreetly, they would arrive two at a time, well wrapped in their black silk *'abaayas* (cloaks) with thick black veils hiding their faces so that they were unrecognisable. At first, they had to be led to the *mikve* but soon they knew the way, for the practice of visiting it quickly became established and proved popular. One of our servants would hand them the key, another nine-inch monster, which they would leave at the door for the *domestique* to lock up with afterward.

The ritual involves stripping to your birthday suit and removing all jewellery. I remember one young lady who forgot to take off her wedding ring and was so worried that she later went to her rabbi to ask what she should do. The rabbi examined her ring finger and found that he could rotate the gold band easily. There was nothing to worry about, he said. Since the ring was loose enough to let the water pass beneath it, she was still considered kosher—clean—and would not have to go back for another three dips!

Baba persuaded his sister and her family to move into our house. This was for company to begin with, for it was hard for us former city dwellers to get used to the ways of the country. One of the most astonishing features of our new life was the fact that we were living in the middle of Baghdad's market garden, which was responsible for providing its citizens with most of their dates and other fresh fruit and vegetables. All around us, the land was being farmed. The open nature of the landscape also meant that it was vulnerable to petty theft: many were the times in the early days when we would wake up to discover that the dates we had carefully picked for our own use and put aside for storage had been stolen, along with any clothes that had been left out on the washing line to dry.

We children thought we were in paradise. We had three *nabqaayi* trees bearing lotus berries, one just outside the house and two further away. We all loved the *khastaaweeyah* date palm by the pathway. It was the ideal tree: big, fat, shady, and easy to climb. We would have our lunch beneath its branches, particularly on festive occasions such as Saturdays or holidays. A round table and canvas chairs were left there permanently, although we hardly ever used them, as we were always on the move, running or playing. But our truly favourite tree was the bent date palm: unlike the others that went straight up—we had more than twenty-five scattered about the grounds—this one grew horizontally so that anyone could climb it, and we could even reach the delicious dates and pick them by ourselves. We took such pleasure in picking and biting into ripening fruit from our trees, be it a fig, grape, plum, apricot, peach, medlar, or mulberry. We had oranges, pomegranates, almonds and walnuts, too. Walnuts were especially prized by us sisters: just before the nut ripened, before the kernel became hard, its juice made an indelible dark-brown stain that we applied to our lips like lipstick (which wasn't to appear in Baghdad until the end of the 1920s). We felt smart and properly grown-up, but it did make our lips chapped and sore. Our stomachs sometimes felt a bit sore, too, after eating dates when they were still green (*khelal el tosh,* we called them), green apricots (*tcheqqel*), green plums (*gawdja*), and fresh lemon with salt. It was a wonder that anything attained maturity with us around: anything growing within our short reach would have been stripped long before the usual time of picking, strictly against parental orders—of course!

The biggest plus arising from Baba's lack of a partner with whom to share the land he had bought was that the lower roof-terrace of our *qasr* could be used in privacy. Sunny in winter, it proved the ideal spot for us to take our lunches. It was cool in summer, having an open aspect, and that was where we dined at night beneath the stars and under the overhanging bough of a mulberry tree positively dripping with fruit. Delicious they were, too.

As before, summer nights were spent on the roof, or *sat-h,* but this time we had lots more space and staff instead of chattering neighbours, chickens, and crowing cockerels. As soon as the sun set, two great pitchers of water would be taken up there so that our drinking water could cool. (Every morning, a man would deliver two big blocks of ice, but as the icebox had not yet arrived in Meso-potamia, they would melt within an hour or two.) The whole family would bed down on the *sat-h-el-'ilee,* the spacious high roof with its bird's-eye view of our surroundings. All the staff, except our Arme-nian maid who stayed with us, had their own *sat-h-el-nassee* lower down on the other side of the house, which we could keep an eye on from our perch. It was *Upstairs, Downstairs,* Baghdad style. Their roof protruded over the *taraar* on the other side of the open-air courtyard that formed the heart of the *qasr.* This was so large that more than two hundred guests and musicians would be able to fit in it when my older sister Fahima had her wedding.

The *taraar* itself was used as a summer lounge, as I have said, furnished with wooden benches on which specially made cotton-filled cushions were placed and everything covered in spotlessly clean white sheets. There were four double windows, deliberately left without curtains or drapes so that they could be flung wide open to let the fresh air in, together with the wonderful scents that wafted in from the garden. These made such an impression on me that still today they remind me of my childhood: orange blossom, jasmine, gardenia, rose. From the *taraar,* you could also watch what was going on in the gardens, which were not just ornamental: as everything else in Baghdad, they had to be useful as well. Because of the difficulties associated with keeping food in such a hot cli-mate, everyone tried to be as self-sufficient as their means would al-low, and growing our own was the best method of ensuring that we ate only the freshest produce. Consequently, to the far left, under the high trellis laden with grapes, two cows and their calves were tethered. To the far right, you could just make out the chicken coop and winter accommodation for the cattle.

Yes, it was the Garden of Eden all right. But we hadn't been all that long in our little orchard paradise—kings of the castle, you might say—before the Great War broke out in Europe, and distant though it seemed, its echoes began to be heard even in our part of the world. This was, after all, the Turkish Ottoman Empire, and when Turkey became a German ally, a huge shadow fell over our lives. All across the empire, men were being conscripted into the Turkish army to fight the British, something that horrified Baba and his friends and placed them in a difficult position, for they admired England.

In 1915, our paradise came to an abrupt end. One day, to Nana's great distress, there came a banging on the door of the *qasr* and men in Turkish uniform took Baba away. He and all the other prominent members of the minority communities were being rounded up and deported to Mosul in the north of the country, near the border with Persia, on suspicion of cooperating with the enemy. Fifty or more young family men from the Jewish and Christian communities—many of them Baba's school friends, as well as two of Nana's brothers, my uncles Ezra and Moshi—made the hard journey, walking or riding mules if they could afford them, under German and Turkish guard.

It was a sad time for my mother to be left with four young children plus me, the baby, and she moved out of the *qasr* to be closer to the family and friends. Terrible hardship was experienced everywhere. Women and children were left behind, neglected and abandoned. Young men hid in attics or basements and dared not venture out on the streets. Many managed to escape to other countries, or to Basra in the south, where the British had established control. Some bought their way out of service with large sums of money, although this was no guarantee against future harassment. Yet they were the lucky ones: the able-bodied Jews who had been mobilised were sent, untrained, ill equipped, and in great haste to the front to fight for the sultan, an ailing ruler who shared few of their traditions or values. Few ever reached it; none came back. Faced with defeat, the Turks had turned on the recruits and killed them all.

Then, suddenly and inexplicably, Baba and the other deportees were allowed home—probably because the sultan's treasury was empty and the Turks, before they faced the final curtain, were trying to get their hands on any savings that people still might have. A number of Jews, together with Muslims and Christians, were executed either because they had deserted from the army or because they could not come up with enough gold to buy their liberty. Finally, when some bankers and money changers grumbled about being forced to exchange their gold and silver coins for newly printed, worthless Turkish banknotes, the Turks' answer was simple: they arrested those who resisted, herded them to the Tigris, killed them, and cut up their bodies before dumping them in the river in sacks. It was Tish'a-Bab, the season of mourning.

What Baba saw and heard when he came back to Baghdad made him realise what a dangerous place our isolated *qasr* would be; we could not possibly return to it and pick up our lives again. But the city itself was no longer safe for a man of military age, and in 1916, fearing what fate might have in store for all of their countrymen, Baba and some friends decided to go into exile again, this time voluntarily. Taking gold with them, the universal passport, they simply took some mules and headed northeast, following the ancient caravan routes, aiming to cross into Persia, today's Iran, and wait the war out in Kermanshah, where Baba had business contacts. It was a hazardous journey, so there was no question of taking their families with them.

It was a wrench for Baba to leave his young family again so soon, but Nana agreed it was the safest thing to do. Before leaving, he made sure that we were all safe and well looked after. There was a man who did the shopping for Nana and ran errands, someone who had known us for many years, who brought our groceries on donkeyback faithfully every morning and was paid by Baba's business secretary. (Later, I remember Baba always complaining that Nana never specified the weight she required, be it an *oka* or an *okiye*—old Ottoman measures, the latter being only a quarter of the former—so consequently we always had too much of everything.) Baba gave his secretary instructions to send him a letter every day with a sentence or signature from every one of his children. Someone always had to hold my hand so that I could add my scribble.

Accompanied by a nomad guide, Baba and his friends travelled for days before coming to the frontier, where they were stopped by some Russian soldiers, allies of the British, who eyed them suspiciously and wanted to take them prisoner. Eliahu Meir, one of the party, who had fair hair and a light complexion, spoke to their officer in English, explaining that he was the group's captain—a "fact" confirmed by Baba, also in English. And so they marched away, looking confident. However, after three days of making hard progress through the mountains, they were set upon by robbers who literally stripped them clean. They took all their money, possessions, and clothes, leaving them with nothing but their underwear. They became lost many times, but eventually, using their common sense, they found their way and arrived at their destination, only to move on again to Hamadan, where they stayed for the remainder of the war.

Childhood

IN OUR FIRST YEARS at the *qasr*, Baba employed a donkey driver to take the three oldest children, Regina, Na'ima, and Salman, to the nearest school in the countryside. Only one mattered, however: Salman. It was important that our brother should have an education, especially in view of Baba's own wonderful prowess and proficiency; the girls just tagged along, as there was room for three on the donkey's back. Salman sat in the middle, protected by the girls.

Regina and Na'ima were lucky to have enlightened parents who allowed them to do that, in view of the almost universal assumption that education was wasted on females, whose mission in life was to raise babies and look after the home. Yet in those days, there was no such concept as further education for us girls: our schooling was considered completed—that word again: *terminated* would have been more accurate—on reaching sixteen, when we would have to stay home to wait to be married off to someone who could be a total stranger, or a cousin if we were lucky. I was fortunate that a more liberal attitude prevailed as I approached the leaving age, and we girls were allowed to stay on, following a *cours supérieur* or, later still, the *cours spécial*. It was more like a club than a classroom, which kept us out of mischief and allowed our parents to say we were still at school "studying," learning cooking, perhaps, or sewing.

What an example Salman had to live up to. In the old days when Baba, much mentally stimulated, had come home with his own grandfather from his day at the synagogue, or *slah*, he had naturally found that his three younger brothers were simply not at his level. But his two older stepbrothers were ahead of him, helping their father, Heskel, in his business and completing their education at the Alliance School for modern European languages. Yemma was determined that Baba, her firstborn and favourite, should benefit from the same opportunities, to give him a head start where she perceived the future to lie. At first, he would not hear of it: he wanted to be like his grandfather. He thought his knowledge of Hebrew was good enough to earn him a living as a *muallem* and it would go against his entire religious upbringing to do anything else. Besides, he argued, what other use could he possibly get from languages?

Yemma eventually won him round by a shrewd device. She gave him something worth all the riches of Babylon in a home that was so crowded and lacking in privacy: his very own locker, complete with key. It seems a small thing now, but in that crowded house, living as they did in each other's pockets, it was the one sure way he could be certain that his siblings would not meddle with his belongings while he was away attending lessons.

The Alliance Israélite Universelle, to give its full name, was founded in Paris in 1860 and opened its doors in Baghdad four years later. It had been going for twenty years when Baba joined his stepbrothers in their last year there. His advanced education was a huge success, bringing him honour as a great linguist as well as a religious thinker. The curriculum included five mandatory languages: Hebrew, Arabic, French, Turkish, and English, in roughly that order of importance. The French influence was very strong in the Ottoman Empire, which explains why we used so many French words in everyday life. Baba did particularly well at French—so well, in fact, that soon the headmaster, a Monsieur Danon, appointed him standby to teach it to the lower grade as well as his own grade should the proper teacher fall ill. By day, my father was absorbed in his studies, as well as keeping a lookout for possible business prospects. By night, using the extremely dim light of a small earthenware container full of oil and water with a thin handmade wick, he studied all the French classics—Victor Hugo, Lamartine, Corneille, and Racine came as second nature to him.

Soon, he was a partner in his father's business and looking around to see how it could expand. They diversified, the enterprise thrived, and all Baba's languages were to prove extremely useful throughout his life. He was considered to be young but knowledgeable when he took his place among the prominent men of the community. He was voted a member of the El-Majlis el-Jismaani, the magistrates' court where Jewish domestic quarrels were settled. He was also an active member on the board of governors at the Alliance, always supporting any improvement and encouraging the employment of teachers from France or England.

When I became old enough to go to school, the donkey rides had to be rethought. Before we had moved to the *qasr*, a man had come every day to our house in Hennouni to take the children to school in the city and then bring them home. Of course, that school had been much better than the country one they were now attending, and Baba decided we should all go back to it. (But not my eldest sister, Regina, who had just turned sixteen and had, therefore, "completed" her education.) One winter, he hired a car and driver to come every morning and pick up those of us who needed to get to the city. Cars were still a novelty in those days and considered relatively dangerous. This one had a permit to carry up to four passengers. All well and good, except Baba insisted on coming with us, too, to get to work, so there was only room for three children again—back to donkey times. We just had to sort ourselves out in descending order of importance: my father, then Salman (though he was third in order of age), then Na'ima, and finally Fahima. No room for me. There was obviously no question of my walking to school alone, so I had to stay home.

It took my father six months to get a permit for the car to carry five passengers instead of four, which was why my formal schooling started late. Far from being the disaster it first seemed, it worked in my favour in the end. Being the baby of the family at the time, I was left in the *qasr* with Nana and the "completed" Regina, some nine years my senior, who took me under her wing as a blessed relief from the task Nana had set her to keep her occupied: embroidering an interminable tablecloth for her trousseau—it was always there for anyone who wanted to contribute and was finally finished when she married a few years later. It was Regina who first taught me that a book, which had seemed to be just paper cov-

ered in print, could tell me many more fascinating stories than the
gardener's wife, whose storytelling held us rapt for hours. Regina
taught me how to read and write and generally prepared me for
school. Many years later she said that I had soaked up everything
she had taught me like blotting paper.

We girls just had to accept our fate: women of a certain social
class simply could not contemplate a career of any sort. So we, too,
grew up in the belief that we would have no alternative but to stay
at home with our mothers once we passed our sixteenth birthday. It
would have been considered degrading for someone of our father's
stature to allow any daughter of his to train for a career. It simply
wasn't done; people might think he expected her to work for a living, or that he could not afford to keep her until she was married.

For the less fortunate, there was the free needlework workshop
in the centre of Baghdad, not ten minutes' walk from the old Jewish quarter. It was established by Nana's first brother, Ezra, whose
philanthropy was legendary. He patronised countless charities but
is best remembered for this workshop, which became known as the
Hagouli Atelier, after the manager he appointed for life. It was a
clever idea to teach needy Jewish girls a way to earn a living without shame or embarrassment. They took on jobs, and richer girls
enjoyed going to the workshop to give their orders and meet their
friends. My school also had a special *atelier de couture* section, set
up in 1923, to teach poorer girls or orphans the practical skills
of dressmaking and embroidery. It was a useful source of bridal
gowns and evening clothes for the whole community. (Among the
most important lessons at school were needlework and embroidery
classes, in which there was a great emphasis on gold embroidery
and brocade fabrics.)

After World War I, Uncle Ezra left Baghdad with all his family and
went to live in England, where he bought a cotton mill in Manches-
ter. As his businesses prospered, he endowed the workshop with
more and more machinery sent over from England. He presented
it with hundreds of sewing machines, but the greatest success was
the pleat-making machine—the first in Iraq. Pleats soon became the
"in thing" as Western costume gradually overtook traditional fashions. Every lady suddenly just had to have a skirt that was *plissée.*

At first my uncle underwrote everything. In addition to being
taught embroidery, needlework, and dressmaking, the younger girls

were given basic reading and writing lessons for an hour or two every day. Everyone who attended the Hagouli Atelier gained in confidence and had a much better start in life than girls who did not. Such was its success that the atelier soon became self-supporting and kept going for many years.

Although, like all other young ladies then, Nana had had no schooling, she had been properly groomed for marriage, being able to cook, sew, and do the difficult embroidery of gold wire on silk. She was considered extremely charming, and in fact, she was best skilled in the gentle art of persuasion. She knew exactly how to coax Baba and get her own way. We daughters also always hurried to do her bidding, and with just a few quiet words, she could defuse the most heated of arguments. Calling on the highest authority, Baba, was a rare occurrence indeed.

We kept my mother's wedding dress for a long time before eventually donating it to a museum in Israel. Made of beautiful cream-silk satin, the long skirt was edged with a long frill, heavily embroidered with gold thread. The fully lined jacket was cut in the princess style, with long, tapering sleeves, a nipped-in waist, and little buttons all the way to the high neckline. Women's fashion was diverse in post–World War I Baghdad. In fact, right up to the 1930s, some Jewish women still dressed like their Muslim counterparts in long robes, wide-skirted dresses and pantaloons, head scarves, and veils, at least outside the house. The veil, called a *khiiliyi*, was made from horsehair to look like stiff black lace: the wearer could see through it even though it covered the face completely. It was worn with an *izaar*, a robe in two pieces that covered the whole body. For everyday wear, it was plain but could be coloured, and for finer occasions, it was made of off-white silk with gold trimmings. The best and most luxurious *izaars* were known as *char-'ali* and came from Persia.

Women of Nana's time also wore gold anklets, *hejel*, which were decorated with bells so that everyone would know that they were wearing gold. Amulets of all kinds were popular as protection against the evil eye, and ones with semiprecious stones were sewn on to children's clothing as a matter of course. On special occasions, mothers and daughters had *dhafaayir* plaited in their hair—

gold leaves would hang from brown ribbons at the end of the plaits.
These were Ottoman traditions, and I remember being dressed this
way as a small child when Nana sent me with my twenty-year-old
cousin to see the first, newly built bridge across the Tigris. I was so
thrilled I was swinging my head from side to side to make my *dhafaayir* tinkle. I soon got tired, however, and started to drag my feet.
I don't know at which point some rascal came up behind me and
cut off my plaits, together with my *dhafaayir.* When Nana asked me
what on earth had happened, I was dumbstruck.

By the 1930s, all Jewish women adopted the *'abaaya* for outside
wear so as not to stand out from the Muslims. This was the common
black robe worn together with a *pooshi* (veil), also in black, tied behind at the level of the forehead. Dressed this way we were completely cloaked in anonymity, which helped to disguise the fact that
we might be wearing Western clothes underneath. Among both men
and women, there was a clash of cultures between the traditionalists,
who would not give up their Ottoman attire, and the modernists,
who couldn't wait to look like Europeans. So we had a situation in
the city where there were weddings with brides dressed like Charles-
ton flappers in sleeveless, relatively short, straight shifts—worn with
blunt haircuts and European cloche hats—while many of the married women guests would be in full Ottoman regalia with their *dhafaayir* and all the rest that went with it.

Before the 1930s, the mere idea of having a haircut was unthinkable, a girl's hair being considered her crowning glory. The only
way to tame such a lot of thick and wavy hair was to wear it in two
ringlet-like plaits. Almost all of us wore it this way, but it was time
consuming and seemed old fashioned. The breakthrough came
when the first ladies' hairdressing salon opened and was patronised
by the younger element—a controversial break with tradition. A
popular song that captured the disapprobation of our elders went,
"Bnayya bettel beit, gassat sha'arha . . ."—"The chaste daughter [of
the house] has had her hair cut! God help us, where will that lead
us? She's taken leave of her modesty."

I have seen a photograph of Nana in the early days of her marriage looking so glamorous, wearing her *char-'ali* of white silk and
gold thread, edged with tiny pom-poms. A big gold brooch with
a hook fastening held it up at the shoulder like a toga. We loved
to ask her about this, and she explained that she had also worn

a substantial golden anklet with little "tinklets," as I called them, together with a gold locket on a heavy gold chain. She was sophisticated, too, for in addition to the gold *dhafaayir* in her hair, which tinkled every time she made the slightest movement of her head, she wore a band of black velvet studded with real pearls around her forehead, which had been made to order by a seamstress expert in pearl embroidery. During the two days it had taken her to make it, she had been closely watched to make sure she didn't pocket anything.

Another outfit I remember seeing her in was the long, royal-blue satin dress heavily embroidered with bows and flowers in all colours of the rainbow. This she wore with a choker formed of several rows of tiny natural pearls, as well as several gold bracelets and rings. It was much admired, and she lent it to many girlfriends for their engagement parties. She was generous and was always giving to the needy, discreetly and without fuss.

After the long summer holiday and all the High Holy Days, in October I was finally really ready for school. I could hardly contain my excitement, dreaming about my red uniform decorated with pearl buttons, for that was the uniform for the *asile,* or kindergarten, in the girls' side of the Alliance Israélite Universelle (also known as the Laura Khedouri School for Girls, built by a great benefactor of Jewish Baghdadis, Sir Eliezer Khedouri, from Shanghai, who had named it after his wife).

I had long hair that I could not manage without Nana's help. Every morning before school, she would take a lot of trouble to make it look nice, combing it carefully and tying ribbons prettily. She wanted to make sure that I had a good start to the day and was well nourished, so she always took the opportunity to make me eat an egg and drink a glass of hot milk, which I hated, but what could I do? The threat was "no egg, no school," and there was the car waiting outside.

Once inside the school, no one was allowed out again until the end of classes, when all two thousand or so pupils left at the same time. The classrooms on the ground floor were paved with flagstones, but the upper floors had marble. The younger children's classes were overcrowded, about fifty or sixty to a class, while the senior ones had fewer girls, around thirty-five to forty. There was a separate building for the young foreign teachers, the *demoiselles,* as we called them. In this residence, they each had a private room with, on the ground floor, a communal kitchen, dining room, toilet, and bathroom.

The *asile* of Madame Sabbagh, my teacher, had about one hundred boys and girls under the age of seven divided into three or four grades, depending on age and capability. Madame Sabbagh, a pretty Parisian lady, had been Mademoiselle Nigri when she had arrived in 1909 to take up her post at the main boys' Alliance as a qualified teacher, but speaking only French, with not a single word of Arabic. Within a year, she had married Monsieur Sabbagh, who was also French and taught at the boys' school—most of the *demoiselles* married similarly. The Sabbaghs soon had a baby boy, Georges, and he joined the *asile* at about the time I was there (he would later become head of the Middle Eastern Center at the University of California, Los Angeles). I was placed in a class with some of the best-graded children, who happened to be mostly girls. We were given Plasticine, drawing paper, and crayons, and a little teaching. Many years later, when I was leaving the Alliance, Madame Sabbagh invited me to have a look at her glass display cabinet. To my amazement, my Plasticine work from those early days was prominently on show.

Madame Sabbagh's technique was to teach us to sing. She played her guitar as she sang, and we had to follow, parrot fashion—and, parrot fashion, we tried to catch words or phrases here and there, obviously with no idea what they all meant. For instance, when the girl beside me whispered into Madame's ear that she wanted to go out for a drink, the "mais oui" that Madame Sabbagh replied loudly sounded to me like "mewi"!

I wanted to know what the French was for "May I go out?" What should have been "Est-ce-que j'peux sortir?" was, to me, "Eski puh so tee?" said quickly. And so it remained to all of us as long as we were in the *asile*. This way, French was easy. More complicated was *bonjour.* In the Arabic alphabet, there is no soft "j" sound, only something that sounds like "dj." Consequently, it became *bondjour,* causing great pain to Madame's musical ears. However, she quickly became our favourite teacher, and in my eagerness to please her and try to emulate her, I hung on her every word. I quickly learned

all the songs. My big achievement was to play with a ball and sing
at the same time:

> Samedi, c'est ma fête,
> je lance ma balle
> je la ratrappe
> je fais un, deux
> je fais le roulement
> et le remerciement.

Total nonsense, but look how it's stuck with me all these years.

One day, Madame Sabbagh brought out her guitar and told us
she had a new song for us. It was "Hatikva," the Hebrew song that is
now the national anthem of Israel. Learning it from Madame Sabbagh, I never guessed that it was in Hebrew, for it sounded just like
the rest of the foreign languages I had been exposed to. Imagine
a world without records, radio, or TV: we could differentiate nothing. Madame Sabbagh's accent didn't change when she sang the
song, so we assumed it was French.

At the start, French was the only foreign language we knew; it was
for school use only, just as children might learn Latin and only use it
at school, not as a living language. A couple of years later, at home,
we acquired a wind-up gramophone and a record of "Hatikva." As
all the family tried to pick out some words of modern Hebrew, I suddenly burst into song. Everybody was flabbergasted. It was only then
that we realised that the song I had learned at school had been in
Hebrew. (Now, that reminds me of the story of the Israeli who went
into a kosher restaurant in New York. A Chinese waiter served him
throughout the meal. As the Israeli was leaving, he complimented
the manager on his Hebrew-speaking Chinese waiter. The manager
quickly hushed him: "He thinks he's speaking English.")

At the end of the year, I passed my exam near the top of the class
and went on to proper school and class nine, which meant that
there were nine more classes to go before my education would be
"complete." So my sister Regina's efforts on my behalf had all been
worthwhile.

Class nine was where the serious part began, the grown-up part.
Away went the red dress; the uniform now was black with a white
collar. And my sudden elevation to this new world coincided with a

big jump in Baghdad's development. From not having any public transport at all, we now had buses passing the *qasr* to take us as far as Rashid Street; any further was impossible, as the streets were too narrow. When river levels allowed, we also had a choice of getting to the city by motorboat, but that was a slow business, heading up-river against the water's flow.

The curriculum contained the usual subjects, but history lessons were particularly relevant. I was awed to discover that, at the dawn of time in this, my ancient land, the Sumerians had invented the wheel as well as the oldest writing system there is—cuneiform script—and arithmetic. They were from a city called Sumer, in southern Mesopotamia.

Besides French, we took Arabic, Hebrew, and English—all from local teachers. The most difficult thing to learn was the Arabic alphabet, for each letter was written in three different ways depending on its position: at the beginning, middle, or end of a word. To us, this meant learning three different alphabets instead of two as in French and English (i.e., capital and lowercase letters). I had already done sums in the *asile*, so maths was not too much of a problem, but starting all those new languages was a struggle. It seemed so pointless: four languages, none of which you could practise outside school. Even the Arabic, which you would have thought would be useful, was, in fact, useless, as written Arabic is totally different from spoken Arabic. Added to which, I was to learn later, each Arab country has a different spoken dialect, which is further subdivided depending on where you come from or even your religion. The pronunciation differs, too, and you will often find that people speaking Arabic from different countries, or even from different parts of the same country, do not understand each other.

English was learned by rote. We had to repeat what the teacher said, and it is only now that I realise what a terrible accent she had. For example, we spent a lot of time repeating "the blue dress" after her, supposedly until we got it right, and by the tenth repetition, we had it down pat: "the blue dree-yes." When she tried to teach us to say "neighbour," it came out as "nag-boor."

I must have done well, for the following year, the teacher congratulated Baba, told him what a bright child he had, and offered to put me two grades higher, to class seven. But instead of being pleased, Baba seemed nonplussed by this news. "Weh hoo weh!"

I heard him splutter (an exclamation we say all the time—which, depending on the tone of voice, can mean anything from surprise and shock to admiration or derision). He said he would have to talk it over with Nana. I overheard them discussing the matter. They were unhappy! If I carried on with the same school record, who knew what would happen? They would end up having me at home at an even more tender age than Regina! In the circumstances, they determined that I should carry on normally. They explained to me that I was very young and so should have fun and enjoy myself. It was not healthy to clog up my brains with too much learning too soon.

Weh hoo weh! School rapidly became too easy for me, and soon I had an ideal opportunity to do my father's bidding.

Sett Farah, our new form teacher, had come from Syria to teach us proper Arabic. I didn't much like her and neither did any of the other girls. She asked us to call her Sett, which meant "miss" or, more elegantly, "mademoiselle," in Syrian Arabic, but in our Arabic it meant "grandmother." We were delighted to obey her and kept calling her Sett for no good reason. She soon found out why we were so giggly, and said, "You may call me mademoiselle," but it was too late and the title of Sett stuck.

She had a loud voice that could be heard by all the other classes when the windows were open, but no one could complain. Her bawling was particularly bad when she tried to convince us that a *bezzoona* (cat) was not a *bezzoona* at all but an *itta*. Well, everybody in Baghdad—Muslim, Christian, and Jew—called a cat a *bezzoona*. We soon learned why she was upset: it turned out that *bezzoona* was a rude word in Syrian Arabic. She was obviously right, because in proper Arabic, the word should have been *itta* or *hirrah,* but it would have been pointless for us to use the new words, as most of our mothers had never been to school. Would we have to teach the new Arabic to everybody we knew so that we could be understood?

A shoe was no longer a *kondra;* it was a *hidha.*

A mouse was not a *jgheidi* but a *fa'er* . . . and so on.

Sett Farah was one of those teachers simply unable to control a class, whose teaching method consists of either yelling at you or making you write things out a thousand times. One day, she stood over me and told me to dot the *i*'s as I went along. Now, I was proud of my slanting handwriting, which I had been meticulously taught the French way, with every letter having thick and thin down- or upstrokes called *plein et délié*. Each mark of the fine-nibbed pen was important, and we learned to distinguish between English and French styles early on. So it was a bit much, this instruction to break my flow just to suit Sett Farah's whim. She would not allow me to dot them later: oh no, every *i* had to have its own dot immediately as it was written. Out of devilment I started dotting all over the place, at random and noisily. Then I offered to fill in an extra page of dots in case there was a shortage. Thankfully, the bell rang for break before she had time to reply.

We looked forward to her lessons so that we could poke fun at her or get up to more mischief of one kind or another. On April Fools' Day, we gave her an old broom in a shoe box made to look like a gift—suitable for the witch-grandma. Once, one of the girls laboriously wrote out her "thousand times" punishment and then sent the entire package by post, addressed to her at the school. On its arrival, Sett Farah was livid because, when she opened the parcel in the teachers' room, the sheaf of papers spilled out with all her colleagues as witnesses. She came into the class trembling with fury. "What is the idea of posting me your miserable punishment?" she screamed.

The culprit replied calmly: "Since you were so insistent, I thought you were in need of it. I posted it because yesterday was a holiday and I thought I had better rush it to you. Is it all right?"

"Need it? Me? Need it!" Sett Farah shouted almost hysterically. "You stupid child, what could I possibly need your punishment for?"

"To use in your toilette, Sett," somebody answered in a low voice, which due to the deafening silence, everybody heard.

Poor old Sett Farah was beside herself. But she was handicapped because she never really knew how to deal with us effectively. On that occasion, she ended the lesson early and marked all our papers with noughts.

Soon after, she made the mistake of giving us an essay to write on the theme "Fifty Years On." Well, she was asking for trouble there—composition was my best subject. My effort said, in part:

> And when I heard that my old teacher Sett Farah had hit upon
> hard times and was suffering, being poor and sick, I went to
> see her and I went by aeroplane. There she was, and I asked
> her: "Do you remember all the zeros?" and she said: "Violette,

I have often thought with regret about those days. Please forgive me. Will you forgive me?" And so I forgave her. And from
then on we became really good friends.

Looking back now, all these years later, I suppose we were cruel to
her, like all high-spirited children of that age.

When I was twelve, my best friend, who was only a year older
than me, became engaged to be married. Her parents promised
her that she could continue to go to school. Well, when she next
came to class she was wearing a lot of scent, and as she walked during break, she left behind a trail of face powder like flour. All the
girls followed her and stared at her as if she had come from outer
space. Instead of congratulating her, I told her what a stupid thing
I thought she had done. She never came back to school. I missed
her a lot, but somehow our relationship had changed and we could
no longer be friends as before.

Games were something that Baba encouraged—he had proudly
brought home a Ludo set that the British had given him—and of
course, we had our dolls to play with. In the school playground, we
skipped rope and played a game called *beeyoot* (houses), similar to
hopscotch, and *shadd 'ayoun* (tied eyes, or blindman's buff), as well
as *mukhutboiya* (hiding place, or hide-and-seek).

But there was one game we would never play, and that was *ka'eeb*,
something we saw on every street corner in the Muslim quarters,
where poor children squatted on the ground in their grubby *deshdaashas* (gowns). The game was played with what looked like large
dice with rounded edges, which were, in fact, sheep's knee bones.
The game basically involved throwing one of these pieces, called
ka'eeb, in the air and grabbing as many of them off the ground as
possible while the first was still airborne. The cunning part was that
each of the *ka'eeb*'s six sides had a value similar to those of dice. No
figures were written on the bone; the value was known from their
natural marking. The game was so addictive that all young boys had
a side pocket bulging with *ka'eeb*.

As a student, I had no special help at home, no coaching. With
so many of us children clamouring for attention, I was simply left

to get on with my studies. At the end of the school year, no one could be sure what our academic future held: the surprises would be made known only when the school reopened for the autumn term. Nevertheless, I enjoyed the summer holidays enormously, as we always entertained a lot and had many guests come to stay. I often had my friends over and we would picnic by the river.

The approach of the High Holy Days meant that autumn and, with it, school would soon be upon us. I was always overexcited at this time, impatient to find out if my friends had realised their girlish dreams. Had this one gone to Hollywood? Had that one become a pilot? What had become of the other one? There was so much to look forward to, so much to hear and tell. My own father had promised that, if I did well, he would send me to Bouffémont Collège, a finishing school in Paris—a dream I had cherished for a long time. And I did do well at school. In the 1920s, the official exams for the French *certificat d'études* were held for the first time in Baghdad's history—and they were held, moreover, at the French ambassador's residence. Male and female candidates were carefully selected from the two Alliance schools, and I found myself among the chosen few. Imagine the excitement: not only could we get an official French diploma; we would also get to visit the ambassador's home. The exam involved a whole day's work, and you had to pass all the subjects to get your diploma: French, maths, history, geography, and science. The results were known immediately: I had done it! But as you will see, I never made it to Paris.

The Shebbath

SCHOOL HOURS were long. Every day, winter and summer, we had classes from seven-thirty in the morning till a break for lunch at noon and then again from two to four in the afternoon. Fridays were different, however, being the eve of the Shebbath—the Sabbath—when we had only the one morning session. Many of my school friends would miss that in order to stay at home—it was the busiest day of the week, with so much preparation necessary.

There was a lot of cooking to do on Friday, and none of the dishes was simple, as food for the Shebbath had to be special. For example, for *lailt el-Shebbath*, the Friday dinner, our meatballs—*kebba*—had to have an outer layer of ground rice, meat, and spices, and our fish cakes—*'eghooq ib-samak*—were coated with rice, fish, and herbs, predominantly dill. In both cases, they had to be as small and as delicate as possible: the more refined the food, the better the cook was deemed to be. We enjoyed *kebba shwandagh*, a sweet-and-sour winter dish of meatballs and beetroot; and in summer, *kebba baamia*, meatballs and ladies' fingers (okra) flavoured with mint and lemon. As cooking on the actual Shebbath was forbidden, at the same time, we also had to prepare the following day's lunch, which would invariably be a slow-cooked meal that could be left in the oven overnight. The most traditional was *etbeet* (also known as *hammiim*)—chickens stuffed with rice and baked with Saturday eggs (*beidh 'al-etbeet*), which were left, unshelled, on top of the chickens as they cooked, with the result that the eggs, when peeled, were brown. The same effect could be achieved by putting them in a saucepan filled with sand, which was left on the embers overnight. Lamb dishes were popular, and for special occasions we had *m-hasha*, vegetables stuffed with minced lamb, rice, parsley, mint, and spices. There was *paacha*, too: lamb tripe stuffed with rice.

Naturally, Nana was queen of the kitchen, but all available female hands were put to work to help Hagouli, our young male cook, and the rest of the kitchen staff. The fuss was incredible, and what a din there was, amplified by the clanging of the *hawan*—the brass mortar and pestle relentlessly crushing all the spices that were to be used in the dishes, a different mix for every speciality. The wonderful scents coming out of that kitchen still haunt me and awaken my taste buds, and I can still hear that *hawan*.

Friday was always the highlight of the week, but there were other times when we children enjoyed being in the kitchen. Every time we entered it, there was something going on that left a deep impression. Before cooking any meat, for instance, Nana would finish the koshering process—it was not enough simply to have the animal killed by a properly accredited *shohet* (kosher butcher). First, she scrupulously removed any white membranes and nonkosher parts. Then she would rinse it at least three times before covering it in salt for about forty-five minutes (thirty minutes for a chicken) to drain any leftover blood. After that, she would rinse it once again, and the meat would then be kosher, ready to be prepared—cut, chopped, or ground before cooking. Kosher meat has to be clean and completely free from blood. The liver must be grilled on an open fire to allow the blood to drain. As a matter of fact, any meat can avoid the salting or draining process if it is to be grilled. The heart had to be cut lengthwise to expose any blood or nonkosher parts within it. After this whole process, Nana then felt it was safe to leave it to the cook to do the rest.

Our cows produced a lot of milk in spring, so we used to make our own butter—and what a performance that was. First, our maid turned the milk into *laban* (yoghurt) before pouring it into the skin of a sheep and adding water to increase the volume by a third. Now came the part that was fun to watch: she blew into the skin, turning it into a balloon. Then, as she sat on the floor with the sheepskin resting beside her, she grabbed the feet and tail with one hand and the shoulders with the other, and rocked the sheepskin backwards and forwards for about half an hour. At the end of that time, butter would float to the top of the *laban,* which she carefully placed in a bowl and removed some of the whey for *shnina,* a salted yoghurt drink like salt *lassi.* She had to repeat the operation until we had five or six pounds of butter.

That wasn't the end of it. To remove any residual liquid, she transferred all the butter to a large pan on the fire and added some washed, uncooked rice. As it came to the boil, the rice absorbed the remaining yoghurt, so that she could finally remove the pure "refined" floating butter to store in Hagouli's *sirdaab* (basement larder) where it remained cool. The rice left at the bottom was not wasted either. After Nana added a pinch of salt, we all wanted a taste of the sour and salty mixture. She gave the rest to the cleaning woman, who added some bread and made a meal of it for her children.

Our kitchen was L shaped. The cooking section had a back door into the garden and an open space for the *tannoor,* a wood-burning clay oven where we cooked our kebab, cookies, and bread, which was like a large pitta but thin and crispy. The rolled-out dough was placed on a hard, round cushion (*malezqa*), baked in the oven, and then, when ready, removed with pincers.

Just outside was a large fenced area with a small pond, where we kept chickens, turkeys, and ducks. To one side of the kitchen was the washroom with a water tap, where the laundry was washed. The floor in this room sloped so that wastewater ran into a drain by the entrance. This room was also used by the staff to wash themselves.

Next to that was a room for our gardener, Djassem, a big, sturdy fellow who remained with us for a good many years. His wife, Fatoom, did not stay the night with him; rather, she returned to her own home and brought him his supper every evening, most frequently lamb with *baamia* (ladies' fingers), their standard fare. Bran bread and raw onion was their lunch—always bran bread, for it was cheaper—accompanied by dates, yoghurt, or a glass of milk.

Naturally, we saw more of Fatoom during the summer holidays, when she gave Djassem a hand. In the afternoon, when she wanted

Gardener Djassem surveying storm damage

to relax, she would sit on the step by the doorway of their room and spin wool to make herself an *'abaaya* for the coming winter. In the spring, sheep-shearing time, she would get untreated fleece at a discount from her son-in-law, who was a shepherd. She would wash and comb it, then turn it into wool thread by twisting it together, a little at a time, and winding it round a spool, the end of which looked like a toy top. On and on she spun, round and round, as if she was playing and enjoying herself. She let me try once, but it really was much more complicated than it looked. While spinning, she would tell us children long tales of chivalry and romance— many based on the *Alf Laylah wa Laylah* (*The Thousand and One Nights*)—and we loved them, for her stories always had happy endings. After a few weeks, when she thought she had spun enough, she would take the wool thread to the weaver, who then wove it into a length of material, enough for an *'abaaya* for herself and a cloak for her husband. How laborious, just for a couple of cloaks.

Beside the gardener's room, there was a room without a door: the cow byre, where the animals sometimes sheltered on rainy nights. We also stored kindling there, next to the fuel room. At the other end of the kitchen was the fire that had to be fed to heat both the water and the stone floor of the *hammam,* the Turkish bath that everybody took, winter and summer, on the eve of the Shebbath in order to be clean on the Lord's Day.

A quick lunch of a simple courgette dish—*qegh'iyyi*—might be
waiting for us before we entered the bath, in which three of us
could fit at a time. As we entered, having left our clothes in the an-
teroom, the floor felt deliciously warm, especially when the weather
was cold outside. There were low benches arranged for us to sit on
if we felt too hot. At the door were placed different-sized wooden
platform clogs called *qabqaab* (after the sound they made) for us to
wear when we returned to the antechamber. That room, like the
kitchen, was L shaped with benches covered with carpets to rest on,
and on its floor were Persian carpets the size of small prayer mats.
On the wall was a silver-framed mirror from Nana's dowry, and in
the corner was a large basket where you would find your towel wrap
and your clean after-bath Shebbath wear.

Nana always took the last *hammam*, after us children. She would
give the girls who could not manage their long hair by themselves
a hand with combing, as she never trusted the maid to do it for us.
My own auburn hair was long, wavy and thick, so after washing it
thoroughly with ordinary soap, called watermelon soap, she covered
my hair with *teen-khawa*—a type of clay from the village of Khawa
(*teen* means "mud")—for a minute or two, and then rinsed it off,
leaving my locks silky and easy to manage until the following Friday.
After my *hammam*, I would go upstairs to dry my hair, sitting in the
sun on the *tarma*—the balcony with a wrought-iron rail that ran
outside the rooms overlooking the square courtyard. In summer in
the breeze, it would dry in no time.

No one then had bathtubs in which you could immerse yourself.
In our old Hennouni days, we had taken our baths in a copper
vessel in the kitchen like everybody else. There had been no gas
or electricity; water would have to be warmed on a wood fire and
poured into the vessel until there was enough for a bath. A hurricane lamp would give us light, for wax candles were expensive and
only used for weddings and other celebrations.

Nana would appoint one of us girls to prepare the table for Friday
night. The *meidi*—the special table setting—had to be ready before
the start of the Shebbath. When it was my turn, I would first lay
a clean tablecloth and arrange two complete, unbroken loaves of

bread, one on either side of the saltcellar, and then cover all this with the special Shebbath covering, beautifully hand-embroidered with gold thread. In some homes, instead of two loaves, they would place twelve pittas under the cover to represent the twelve tribes of Israel. I would then place a silver beaker of raisin juice on the table, along with its cover, waiting for Baba to recite a blessing over the lot. Nothing else should be on the table until after this blessing. We used the same word—*qeddoos*—for both the blessing and the nonalcoholic juice we used in place of wine, made from raisins that were soaked overnight in winter or just in the morning in summer because it could easily turn sour in the heat.

Once the *meidi* was set and just before the sun went down, Nana would light, not the symbolic candles used today, but the *qerraayee,* a glass bowl of water into which sesame oil was poured and five homemade wicks were placed on wire supports. The wicks were made of cotton wool wrapped around special thin twigs cut from the stems of palm leaves, which burned slowly. The lighting of the *qerraayee* had special meaning. It had to be done before the sun went over the horizon, and it meant the start of the Shebbath and twenty-six hours of prohibition, summed up in two words: *do not.* Almost everything was "do not—it is not allowed." So, as the time approached, Nana would sound a warning (every minute, it seemed) by shouting: "Time for *qerraayee,* time for *qerraayee,* hurry up, the sun is setting, we are late!" (In other houses, boys would call out: "Saagh waqt il-shi'la. 'Sh'uloo 'sh'uloo!"—"It's time for the lighting. Light it, light it!") And almost every time, one of us would beg for another minute, to finish writing or some other trivial matter. Once the *qerraayee* was lit, there could be no more writing, no more work. It was the only light by which we could see to read before going to bed, and its feeble glow would last until well after midnight. In the late 1920s, kosher candles began to be produced in Palestine, and eventually these replaced the *qerraayee.*

Finally, as the sun was about to set, Nana would put on her prettiest head scarf and recite the *berakha* (blessing) as she lit the *qerraayee.* Then, inaudibly, she would whisper her own personal request that only the One above could hear, before turning to all of us present and saying, "Shebbath Shalom."

On Fridays, Baba would come home early, take his *hammam,* then make his way to the *slah,* the synagogue he had built at the end of our garden soon after we moved to the *qasr*. Without it, he would have had to go into the city on foot to pray, for once the Shebbath started, no transport was allowed—even the animals had to have their day of rest. In modern days, the extremely religious have extended the rule to motorised locomotion.

At the same time as building a synagogue, Baba had purchased the land across the road from us. This he then parcelled and sold off as building plots. Soon many of his friends came to live in our neighbourhood, easily persuaded of the wisdom of the move by the attraction of having both the synagogue and the river within easy walking distance. The closest to us on the river were Eliahu and Rahma Khazam, who bought the Naqiib's property and moved in with their family, and when my eldest sister, Regina, was married, she was one of the first to build a beautiful home just across the road from us. The area eventually became popular, but at the start not many people attended our *slah,* and Baba often came home early because there had been no *minyan,* or quorum.

When he returned from *slah,* we were all ready, standing in place with our heads covered. As he recited *qeddoos,* standing with the glass of *qeddoos* wine in his hand, we all responded "amen" in unison in the appropriate places as well as at the end of the blessing. Then he would take the first sip before passing the wine to Nana and the children in turn. We all rushed to kiss Baba's hand, and he blessed us by putting his hand on our heads and saying in Hebrew: "The Lord keep you." We then kissed Nana's hand. (Kissing your parents' hands was both a sign of respect and submission. Only the very young got to kiss and be kissed on the cheek.) The ceremony continued with Baba going to wash his hands, after which he removed the cover from the *meidi* and pinched off a piece of bread for each one of us, which he dipped into the salt while blessing God for giving us bread. The saltcellar, from Nana's dowry, was made of silver with a special tilting lid.

After eating this double-blessed bread, the ceremony of ushering in the Shebbath was over. Now at last we could lay the table with plates and cutlery and sit down to the best dinner of the week. All the good food that we did not have time to savour during the other six days—the best sweets and any new-season fruit—was saved for the Shebbath. Traditionally, we started with *marag eb-jiij,* chicken soup with lots of chickpeas and rice. We always had rice. Rice was the staple of any meal, and everything else was just an accompaniment. We then had the *kebba* or the fish cakes, and for salad we had sliced cucumber marinated in homemade wine vinegar with fresh mint and garlic, as well as a mixed salad with lemon and salt—no oil. (No one ever used salad oil in Baghdad; instead, much of our cuisine was based on sweet-and-sour principles, using date syrup and a great deal of lemon, dried lime, vinegar, tamarind, or sour pomegranate juice.) After dinner came the most convivial part of the week, when the whole family sat around the table and sang *sbahoth,* songs of praise.

The following morning, the Shebbath, the men would be greeted on their return from synagogue with the wafting aroma of the *et-beet* that had been left to look after itself overnight. The eggs were now hot and brown, exuding the most appetising smells. On a cold winter's morning, they were irresistible. Today, Saturday eggs have passed into Israeli cuisine.

My favourite time of all was Purim, which we called Mjalla, the holiday when our people commemorate their deliverance from a massacre planned in the days of the Persian Empire. To us in Baghdad, its celebration was especially significant, for Babylon had been part of that empire, and therefore the events of Mjalla would have involved our direct ancestors.

Our excitement began around the end of January or early February, as the trees were showing their first blossoms, signalling the end of our short winter. It was now the New Year for Trees—Tebq'e Essejagh—and our dining table was spread with all kinds of dried fruits such as figs, dates, prunes, apricots, and sultanas, as well as nuts. We said a blessing before dinner as if to say goodbye to them and hello to the fresh variety we knew would be coming along soon. With spring in the air, we didn't have long to wait until Purim. The reason we children looked forward to it so much was that, of all the holy days in the calendar, this was a time when almost everything was allowed and nothing was *assoor* (forbidden)! We got to wear disguises, we got to eat lots of pastries—and we got money!

The deliverance happened during the reign of King Ahashwerosh (Xerxes) of Persia, who reigned over all the land from India to Abyssinia. Mordekhai the Jew was his good minister, who allowed his orphaned young cousin Esther to become his queen. She was so beautiful that the king fell madly in love with her and did all he could to please her. Then, one day, along came the evil Haman, who wormed his way to the top as equerry to the king. Mordekhai refused to bow to him, and this so stung Haman that he somehow obtained a decree allowing him to have all the Jews killed. In particular, he planned to make an example of Mordekhai and have him hanged on gallows in the middle of the main square. All the Jews, old and young, were crying, fasting, and mourning, knowing that they would soon be exterminated. Mordekhai, accepting his fate (which seemed predestined), managed to get to see Esther to say good-bye.

Now Esther herself was crying and started to fast. The king became worried and asked what was causing her such distress. She told him the story and begged to be allowed to die with her people.

"But who," asked the king, "is going to kill your people?"

"Haman, Sire," came the answer from Esther's pretty mouth. (Her loveliness still took the king's breath away.)

"I promise you I'll give him a good dose of his own medicine. Dry your tears and you will laugh for the rest of your life," said the king. "That villain Haman has taken advantage of my patronage."

King Ahashwerosh must have had a good sense of humour. He ordered a big banquet and, with Esther sitting at his side, summoned Haman and said: "I would like to honour a man whose service I value. How do you suggest I do that, Haman?"

Haman's chest puffed out like a frog. Surely, this honour was for him, and soon he would be invited to share the king's succulent food. His mouth watered with anticipation. It must be that he was about to be named the grand vizier, the king's right-hand man. What joy!

"Your Majesty, dress him in cloth of silk and gold and let him ride your favourite stallion with an escort of attendants on horseback. Have the town crier call: 'Make way, make way, for here comes the King's favourite by royal command!'" replied Haman. "Invite the whole town to the procession with drums and trumpets, and have sweets and coins tossed to the children."

"And so it shall be!" said the king. "Haman, I command you to perform the town crier's job. Mordekhai the Jew will ride my best stallion just as you have described."

And so it was that Mordekhai was honoured with a magnificent procession, complete with clowns and acrobats, plus sweets and handfuls of coins distributed to the crowds that lined the street, followed by another lavish banquet. It was Mordekhai who became the grand vizier, and the king decreed that Haman and his sons should swing from the same gallows that the equerry had had prepared for Mordekhai in the main square—and all our people rejoiced.

And so came the end of Haman Harasha'—Haman the Evil— who was short and bald with a bushy moustache and beard and (famously) oversized ears. We celebrated with lots of pastries, including some triangular ones called *oznei Haman* (Haman's ears), and *massafaan,* a kind of marzipan, and *shakarlama,* a type of shortbread that was the best and richest of all, with lots of fresh butter and sugar.

On the eve of Purim, the whole story—the Megillah (the book of Esther)—was read in the synagogue and also at home. When Baba returned from the *slah,* he would give us as many coins as our little hands could carry. This was called *dmei Purim*—lots of new coppers to play cards with, some silver and one gold. We would keep the gold coin for a while, then pass it to Nana to keep for us. I remember Nana had a secret drawer full of them in different sizes.

We children loved to wear our disguises. Most girls were Queen Esther, of course, and the boys were King Ahashwerosh or Mordekhai. We would burn an effigy of Haman on a bonfire in the garden, but this custom was dying out in the old quarter, where many accidents had happened and it was getting dangerous.

Drummers and trumpeters went from house to house early on the morning of Mjalla. They walked all the way to our home in Karrada and stood in the courtyard and played loudly, singing the praises of Baba, how generous he always was, and "please God" might they come again to play at the weddings of his children, whose names they called out one by one—information they had obtained from whoever happened to have opened the door. We liked to toss them some of our coins, which the musicians' children would pick up.

After dinner we cleared the big round table and brought out the playing cards. The traditional game was *naqsh-y-hood,* played like vingt-et-un, to stimulate arithmetic in a child's mind. We would all participate, with Baba dealing, playing with real money to make it more dramatic. A much simpler card game was *dossa,* where you gambled on an unseen card. Because our family was large, Mjalla was an occasion for much merriment.

Iraq

WITH THE INNOCENCE of childhood, my sisters, brother, and I were growing up oblivious to the dramatic events unfolding in the big world around us. Although my elder siblings had been aware of the Great War because Baba had left us for safe haven in Persia, we never questioned why Britain was struggling to conquer Mesopotamia from the Ottomans. It was only as we grew up that we realised it was a question of oil—the blessing and curse that has oozed through the centuries to this day. Because of it, as we enjoyed our days at the *qasr* and struggled with our schooling, not just our own futures but the fate of the entire Middle East remained in the balance.

The Venetian traveller Marco Polo was the first European to see oil surface, as he followed the Silk Road through Mesopotamia in the thirteenth century. Of his discovery, he wrote: "People come from distant parts to procure it." What a prophetic observation that turned out to be.

By the time he reached our city, "anciently called Babylon," it was in the middle of a golden age as a banking centre at the crossroads of international trade routes taking its citizens, mainly Jews, to every corner of the known world. In his *Travels*, he described this, the noblest city in the region, with its silks shot with gold, its damasks and velvets, all being shipped to and from the sea via the river Tigris.

A stream of oil flowing in northern Iraq

My people had arrived in Mesopotamia in biblical times, and since the country became part of the Muslim Ottoman Empire in 1534, we had enjoyed protected minority status as the People of the Book, believers in the one true God. During Baba's and Nana's lives in the nineteenth century, our communities in the three *vilayets* (provinces) from which the country was formed—Mosul in the north, Baghdad in the centre, and Basra in the south—grew steadily in number and prosperity, with everyone living in large family groups, in harmony with our Muslim and Christian neighbours. Our top businessmen were respected, leading citizens, enjoying privileges associated with the uppermost ranks of society, dominant in the commercial, financial, and cultural life of the country, contributing greatly to its development.

In 1908, shortly before I was born, large deposits of oil were discovered in neighbouring Persia, and the prospects for Mesopotamia caught the West's attention. The country held great promise, and the Anglo-Persian Oil Company obtained drilling rights across half a million square miles of Mesopotamian sands.

Germany already had a firm footing in Mesopotamia when World War I broke out in 1914, so it came as no surprise when the Ottomans decided to take sides with Berlin. This posed a threat that London could not ignore. An Anglo-Indian force landed at Basra to protect Britain's route to India and the supply of oil on which its navy depended. The troops' advance towards Baghdad was difficult. In summer, soldiers fell victim to heat, flies, and mosquitoes; in winter, they froze. In the rainy season, when the rivers flooded and dust turned to mud, they were bogged down. They suffered some major defeats before marching into Baghdad in 1917.

When the forces arrived, the Indian soldiers and the Tommies— *N'gléz* we called all of them—showered us local children with coins in a bid to make friends, and everyone celebrated. There were annas and rupees and chocolates and chewing gum—Wrigley's best— and all kinds of novelties.

Britain became the supreme power in the Middle East, either occupying or influencing every nation. It imposed colonial rule on Mesopotamia with a civil administration like India's, obviously intending to stay for a long time. But I now realise that they didn't have such a smooth passage: there were armed uprisings in the Kurdish north, and in 1920, the unrest turned into a major insurrection across central and southern parts and was crushed only after great loss of life. The Great Revolution was how the rebels saw it.

The fate of the Middle East was finally sealed by the League of Nations' formal acknowledgment of the "mandates." To the victorious British went Mesopotamia, Transjordan, and Palestine; to the French, Syria and Lebanon. And at a conference in Cairo the following year (1921), lines were drawn in the sand and a new country—Iraq—emerged from the broken pieces of the sultan's empire. The decision forced together the three old Turkish *vilayets*— Basra, which was primarily occupied by Shi'a Muslims; Baghdad, which was Sunni; and Mosul, which was Kurd—which had been kept separate under Ottoman rule. They had never been linked like this before; their people did not like each other. In fact, the only thing they had in common was a dislike of central control. What a mess.

The British decided that Iraq should be a kingdom, with a monarch that London could rely on, and to this end, they brought us a ruler from Arabia, King Faisal.

The people were outraged. It seemed that the British were deliberately pursuing a divide-and-rule agenda by forcing them to live together and create an unstable nation, with little regard for the wishes of its citizens. Britain had failed to honour the promise of independence it had made to all Arabs in exchange for their support in fighting the Turks and insulted Muslim pride. On top of everything, everywhere in the Muslim world there was frustration and anger at Britain's other pledge—in the Balfour Declaration of 1917—to give Palestine to the Jews.

While all this was going on, my community represented almost 40 per cent of the population of Baghdad: 80,000 of a total of 202,200 according to the last Ottoman yearbook in 1917. There were also 12,000 Christians, 8,000 Kurds, 800 Persians and 101,400 "other" Arabs, Turks, and Muslims. For us, nothing had changed: we felt ourselves secure and integrated, rooted in the country as we had been since biblical times. We were truly indigenous, here for a thousand years before the Arab-Islamic conquest. It was our home! And we enjoyed a neighbourly relationship with the other communities. Each adult could speak three versions of Arabic: the written or formal, as used in official business; the local Iraqi Arabic, used when speaking with Muslims; and Judeo-Arabic (Arabic in Hebrew characters), a dialect that had evolved over the centuries and included a vocabulary borrowed largely from Hebrew but also, for good measure, from Turkish, Farsi, and a sprinkling of European tongues [see the glossary at the end of this book].

Within our community, the majority believed that they had much to gain from the coming of the British. And for their part, the British saw that there was much to gain from befriending us, with whom they had already had contact during a century of trade under colonial rule in India. They were impressed by our business acumen and adaptability, our command of English, and the fact that we knew how the British system worked.

Our people had lately become full citizens under Ottoman rule, enjoying equal rights and duties with the Muslims. Intercommunity relations were cordial and cooperative, with mutual respect for religion and culture. However, neither community encouraged deep fraternisation, and each was wary of the other, though we lived side by side in peaceful coexistence, equally subjugated, first by the Ottomans and now by the British. The thought of any transfer of power to the Arabs filled us with apprehension. There was such an "instant connection," as one observer has called it, between ourselves and the new power that we even petitioned for British citizenship. The request was denied and we were given an either-or choice: we could remain "Ottoman" and be treated as foreigners in our own country or become Iraqi subjects. We all elected to become Iraqis and abide by Muslim rules.

When Faisal was proclaimed king, we held a festive reception for him at the Great Synagogue with many notables from all religions present. Describing the Jews as "the moving spirit among the inhabitants of Iraq," he kissed a Torah scroll and declared that, henceforth, there would be no discrimination between Muslim, Jew, or Christian. We took great heart from this.

Such was the integration and progress that by 1926, when the Baghdad Chamber of Commerce's administrative council was founded, Jews accounted for one-third of its members. So important were our menfolk that when they shut their shops, banks, and businesses for the Shebbath, commercial activity in the main street ceased. Non-Jewish shopkeepers closed for lack of customers. Bazaars emptied. In this predominantly Muslim land, Saturday, not Friday, was in effect the holy day.

Changes

I'M SORRY BABA was not there to witness the historic moment when the country finally fell into the hands of the British, as it was seen as such a blessing. It had been particularly hard on my mother, having to worry about Baba's safety at the same time as raising the five of us (my sisters Daisy and Marcelle didn't come along until after the war).

In 1917, as soon as it was thought safe, Baba made his way back to Baghdad. He told us the story of his escape and about life in Kermanshah and Hamadan, where he had visited the shrine of Esther and her cousin and guardian Mordekhai, the heroes of our Purim story. And then, just as we were starting to draw breath, we found ourselves turfed out of our home!

Our handsome *qasr* was one of the first buildings requisitioned by the British, who pinpointed it as particularly suitable for their needs because of its riverside location. It meant that they could unload their equipment directly from the water, using boats as transport—roads were mostly still unpaved and pitch black at night. They intended to create a military school there, and as they began to transform it, we had to move out, back to the city, where we took rented accommodation.

COURTESY OF THE IMPERIAL WAR MUSEUM (IWM Q24168)

Victorious Anglo-Indian forces entering the city, 1917

From the grandeur of the palace we now found ourselves in a modest house in the Kutchet el-Nasaara district, the mainly Christian quarter (Nasaara means "Nazareth") off Rashid Street, the principal street or boulevard. It was where Baba's parents had their big house, after moving from Hennouni, but in contrast, ours was sandwiched in a narrow lane bustling with tradespeople and vendors trying to sell all manner of things. I never tired of looking down from the first-floor window and watching the scene below: the cobbler producing an endless stream of nails from his mouth as he hammered them into shoes; the ice-cream seller, *abul booz donderma,* shouting how refreshing his ices were; and *abul shaadi,* the man with a monkey playing a miniature tambourine and acting the coquette, pretending to be a bride lying down on her bed. We all threw money to the monkey, which he collected in his cap and gave to his master.

The milkmaid came by with her cow and milked it for us on our doorstep just as before in Hennouni. A nice homely touch, but it only served to remind us that, as the country had been going forward, we had gone backwards after leaving our wonderful *qasr* and our own cows.

Well, we accepted our lot philosophically in our temporary lodging, and with Baba now safely home, things were starting to look up. In Baghdad, any literate or even semiliterate person could look forward to a career, and as most Jews had some schooling and could at least read and write, their living was virtually secure. They were in great demand as clerks and supervisors in the civil service, and surely Baba must have been tempted to go that way. But he chose instead to return to what he knew best—trading—and reactivated the business he'd had to leave so abruptly.

The British returned our property in 1919, and we were allowed to move back to the *qasr*. Originally, when we had been forced to vacate it and move to the city, the disappointment for us children had been tempered by the discovery in our rented home of a great big box of toys and games that a Turkish family had been obliged to leave behind in their haste to depart. Now my whole family discovered something truly wondrous. We had suddenly been propelled into the twentieth century: the British had wired the *qasr* with electricity—we had light! There was an electric light in every room, plus, we could scarcely believe, electric *punkahs* (ceiling fans) that worked at the press of a button. We were totally entranced by this magic, and as life began to revert to normal, the benefits of the cooling breezes created by the fans made all the previous upheavals seem worthwhile.

But there was still a world of difference between our life then and what we have come to expect today. In winter, when it turned cold, the supposed great comfort of our *qasr* was, in fact, pretty questionable. For example, in the dining room, we had a wood fire, a Persian carpet on the floor, upholstered chairs, and a very large square table that we all used to fit around (something else the British had left behind: it seated twelve). But it was a long walk from the kitchen at the other end of the house. Consequently, and to my father's utter annoyance, no matter how hot the food was when it left the kitchen, it was always cold by the time it reached our table. Hagouli had to dish up the soup in the tureen, walk the length of the house along the open cloister, climb the stairs to the first floor, then take another long walk through the terrace area before finally reaching us. Even with the help of a maid, it took several journeys before all the different dishes were served.

I have already mentioned that, at the house where we had lived previously, our water supply came from the Tigris, hauled up in goatskins. At the *qasr*, it was at last on tap. Nevertheless, our sanitary arrangements were just as primitive as before. Piped sewers were yet to come; we had a septic pit, like everyone else. Toilets were therefore placed as far away from the main rooms as possible. In this respect, ours was no different from all the other homes in Baghdad. Our toilets were completely detached from the main building, but we did have two and they were housed in the area beside the laundry room and fuel room. It was always a problem if you wanted to go at night, worse still on a winter's night. When we eventually got proper plumbing, we had several built, as if to make up for past deprivation: one on the ground floor, two on the first floor, and one on the roof, as well as the staff toilet in the garden by the kitchen.

Soon after we moved back to the *qasr*, one late summer's evening as darkness was falling and we were all assembled around the golden tea samovar placed in the centre of the big table, we heard a sudden scream of distress—so loud that it could have been coming from next door. But there was no next door; we were miles from anybody, and that fact made this screech even more disturbing. "Yaboo-ooo-ooo! Yaboo-ooo-ooo-ooo!" it went. It came again, this time accompanied by a cacophony of shouts and banging metal.

We rushed to the terrace to see what was happening. In the light of oil lamps we could see that hundreds of people had gathered on the riverbank, the women carrying their belongings bundled inside their *'abaayas*. Everyone was barefoot and carried pots and pans, plus sticks, buckets, tins, skewers, and huge metal ladles to beat out a really tremendous din. Villagers seemed to be gravitating to the river's edge from all over the area—fathers, mothers, brothers, sisters, uncles, aunts, grandparents, and even babies—shouting alarmingly or singing out of tune, a rhyming verse that we couldn't quite catch at first.

Then we got it. The verse was a threat to the wicked whale ("Ya hoota ya mal'oona!") that had jumped out of the river and swallowed the moon in one gulp!

At the sound of the word *moon,* we looked up. Sure enough, there it was, suspended as usual over the city. But then we heard the next verse: the moon was bleeding! It was true—it had taken on a reddish tinge. The song went on: "If you don't release our beloved moon, we will break your eardrums with our noise!" And the caterwauling and banging and beating started again, if anything even more intense and penetrating.

We covered our ears. It took them a good hour to convince the whale to get sick, throw up, and release the moon from its stomach. After it was restored to its normal bright self, flooding the beach scene with moonlight, the applause and sounds of joy went on until midnight. "La-la-la-la-la-la-la-la-la-la-la-la-la-la!" went the ululations (*halaahil*), with these simple people congratulating themselves on their achievement and hard work.

Baba explained everything to us: on this occasion, it had been an eclipse. But this strange ritual would be repeated whenever the full moon appeared reddish, taking in the dying rays of the sun at nightfall as it sank over the hot desert.

We had been back at our *qasr* only a couple of years when King Faisal gained the throne and decided that he needed a *qasr* of his own. We were given to understand that he rather fancied ours—it was not for sale!—and that he would be visiting to have a look. Baba thought about it but decided that he liked his *qasr* too much to move out again. To avoid giving offence, he made sure that he was out of the house at the appointed time.

We children were all at school except for Regina and Marcelle, the toddler, when His Majesty and the royal entourage arrived, their carriages coming up the drive from the river. It was left to Djassem, our gardener, to welcome them. Nana did not make an appearance because she would have had to wear an *'abaaya;* Regina did not show her face because it was not seemly for a pretty young lady to meet men; so the only family member they met was the youngest, Marcelle, a lovely little girl, all ringlets and mischief. The king really took to her. He picked her up and gave her a kiss on the cheek.

We never heard another royal word about our *qasr,* but a couple of years later I had a chance to see His Majesty myself. He visited our

*King Faisal and
regal pet in his
palace courtyard*

school to impress upon us that he considered the Jews as friends,
good and loyal subjects. By then he had found the *qasr* he had been
looking for: Umm Habib Palace, an old Abbasid house on the banks
of the river. However, when the royal residence was flooded in 1926,
the king had to move temporarily to the house of Menahem Daniel, Baba's friend, a prominent Jewish merchant.

Our *qasr* was at its busiest at Pessah (Passover), the most difficult
of all our festivities to observe properly in terms of preparations. Not
a speck of flour or crumb of normal everyday bread, pastry, or any
other product that contains flour can remain in the house. To carry
this decree to its natural conclusion, the only way to be absolutely
sure is to clean with meticulous care every single room, each and
every cupboard and drawer, every nook and cranny. In our house,
and in every other Jewish home in Baghdad, this amounted to a
spring clean of gigantic proportions. Every room was completely

emptied, washed, and scrubbed; even the ceilings were given a brush with a branch from a palm tree. Then all the cupboards, drawers, and boxes, even those in remote parts of the house, were cleaned and checked. We called it *ta'aziil 'iid leftiigh,* "sorting for Pessah." Once a room was cleaned, it was out of bounds to us children in case we forgetfully munched on bread or a biscuit.

Pessah is the celebration of our people's departure from Egypt, led by Moses (Moshe Rabenu). For a long time, Moses begged Pharaoh to let his people return to Israel, but as the Israelites were useful slaves and Pharaoh was fond of Moses, he could not bring himself to agree. To persuade him otherwise, the Lord visited the ten plagues upon him and all the Egyptians. Finally, after the terrible tenth and last plague, when all Egyptian firstborn sons were killed, Pharaoh agreed to let the Israelites go. Worried that he might change his mind yet again, they left with their families in such a hurry that they took as *zewwada*—provisions for the long journey—bread they had grabbed from the oven without giving the dough time to rise. In memory of their escape, we celebrate their departure to this day by eating unleavened bread (*massa*), just as they had to do, for one whole week.

As it happened, Pharaoh did indeed change his mind, and with his mighty army he chased after Moses and all the Jews to turn them back. They were already at the Red Sea with no means of getting across, effectively trapped, when the Lord showed His hand again, splitting the sea asunder so that the Israelites could cross to the other side, walking along the seabed. When Pharaoh tried to follow, the sea came together again; many of the Egyptians were drowned and the rest turned back.

When I was just a child, you could not buy kosher *massa* for Pessah. Every household had to prepare its own, enough to keep going for a week. Our family was large, we also had some Jewish staff, and we could certainly expect a lot of friends to drop in, which meant we had to prepare a huge amount of bread, right from scratch. So, in one of the cleaned rooms, *takhta* (low stools) were arranged all around an immense circular tray, more than a yard in diameter, for those who wanted to help clean the *shmoura* (wheat). About twenty pounds of wheat at a time was poured onto the tray to be picked clean, handful by handful, to ensure that it contained no foreign bodies or seeds from different plants and so was kosher for Pessah.

It was checked carefully three times so that there would not be the slightest doubt that the wheat was pure. It took a week to clean enough for our needs, but it was enjoyable, as everyone helped, daughters and domestics, cousins and aunts, and even neighbours on a reciprocal basis, telling stories, laughing, teasing, and joking. (As if all this trouble were not enough, some of the most religious in the community went so far as to ensure that the wheat came from a particular field.) Only then could the wheat be taken to be ground into flour at the mill.

When Baba was a child, living in the big family house in Hennouni, he would make his grandfather Hayim promise to wake him as soon as he rose at about four in the morning so that they could go to the mill together to grind the wheat for the *massa*. A porter from the neighbourhood would come at the appointed time to carry the wheat, and a servant would also accompany them, leading the way with a *fanoos* (lantern). Being so early at the mill meant that they were the first that day to use the equipment, which had been specially cleaned for Pessah. As Hayim was a rabbi, it was even more important to be sure that his *massa* was 100 per cent kosher.

Baba was excited to be allowed outside the house so early in the morning. It made him feel important, particularly if he came across any of his friends. By five in the morning, the streets were as crowded as during the daytime. It was festival time in the Jewish quarter and everybody was rushing about shopping and making preparations—a ritual that nobody dared (or wished) to miss. The whole neighbourhood would throb with activity, and even the Muslims would get in on the act, doubling their prices for goods and services—and getting them.

The mill was much the same as the ones used throughout history, the classic biblical kind you still see in Egyptian, Greek, and Roman ruins. It consisted of two massive round stones placed one on top of another, the grain to be ground being passed slowly through a hole in the centre of the top one. Attached to this stone was a heavy pole, the other end of which was attached to a poor, harnessed, and blindfolded donkey. Baba loved seeing the donkey going round and round, but mostly he looked forward to getting a ride on it. It would start its endless walk, watched by the miller with a stick in his hand, and whenever its spirits flagged, its master would give it a little prod, underscoring his encouragement with the cry, "Diikh!

Diikh!" The ground wheat, now flour, would fall to the floor from where it was gathered up and be put back into its original sacks.

They used to tell a story about a mill donkey that was getting old and slow. His master, Shemwel, decided the time had come to sell it; a Muslim, Mahmoud, bought it. However, after a couple of days the donkey lay down and refused to budge. Annoyed, when he finally managed to get the animal moving again, Mahmoud determined to return it to Shemwel and demand his money back.

Shemwel saw them coming and knew what the problem was. He took one look at the donkey and fell about its neck, caressing it like a long-lost loved one. "Oh my poor friend!" he said. "What have they done to you?" He looked at Mahmoud accusingly. "We used to love this donkey. Why have you been cruel to him? He has been good to us these many years—almost one of the family—and we never had cause to complain."

Mahmoud described the donkey's stubbornness and laziness.

"But he is a sabbatical donkey! On the Shebbath he rests, like us! If you made him work on the Shebbath, obviously he would become obstinate. I do think you had better give him back to me."

When Mahmoud saw that Shemwel genuinely seemed to love his donkey and wanted him back, he was confused. "I am so sorry," he said to Shemwel. "I had not realised he was a sabbatical donkey, and I now have a guilty conscience because I made him work on his day of rest. I must be allowed to keep him and make it up to him. I promise to take great care of him in order to clear my conscience for making him work on the Shebbath!"

The other story I liked, which also had to do with grinding wheat for flour, was more of a domestic drama. Quite apart from the big mill I just described, every household had a smaller version of its own. This worked on exactly the same lines as the large one, but rather than being driven by a donkey, it was powered by hand crank and milled grains a handful at a time. This was heavy work, and most housewives were happy for 'Amsha, an elderly Arab widow, to come and do the job for them. She went from house to house, arriving in the evening and leaving at daybreak, having worked all night so as not to get in anyone's way. Nobody ever knew what she did with her days.

Well, in one such house lived a pretty young woman, Yasmina, with her husband and her six-year-old son Hassan. Every morning a *laala* (a man who would chaperone children to school) would go along the street collecting all the children, including young Hassan. And every morning, this *laala*'s passion for Yasmina grew as he tried to catch her eye. One day, he slyly said to Hassan on the way home: "When you get home, Hassan, tell your mother that you have a message from the *laala*, and that it is "ahem!" He hoped Yasmina would understand.

The next day, to his great joy, it appeared that Yasmina did indeed seem to understand, for Hassan said, "*Laala*, Mother said, 'Ahem! Ahem! Thursday, seven-thirty.'"

The *laala* could not believe his good fortune. When he arrived at the appointed time, there on the veranda, in a gentle breeze, was a lovely table laid out with *mazza* (a selection of appetisers) and Yasmina standing there, looking lovelier than ever in a flowery *bournous* (gown). His happiness was complete when he learnt that Hassan was already in bed. Here was his big chance.

Hardly had they settled down when three knocks could be heard at the door. "Ya Allah!" exclaimed Yasmina. "It's my husband! What shall we do? He is a big man and he is sure to kill you. It is best if you disguise yourself. Here, wear 'Amsha's *'abaaya* and sit in the kitchen and grind the wheat." And as she talked, she pushed the *laala* into the kitchen where everything had been prepared, not giving him a chance to argue. Then she opened the door to her husband.

"What can I hear?" he said after a while. "Is 'Amsha here tonight? But this is Thursday, it is not her night."

"It *is* 'Amsha. She is in great demand at the moment and tonight was the only one she could mill for us," said Yasmina.

Inside the kitchen, the *laala* continued grinding the wheat furiously, handful by handful, not daring to stop for fear of attracting attention. No doubt, too, he was grinding his teeth while he listened to Yasmina's husband eating and laughing instead of him. By midnight, tired and fed up, he was perspiring profusely in the woollen *'abaaya* he was wearing on top of his own *deshdaasha*, but he had finished grinding the whole bag of wheat. It was only then that Yasmina let "'Amsha" out and the *laala* fled home, hungry, thirsty, and angry.

One morning about a week later, Hassan said to the *laala* on the way to school: "*Laala*, my mother said, 'Thursday, seven-thirty. Ahem! Ahem!'"

"You little rascal," said the *laala*. "You must have finished your flour."

Soon after we moved back to the *qasr*, the situation improved dramatically. First, the religious authorities (Rabbanut) made flour available that was certified kosher for Pessah; and second, the mills became mechanised. Even then, it took years to convince everyone to buy the ready-made flour and not to grind it in the stone mills themselves.

With ready-to-bake flour, things became so much easier. Nana would take charge of the operation like a conductor. We set ourselves up in the shade in the open space outside the kitchen, and it being late spring, the air was heavy with the heady scent of orange blossom. We all gave a hand. Hagouli would do the kneading first, only about two pounds at a time, working quickly using only flour and water—no salt, no fat, no yeast, and no spices. We took this dough from him as soon as it was done so that it did not get a chance to rise. One of us rolled it into a long rope about an inch in diameter. Another cut the rope into one-inch bits, and yet another kneaded these into small circles. These were then stretched a little, ready for Nana. Sitting on her low *takhta* with her busy rolling pin, she meticulously rolled out the circles until each was paper thin and the size of a pizza today. Then one of us quickly whipped it off the table and handed it to Zahra, the baker.

Zahra's job was to take care of the clay *tannoor* oven. She lit a fire at the bottom and, once it was hot, wiped the inside with a wet cloth to remove the smoky deposit before sticking the rolled-out dough onto the inner wall. She had to be extremely vigilant and quick, as the thin dough circles browned fast. The finished items were called *jeghaadeq*—pronounced just like the sound they made when you bit into them: "jraduck!"—or, at Pessah, *massa*. Still hot, they were arranged in a *zembiil*—a deep basket made of woven palm leaves—to cool off. The whole production line worked like clockwork, with everyone knowing his or her job. When one *zembiil* was full, it was taken to be stored in the specially cleaned room along with all the other *kasher lil-Pessah* food. But we children were often distracted from our tasks, running around, picking fruit, going to look at the cows or the chickens—so much to do and no time to get bored.

Before every Pessah, Zahra spent a week building us a brand-new *tannoor*: bell shaped, about three feet high, and with walls an inch thick. It took her a week. She started by carefully arranging a couple of layers of clay that served as a base. This was allowed to dry over-

night, and the following day she added three more layers, each
about an inch high, to make the wall. This dried overnight, then
four more rows would be added the following day, and so on. This
way it did not collapse. When the oven was complete and dry, it was
carefully placed outdoors in the recess between the kitchen wall,
the washroom, and the garden fence, under a tin roof to protect it
from any rain.

At breakfast on the eve of Pessah, we ate normal bread for the
last time. Baba waited for everyone to finish, and then, with a small
blessing, he lit a fire in the stove to burn any that was left over; after
that, all food that was not kosher for Pessah had to be disposed of.
No bread, biscuit, or wheat product was allowed anywhere inside
the house. Together with all the provisions from our pantry, we put
away all our everyday plates, cutlery, pots, and pans in a small storeroom. This we locked and gave the key to Djassem, as if the room
and its contents belonged to him. It was called the *hamess* room.
But even this room was cleaned up. And, at the end of Pessah, we
bought the key and the contents back from Djassem for a small
amount of money. He could have charged much more, for we had
to get it back at any price.

All our *kasher lil-Pessah* vessels were stored in another small room
called a *kabeshkaan,* which you could only reach by climbing a lad-
der, for it was like a cabin fixed to the wall above the *tarma* balcony.
It was purposely kept inaccessible so that everything would remain
clean until the next Pessah, but we children were always curious to
see what was in there and fought for our turn to climb up that lad-
der. (Some everyday saucepans could be used during Pessah, but
only if you first washed them clean, then dipped them in boiling
water with a pinch of salt and some pebbles—a procedure called
'aghala.)

It was all thrilling to us children. We also greatly looked forward
to the long evening celebrations—at school for the previous six
weeks or so since Purim, we had been practising the singing and
readings for an hour every day. Each chapter of Scripture was sung
first in Hebrew (taught to us by an elderly rabbi), then in Arabic,
each to a different tune. The stories they told sounded like fun,
and we would tease anyone who made the slightest mistake after
all these efforts. On Pessah nights when we were still living in Hennouni, you could hear voices in the neighbourhood and guess how

far into the Scripture those around us had read. It was like a badge of honour if you could boast to your friends that you were still at table at midnight.

On the last day of Pessah, it was traditional to eat a lot of dairy produce and *halba,* a special green bean. Finally, we would take a small branch of green *zdab,* a variety of myrtle, and gently touch one another other with it, wishing each a "green year"—I'm not sure why. Of course, we children took the opportunity to hit each other and run away.

Baghdad seemed so wonderful to me then. Originally there had been only one main road: Rashid Street, named after the legendary caliph of Scheherazade's times, Harun al-Rashid. Everyone knew it simply as the Jaadda, or "road." It was unpaved—dusty in summer and muddy in winter—and as wide as three *'arabaana* (horse-drawn carriages). It ran parallel to the Tigris for almost two miles, from southeast to northwest—that is, from Baab el-Shargi to Baab el-Mu'Adham, where the heart of the city and the *souq* were. That was called the Meedan, and most Muslims lived around there. Several short side streets led to the boat and *guffa* stations on the river and to the area where you could buy fresh fish.

Sayyed Sultan 'Ali Street, where we would board the boat to go home after school, was next to the old bridge which linked the city on the left bank to the underdeveloped right bank. It was a crude affair, consisting of a long row of skiffs that rocked with the river's flow. They were tied together, but a passage could be opened in the middle so that larger boats could pass when necessary.

Something like it had been in this position, spanning four hundred yards of river, for more than five hundred years: there is a lovely illustration of it by a fifteenth-century Persian artist. Few people ventured to the right bank, Dhaak el-Sob—literally, "the other bank"—where there were just some scattered *qasrs* and nomadic tents lived in by farmers and gardeners who sent their produce to market by boat or *guffa.* Often buyers from the *souq* made the trek there, hoping to haggle the price down. In summer, the farmers set up reed huts by the river, where they could enjoy a short holiday with their families. They were known for their generous hospitality.

From Baab el-Mu'Adham, there was a tramway that I would love
to have ridden. The horse-drawn double-decker carried Muslims
the two and a half miles to their mosque at Kadhimain.

Halfway between the two Baabs (a *baab* is a door or gate) was
Kutchet el-Nasaara, where, despite its name meaning the "Christian
Lane," many of our people lived, as we did briefly after the British took Baghdad. Hennouni was to the north, and surrounding it
were poorer areas such as Sheikh Sehaq, where both the Jewish and
Muslim destitute and dispossessed lived and where the better-off
Jewish community would pour out their charity. For example, when
someone recovered from an illness, it was customary for the happy,
healthy family immediately to arrange a luncheon for Sheikh Sehaq residents. In this quarter was a shrine to the wise rabbi Sheikh
Ishaq, who is venerated even by the Muslims (who claim he was
the treasurer of Muhammad's cousin) for his wisdom in religious
matters and so given the respectful title of *sheikh*. There was an

COURTESY OF THE BRITISH LIBRARY

FAR LEFT. *The bridge of skiffs, 1920*

NEAR LEFT. *The bridge of skiffs as depicted in a Persian miniature from 1458*

even more overpopulated and poorer quarter called Taht el-Takya where the houses had no locks, not even on the front doors, just simple wooden bolts that made the doors only slightly more difficult to push open.

But no matter how poor people were, there was always someone worse off, and equally there was always someone who coveted what little one had. This gave rise to plenty of stories. One in particular I remember concerned Ahmed and 'Aysha, a married couple who had been the victims of several burglaries. The next time the thief entered, though, they were ready. As he crept into the house thinking he was unobserved, 'Aysha asked her husband in a loud voice: "Where did you finally hide the money?"

A horse-drawn double-decker tram of the period

MATSON PHOTOGRAPH COLLECTION, LIBRARY OF CONGRESS

"Never you mind," he replied. "This time no one will find it. It's in the crack in the wall behind the lavatory. No one could possibly guess it's there."

What an easy job this is going to be, thought the intruder as he made his way to the latrine, a stinking hole in the ground behind the house. Ahmed and 'Aysha watched him go. Just in front of the lavatory was a dry well where they had prepared a trap by leaving it only loosely covered. Of course, the thief fell in and couldn't get out—and when Ahmed and 'Aysha invited everyone to come around and peer down at their captive, they became the toast of the neighbourhood.

Another story I liked involved a Jew, Eliyahou. Making his way home through the narrow alleyways, he was confronted by two Muslim thugs who stripped him of all his possessions except his gold ring, which was too tight to remove.

"Count your blessings," huffed one of the assailants, pointing to the sky. "We fear Allah, otherwise we would cut off your finger to get it."

"Blessed be Allah that you fear him!" replied Eliyahou. "The money you took was my month's wages to feed my family. If you truly feared him, you would hand it back." And, shamefaced, his two attackers returned everything.

Eliyahou felt relieved, but the experience had unsettled him. Worried about getting home, he said: "Would you mind escorting me down the road to the main street in case I meet a thug who does not fear Allah?" And so they did, knowing that there was always a street gang waiting for the next easy victim.

I remember that all the buildings lining Rashid Street were uniformly residential and two storeys high. Some people converted a ground-floor room into a shop or store, but there were no display windows, just the open front. There were no grocery shops, certainly no restaurants, and initially, only one pharmacy—Gourgi el-Azachi (Gourgi the Pharmacist)—though later he had competition from an Armenian called Karikor. Everybody locked their shops firmly at night with a double lock, using keys that weighed a pound or more and measured about nine inches. Two hands were needed to lock or unlock these doors. This type of security was necessary as insurance was nonexistent. In 1924, everyone was left speechless on

Rashid Street in 1928, with traffic driving on the left, British style

COURTESY OF THE SCRIBE

hearing that an insurance claim for a shattered pair of spectacles, which had been broken accidentally, had been paid in full.

In those days, our medical knowledge was not up to date, and medicines and other pharmaceuticals were quite basic. We had few doctors, and not only were they unqualified but they were proud to tell you so. Some 90 per cent of the population consulted a *wassaf*—a potion seller or quack—before trying to find a "real" doctor and paying him a fee, although that was modest by today's standards. A consultation cost only four annas, tuppence in old British money (equivalent to eighty pence today), but an English doctor could command two rupees (three shillings, or six pounds today) at his clinic and five rupees (eight shillings, or fifteen pounds today) for a home visit. The *wassaf* would give you a concoction we called *wassfa* (prescription). I can't remember what was in it, but most of the time it worked, by pure coincidence I'm sure.

In the circumstances, it was not surprising that the cures most people chose were homemade, and as you might suspect, we all had our own favourite remedies. Anyone with bronchial problems or chest colds would have their chest rubbed with heated oil, and we all kept supplies of distilled orange-blossom water for stomach upsets. For sore throats, we relied on a mixture of hot lemon juice and honey, just like today, and homemade vinegar was considered the best antiseptic. We also used it to help with digestion—ginger, too. For scorpion or snake bites, or for any skin problem, we would cut a fleshy cactus stem and use the gel that oozed out as an antidote. Most of the spices we used in the kitchen had known healing properties: turmeric, cardamom, pepper, saffron, nutmeg, cumin, cloves, and cinnamon. Other unusual remedies were infusions using the tender leaves of the Seville orange tree to help the digestion, dried violet flowers to lower a temperature, and dried powdered limes to cure a sore throat. But, first, if we had an ache or pain we would keep the sore area warm by wrapping it with a woollen bandage or scarf. Surprisingly, it often helped.

If a child fell sick or had a temperature, a mother would turn to one of two tried and tested home brews: either goat's milk (some went so far as to keep a goat, just in case) or a sugared infusion of

dried berries and violet flowers. If she suspected the child's illness
was due to the evil eye, she would dig a hole in the ground outside
the house by the doorstep, pour a glass of water in it, then massage
the child's hands, feet, forehead, and sometimes the whole body
with the mud from the hole. As a last resort, she would call on the
great Muslim healer Mullah Juwad, whose remedy was supposed
to be infallible. He lived in the Karkh across the river by the old
bridge, a long way from the Jewish quarter—say, forty minutes or
more by *'arabaana*. Mullah Juwad would read a sentence from the
Qur'an, blow on the face of the child, and write a blessing from Allah on a piece of paper that he would fold and give to the mother
to sew on the child's pillow, like a talisman. He would also give her
another seven bits of folded paper, one for each day of the week,
which she had to soak in water that the child would then have to
drink. There was no fixed price; you paid what you could. Many
were so grateful that they went back to give him presents.

For adults, too, there was one last, desperate course of action if
other potions failed: to seek the Light of God. That really was the
name—Noor-Allah—of one of our best-known doctors, who was re-
puted to have an infallible cure for everything. In reality, I believe
he only ever prescribed one of two medicines: either a mild mixture of coloured barley water or a powerful laxative—castor oil (his
preferred solution in 90 per cent of cases).

Jokes used to circulate about Dr. Noor-Allah, all probably based
on truth. For example, one day as he was sitting puffing on his *nargiila* (hubble-bubble), he noticed Selim standing nearby.

"How is your father today, Selim?" he asked.

"God rest his soul, he passed away last night," replied Selim.

"Did you at least give him the medicine I prescribed before he
went?"

"Yes, I did."

"That was very lucky," said the doctor, breathing a sigh of relief.
"God only knows what would have happened if he hadn't taken it."

Rashid Street was a wonderful stage. Old women could be seen
sitting by large pots of long string beans (*lubia*) boiling in water,
selling chunks of dry bread and the right to dip them into the tasty

liquid. Each piece was tied to a differently coloured thread, and after the bread had soaked up enough juice, she would ask: "Khei-tak?" ("Your thread?"—meaning, "Which colour is it?") Not unlike the idea of fondue today.

Further down the kerbside, a man would sit, singing alongside a pot of boiling water into which he'd put some sheep's tripe and head bones. Like the bean lady, he was selling the right to dunk bread into his so-called excellent *tashrib* (broth) and the same colour code applied. A quick wit, he would shout: "As I was singing to the *tashrib*, 'Whoever tastes you will always return!'" Any complaints were met with a quick rebuff: "Gulp it down and praise your Allah!" he would say. And if, as was often the case, someone found a piece of rag instead of tripe, he would challenge the customer with: "What did you expect, a silk handkerchief?"

Which leads me to ask: what is it that rich people in Baghdad blow tidily into their clean handkerchiefs and the poor dispose of in the middle of the street? In the pocket of their *zboon*, a belted cotton gown, Muslim men carried a large, red, printed handkerchief—not for the usual purpose of blowing their nose, for they had a certain way of doing that deftly, directly into the street, without a mess. With its corners tied together, the handkerchief was used as a bag to carry home any fruit or vegetables they purchased. There was no wrapping paper at all. The main shopping would go into a *zembiil* basket. Jewish men carried either a white or a striped hankie or possibly even two: one for shopping and one for nose blowing.

Occasionally on a wide corner you would see a man sitting on the pavement, fanning a charcoal stove, selling kebabs. Once you caught a whiff of the marvellous smell you couldn't help but feel a craving. Barbers set up shop on the same pavement, offering the same range of interesting services—shaves, haircuts, dental extractions, boil lancings—that we were used to seeing in the alleys of Hennouni. Again, there was no privacy.

The jostling pavements were chockablock with pedestrians trying to scurry past street sellers carrying their wares in baskets on their heads or on the backs of donkeys, or dodging people with old-fashioned iron scales for weighing their produce with rocks as I've said before. With lovely voices, they sang the virtues of their fresh radishes, their lotus berries, or their *gargaree* (hard-candy sweets), saying all kinds of things to draw attention to the wonder-

*A roadside
kebab seller*

MATSON PHOTOGRAPH COLLECTION, LIBRARY OF CONGRESS

ful nature of their food. "Sell your mother and buy some!" they
would cry. "Come and buy my sweets like honey!" "The pieces are
big—my master was drunk when he cut them!" "Bee'a el-Ummak
wu-shtaree!" "Umm el-'asal!" "Stayee sakran u qassa!"

Not everyone sold products at rock-bottom prices. There were
one or two more upmarket places where better-quality fare could be
procured at correspondingly higher rates, so you had to give your
"shopper" strict instructions about whom to patronise. Most people
had a trusted shopper, a *meswaqchi,* who came every morning to take
your order (ours was called Aboudi), or the *abul beit* (head of the
household) would do the honours and employ a *hammaal* (porter)
to run the purchases home.

In Baab el-Agha, just by the old bridge, a self-important green-
grocer stationed himself in his smart green *'amaama* (a turban worn

Unloading
watermelons

only by the descendants of the prophet Muhammad). He liked to shine his apples, oranges, and watermelons to make them look even more appetising in the heat of the day, knowing that because of his good location only richer customers would come his way. He would shout out his message: "Ala al-satchiin! Ala al-satchiin!"—literally, "by the knife!" meaning that he was prepared to cut a small triangular window in a watermelon for potential customers to see its quality. There is no precise method of knowing when a watermelon is ripe, particularly early in the season when growers are in a hurry to get their produce to market to take advantage of high prices and may pick them too soon. Pink watermelon flesh is likely to be insipid; what you are looking for is a deep red colour—and, clearly, by accepting the offer to peek into the heart of the watermelon, a buyer was honour bound to buy it if it was red, just as he could decline a pink one.

On one particular morning, the vendor had a possible buyer, so, true to his word, he cut out a triangle from the biggest melon in his pile—and, to his dismay, saw that it was barely pink. This could mean the total loss of a large, early-season watermelon. The customer lifted his eyebrows to signify "no, thanks." The seller, who was a big and burly man, quickly replaced the triangle in the melon to make it look whole again. Holding it out to the customer and smiling fiercely, he whispered: "You had better pay up, or this very knife will open a little window in your heart!" And with that he turned back to the street and began again: "Ala al-satchiin! Ala al-satchiin!"

Going towards the southeast, by the time you reached Baab el-Shargi—the "East Gate"—houses were few and far between. This was the site of the smelly town refuse tip until around 1930, when it was covered over and replaced by Park el-Sadoon, the first playground with swings for children and benches for the grown-ups. You had reached the city limits, but the large open spaces with orchards and market gardens were soon to be developed. At this point, Rashid Street divided. If you went to the left, it would lead you to Karrada, Sab'e Qessoor, and Zweeya, winding its way along dusty, unmarked paths used by donkeys, mules, horses, and shepherds. On the way were a few scattered tents, reed huts, and mud-brick nomadic homes. Coach drivers—the *'arabanchis*—always grumbled and swore when they took us along here to get to our *qasr*. The state of the road was certainly not doing their coachwork any good, and it did not improve until some time after the war.

If you took the road to the right, you would be on a straight street called the Saddah (now Abu Nuwas Street) that followed the riverside, lined with *qasrs* overlooking the water. It was so narrow that just about one *'arabaana* could go through at a time, with no room to turn around. So the driver had to go another mile before he could return on the back street. Not surprisingly, the Saddah was used mostly for walking. People would go there for their promenades, relaxing during their leisure time or on Saturdays and holidays. It was common to spend a whole day there, picnicking with family and friends to the accompaniment of music, which played an important part in our lives. In fact, during the first half of the twentieth century, Jews were virtually the only instrumental players in Iraq, and we had our own brand of music, called *maqaam,* while troupes of female musicians—the *deqqaaqat*—sang and played tambourines at wedding parties for tips. When Iraq Radio started broadcasting in 1936, the music was always live; only one of its musicians was Muslim, and nearly all of the members of the Baghdad Symphony Orchestra were Jewish. This had consequences: since no music could possibly be broadcast on Yom Kippur and Tish'a-Bab, that meant absolutely no music on Iraq Radio then.

Our *qasr* was about two miles along the Saddah, and in time, many of our acquaintances built similar residences there, right up to Sab'e Qessoor, where my future husband lived, some distance away. Then they even developed further, right up to Zweeya where the Tigris becomes Shatt Grara, forming a large curve that curls around Karrada. Some of our good friends built a huge *qasr* at Shatt Grara. The children went to our school, so we often visited each other. But because transportation to school was so awkward, they used their *qasr* only as their weekend country residence and spent the rest of the week in Baghdad itself.

Almost all the residents on the riverside were from our community; they moved there gradually after World War I to avoid the ravages of the floods. This may sound contradictory, but I suppose the fact that our district was underpopulated and the buildings were substantial gave all of us a feeling of security lacking in the overcrowded parts of the city. Nowhere was immune from risk, the floods of the Tigris being notoriously violent, sometimes costing many lives and causing other terrible effects such as the cholera epidemic that had persuaded Baba to build the *qasr* in the first place.

Baghdad had no river defence system. Most efforts to control the waters in the early days were primarily concerned with irrigation, the most impressive improvement being the construction of the Hindiya Barrage, started in 1914 and completed in the early 1920s with the help of the British—but that involved diverting the other great river of Iraq, the Euphrates. Every spring from March to May the melting snow rushed from Turkey's and Iraq's northern mountains, swelling the twin rivers and accounting for more than half their annual flow. It gnawed away at the land, and the reasonably wide pathway between the river and the *qasr* that Baba had built became narrower. An attempt was made to stop this by embedding some firewood bundles in the riverside. It was only after the war, when we reoccupied the *qasr,* that a reinforced concrete dyke was created, with a concrete staircase of about twenty-five steps to give access to the water. From that time on, the path was protected.

The road to my school was always quite an adventure. Leaving Rashid Street, there was a good fifteen-minute walk through a labyrinth of small narrow lanes before arriving at the Shorjah. This was—and, for all I know, still is—a covered market area, full of all sorts of scents of fresh fruit, vegetables, spices, and herbs. There was also an enormous number of flies that you were always having to bat away. The market was stiff with people going about their business, that of the villains and rogues being to pinch bottoms with impunity in the crush. It was impossible to escape their attention.

Beyond the Shorjah the road forked, with one prong leading to the 'Alaawi, the wholesale market for commodities, and the other to the boys' school and the Roundabout. This was where all the stationery and haberdashery shops were located, also vendors sitting on the ground selling homemade 'alootcha (a sticky sweet) and semsemiyee (caramelised sesame seed). One day my Uncle Moshi, a gambling man, stopped at the 'alootcha man's pitch, where he had two big trays on display. Fancying a piece and seeing that the vendor was swishing the flies off his confectionery, he made him a wager: he would give the vendor twenty rupees if the next fly landed on the left-hand tray, but if it landed on the right-hand one, he would win both trays. The vendor, seeing an opportunity to make much more money than the two trays' worth combined, accepted the bet. A crowd of men and boys soon gathered. The man stopped waving the flies away. And the next one landed . . . on the right-hand tray. Uncle Moshi's joy was complete when he distributed the winnings among the onlookers.

The most popular pitch was that of abul 'ambah (the pickle man) who sold nothing but the snacks we so much enjoyed—the mouthwatering laffa 'amba, a pitta-like bread wrapped around some mango pickle which most of us bought for lunch. Sometimes as a special treat he would dunk the whole wrap in his pickle bowl for us.

In the same lane, I loved watching the tcheraakh khashab—wood turner—who worked on a kind of lathe making poles for our bannisters, spindles, chair legs, and so on. But best of all, on the right-hand side of the lane as we went to school was the man with the sandouq el-welayaat: a magic lantern (the name literally means a "box of the countries"). It was truly magical. It had a narrow front with a big lens fixed on each of its other three sides. Inside was a scroll, with pictures lit by a lantern. The man turned the scroll and narrated a story about each picture, starting every time with "Shoof 'indak Ya salaam!" ("Look here, what a wonder!"). I can still remember some of them, all to do with the Ottoman days: "Shoof 'indak Ya salaam! This is Istanbul with its towers and castles . . . Here is 'Antar with his beloved 'Abla! This is a German gun . . ." And so on. It was cinema to us.

The boys' school was spacious and airy with a proper playground, and there were French and English teachers from Paris and London. All the pupils dressed in suits and ties like their European coun-

Inside the Shorjah market

terparts. It was a palace compared with the *midraash* opposite, the
elementary school for less-well-off Jewish boys that was subsidised
by our community. Next to the Great Synagogue, which dated from
the fifth century, it had been established to provide free primary
education and a hot lunch for all Jewish boys. Before it was built
in 1833, youngsters had to learn the basics of Judaism and Hebrew
from private teachers, which meant that the poorer ones who could
not pay remained illiterate. Midraash boys were dressed in a *zboon*
and rough calico underpants. They wore shoes or sandals without
socks, invariably hand-me-downs that were mostly too big. Richer
families provided their lunch, which consisted of rice coloured yellow with turmeric and flavoured with sesame oil, fried onion, and
crushed cumin seeds. Classes were enormous, with up to two hundred boys crammed in a dark room with one teacher. They had the
most primitive sanitation arrangements, and as can be imagined,
with such overcrowding, the entire place stank. Even the street outside wasn't immune: it was impossible to walk past without holding
one's nose and even covering one's eyes. The Education Department sent an inspector one day to check if the *midraash* was teaching English. Seeing a stranger, all the boys went silent, staring at

The bustling market scene

him. He stared back. A powerful smell of urine assailed his nostrils. In a hurry now, he turned to the teacher and said, "If you can manage to keep their attention in this way, then you surely deserve to pass muster." And he left, as fast as he could. I heard this story from the inspector himself.

Another important boys' school near the centre of the city, Madrassat Shamash, was founded in 1926 by a rich relative of my future husband as a thanksgiving for being saved when the ship he was sailing on sank in the Mediterranean.

Opposite the Great Synagogue, where the road widened, came the imposing girls' school. This was my school. A semicircle of shiny metallic characters formed an inscription above the big double gates: Alliance Israélite Universelle. To reach the entrance, you had to go through these gates and onto the paved path, lined on each side by a strip of lawn around which were large terra-cotta flowerpots and hedges. This little garden was the pride and joy of the *hajji* (Muslim pilgrim) who looked after it. We called him "the Afghani," a big, burly man armed with a whip that he cracked to shoo away undesirables. He lived in the small caretaker's apartment to the right of the gate, where he placed a pottery water jug that was cooled by the night air and so kept its contents fresh all day, quite an attraction when the only alternative was lukewarm tapwater and the ambient temperature was a scorching one hundred degrees Fahrenheit in the shade. Rich girls paid him for the pleasure of having a cold drink from his jug.

Past the Alliance was Hennouni, where we had lived before the move to the *qasr*. This was where all the kosher food shops and stalls were and where the entire Jewish community shopped for meat, chicken, fish, and bread. After Hennouni came Sheikh Sehaq and then Abou Siffain (the name literally means "Of the Two Swords"), a disreputable area where the poorest lived, both Muslims and Jews. I would guess at least 90 per cent of them walked around barefooted. Once a year, however, even the most destitute Muslim would invest in a new pair of *yamanee* for Ramadan. This boat-shaped footwear is a cross between a shoe and a slipper, made from sheepskin, never worn with socks, and invariably dyed vivid red. It was chosen not for its comfortable fit but for how loudly it could be made to squeak—

Shoe sellers in the souq

its wearer anxious that all around should know that he was not a barefooted man.

Unfortunately, all footwear has to be discarded at the door of the *jaami'* (mosque) when going in to pray, and it is forbidden to carry it in—the footwear caretaker positioned at the door sees to that. This situation always resulted in the *yamanee* being stolen if they were new. The caretaker obviously had first choice: nobody with new ones ever stood a chance. He had a deal with the cobbler around the corner, to whom he promptly passed the footwear, to be resold to the next poor fool. Second in line for a decent-looking pair of *yamanee* was the villain who had entered the *jaami'* bare-footed in the first place, fully intending to pick up a pair on the way out. Only the oldest and most worn-out *yamanee* were left for the last to come out of the mosque.

There was a story told about one worshipper, Fuad, who worried about losing his new *yamanee*, which he had just bought for the *'iid* (feast). He wrapped them in a piece of paper and made it look like a parcel. At the door, the footwear caretaker, suspecting it might be a new pair of *yamanee* being smuggled into the mosque, asked him what he was carrying.

"The law for the protection of *yamanee*," came the smart reply.

At the mention of "law," the caretaker thought it best to let it go, visualising him to be a government official and himself ending up in prison. So Fuad saved his *yamanee* and wouldn't wear them until the *'iid* began, after the prayers.

On his way home with his parcel under his arm, he suppressed a grin when he thought how he had tricked the caretaker. He also thought how wise he was not to be wearing his *yamanee* at that par-ticular moment in that muddy street because, as everyone knew, getting them wet would lessen the squeak. His head full of these thoughts and unable to see where he was putting his foot, he stepped on a rusty nail and his foot started to bleed. As he sat examining the damage, he whispered a fervent prayer: "How can I praise Allah for guiding me and keeping my *yamanee* intact in the parcel? This rusty nail would have ruined my new *yamanee*. Praise be to Allah! A miracle, to sacrifice me and keep my new *yamanee* safe."

There was also the story of the *sayyed* (dignitary), so smartly dressed in his green *'amaama* turban, his plush, brown, heavy wool *'abaaya* trimmed with gold braiding, and his new *yamanee*, rhythmically squeaking as he strode in the middle of the road. His portly build made him miss the banana skin casually discarded in his path. He slipped and fell heavily on his bottom. A youth saw this mishap and couldn't hold back his laughter. When their eyes met, the youth stopped short and said solicitously: "Did you fall down, *sayyed?*" Gathering all his strength, the *sayyed* pulled himself up and started hitting the youth left and right. "What did you think I was doing, sitting in the mud? Cooling my bottom?"

I enjoyed these stories so much, even though they were ridiculous, as they conjured up the old days of the sultanate. They always started with the phrase "b-iyyaam el Osmali"—"in the days of the Ottomans"—so you had a pretty fair idea of what was coming: they were mostly about gullible people with little education being made to do silly things. The point was to highlight the humble expectations of the period rather than the stupidity of the individual.

High Holy Days

THE SCORCHING SUMMER never seemed to want to end. And right in the middle of it, just when we felt we were on fire, came Tish'a-Bab, the ninth of the month of Av, a three-week period of mourning when, by chance, most of our own tragedies (like Baba being deported) occurred. It was during Tish'a-Bab that Babylonia's King Nebuchadnezzar razed Jerusalem and destroyed Beit Hamiqdash, the Temple that housed the tablets—the original Ten Commandments brought down from Mount Sinai by Moshe Rabenu: Moses.

Some 1,200 years earlier, our patriarch Abraham Abinou had journeyed to Judea in the Promised Land from his home in Ur in Babylonia (Mesopotamia) to found a new nation that, he was convinced, was destined to bring the knowledge of God to the world. In Judea, the migrants became known as Hebrews, from the word 'ebher—"the other side" (of the Euphrates). So when Nebuchadnezzar captured the Jews and brought them back to Mesopotamia as slaves, initially to dredge the irrigation channels of the twin rivers, they were, in a sense, returning home. And so began the period known as the Babylonian captivity.

Now, Moshe Rabenu had warned that the tablets were sacred, that the Almighty would take his revenge on anyone who desecrated them by so much as touching them. So sacred were they that a man had to immerse himself in the *mikve* before handling them. Sure enough, as foretold, Nebuchadnezzar was punished. He went mad and had to live in the forest among the beasts for the next seven years until he came back to his senses and he returned to the throne of Babylonia.

One day the king had a powerful dream about a statue with feet of clay, which no one in his court could interpret for him. Eventually, one of the captives, Daniel, was recommended and sent for. And this is how he interpreted the dream: "The statue is nothing less than the image of your empire. It will collapse under the slightest tremor." And so it happened, for shortly after Nebuchadnezzar heard this, Babylonia, the capital of the empire of Hammurabi, was vanquished by the Assyrians, to be followed throughout its history by many other peoples.

Although Babylonia was their ancestral home, in their hearts our people longed only for Jerusalem. In the sixth century B.C., the prophet Ezekiel, whose shrine still exists in Iraq, restored their spirit—one day, he prophesied, there would be a national rebirth. Meanwhile, over time, the exiles from Judea progressed. From their origins as peasants, settlers, cattle breeders, farmers, and tradesmen, they became merchants, traders, financiers and bankers, and even scientists—the professions familiar in our community today—and set up an important scholarly religious centre. They reputedly constituted the largest Jewish community in the world, and gave us the compilation of laws and tradition known as the Babylonian Talmud.

Babylon is still there, in ruins sixty miles from Baghdad. It was destroyed by all its successive conquerors—Saddam Hussein included, who vainly put his name on its walls—and never recovered. Many of the treasures discovered there by British archaeologists after World War I can be seen in the British Museum. Cuneiform inscriptions first deciphered by them have served as the basis for translating other ancient texts that have given us much information about those times.

I remember visiting the ruins when I was a teenager in 1925, when we all climbed up on the great Lion of Babylon for a photograph. The lion's face was greatly mutilated by soldiers during World War I, as they believed the legend that he was stuffed with gold: the gran-

British soldiers on the Great Lion of Babylon, 1920

ite was hard to break, so they gave up in disgust. Further south, in Ur, Abraham's homeland, we saw the remains of the Tower of Babel that the Hebrews had built when they tried to reach heaven. Some say that this high tower collapsed, still incomplete, because those building it all spoke different dialects and couldn't understand each other. Others say that the Almighty, irritated by their presumption, deliberately made it crash and gave them all different languages so they could never undertake a similar operation again.

Back in Judea, Beit Hamiqdash (the Temple) was carefully rebuilt—only to be demolished again in A.D. 70, this time by the Romans. Once more, a catastrophe occurred during Tish'a-Bab. All that remains of the Temple now is just one side wall on which Cabalist marks can still be discerned. It is known in the West as the Wailing Wall because of all the tears that have been shed over it. We still consider it our holiest shrine, and people make pilgrimages there to pray and leave requests written on tiny bits of paper in the sacred language. These requests are squeezed in between the cracks of the massive rocks that form the wall, with the hope that the wind will suck them up and deliver them directly to heaven.

So, there we were in Tish'a-Bab, roasting in the hottest part of summer during a period whose name was synonymous with bad happenings. If someone was unfortunate or unlucky, we called him or her a Tish'a-Bab, and even if something was going well during Tish'a-Bab, you had the uneasy feeling that it was such an exception, it could not be right. Everyone observed Tish'a-Bab because we were all too superstitious to do otherwise. During Tish'a-Bab, we never wore new clothes. It was forbidden to cut a new dress or buy a new outfit, or make a new deal or buy a new house. You could discuss a new business deal but not conclude it, unless your negotiations had begun before the three-week period. Oh, and you could mend old clothes. But that was about it. If in spite of that you went ahead and things then went wrong, people would wag their finger and say, "We warned you!"

During Tish'a-Bab, we all used to listen with tears streaming down our cheeks to the moving voice of a young girl singer who sang the tragic "Story of Hannah," about a woman who refused to denounce God at the fall of the Temple and, at the mercy of the infidels, had to watch as all of her seven sons were slaughtered in front of her, one by one. It was said that if you were moved enough to shed a tear for Hannah you would have a good year ahead of you without tears or sorrow. "Esmaoo sautie, qualet Hannah we-nzuroo ma jaraa lee . . ."—"Listen to my cry," Hannah said, "and let me tell you what happened to me . . ."

During Tish'a-Bab, mishaps happened in our lifetime, too. Once, some youngsters ignored the superstitious restrictions and decided to go rowing on the river. Only yards from their house, their boat suddenly capsized and they were engulfed in a *ghuwwasa* (whirlpool) and drowned right in front of their parents. A few years later, in almost exactly the same spot, again during Tish'a-Bab, ten men— all family men known to be strong swimmers—drowned when their boat started turning in a circle and disappeared, sinking without a trace, never to be seen again.

During Tish'a-Bab, the sky is endlessly blue. Not a single cloud can be seen to break the monotony. Not even a little puff cloud. There is no wind, no breeze, not a breath of air. The days are the longest, with the sun in full glare, burning and blazing, and nowhere to hide, day after day, night after night. These are the days of the tall, slim, dark, and handsome palm trees reaching for the sky, carrying their fruit with their request firsthand to heaven for maximum heat to ripen their delicious dates. If, by some chance, a suspicion of a hot breeze crept down to fan us humans, the palm trees immediately complained, arching their slim bodies, hair flying in the air, in order to seduce the heavens. Then, obviously beguiled, the ventilator immediately switched off. The date palms loved a blazing furnace, the hotter the better.

For us down below, it was Tish'a-Bab. How enviously we watched the palms' frisky movements, clapping their hands as if to mock us that their eloquence surpassed our own, teasing us while we roasted and slowly went out of our minds. Sometimes you would turn to see if there was a fire burning behind you. If you dared to venture out in the sun without a hat, you could almost feel your brains cook. You had to take short breaths—breathe too deeply and your nostrils burned. If you touched a nail fixed to the door, you could burn your finger. The shade temperature hovered between 104 and 113 degrees Fahrenheit and sometimes rose to 122 degrees.

No ice. The iceman would not deliver in such weather, and as I have said, we had no electric fridges, not until the late 1930s anyway. No music and no entertainment were allowed. But the city was developing: we could hear a distant gramophone and a song wafting towards us, ceaselessly sung by Farrouh, "Khadri-etchay Khadri," about a girl who swore that she would not brew tea for anyone unless her lover came back to her.

No school. It had closed for the summer two weeks earlier. No appetite, and anyway, with the kosher abattoir shut for twenty-two days, vegetarian food was all we could eat—dishes like *sembousak el-taawa,* samosas filled with chickpeas and fried onions, and *kichree* (kedgeree, made of lentils, tomatoes, and rice) with *laban* topped with fried garlic, onion, cumin seed, raisins, and almond flakes. This was the "mess of pottage" that Esau had found so tasty he sold his birthright to his younger brother Jacob for it, which is why it is eaten in this time of mourning. No chicken, no meat allowed. Breakfast could keep us going all day: aubergine fried with onion and tomato with added grated white cheese, laid in a pitta to make a *laffa* wrap.

No weddings, no engagements, no parties. In the country, the fields were littered with the stinking carcasses of dead animals—horses, donkeys, cows—overcome by the heat, left rotting for the feasting, buzzing bluebottles. Some were pushed into the Tigris, which was at its lowest, and many was the time that one, smelling unbearably, would get stuck on our shore until someone from the *qasr* prodded it off again, sending it downstream. Small islands appeared in the middle of the river, and at times it stank, too, when a dead fish floated on its scummy waters. Heaven knows how hot it was in the sun, maybe 130 degrees Fahrenheit or more. No one had a thermometer. Even so, we would all gravitate to the *daghboona* corridor of the *qasr*, leaving the front door open in the forlorn hope that some fresh air might come from the river to cool us. But instead it was the flies that came in. Even they seemed to be suffering from the heat as they lazily buzzed around, making easy targets for our fly swats. We always had several of them lying about ready for action, and the chance to show our prowess in using them. A *qettaala* (killer) was made out of handwoven palm leaves on a stick, and I can still see Baba, the grandmaster, stalking his next victim purposefully.

Did I call the *daghboona* a corridor? It was huge. Two hammocks could fit in it, as well as two settees on each side. Our large black guard dog, Sabb'e (Lion), would try to cool himself by the door, always on the alert with a warning growl for anything suspicious. Even in normal times, Nana loved to spend time in the *daghboona*—alongside Regina's endless tablecloth—so you knew where to go if you wanted a chat or some advice. The fishermen also knew where to go if they made a good catch, anticipating correctly that my mother would pay a good price for a nice big fish that was still wriggling.

We children sneaked into the *mikve* to cool ourselves, but our parents did not encourage us, for coming out into such heat from such a cool underground pool could have damaging side effects. To be confined to bed was a trial for everyone, and this was the time of year when many people caught dysentery, had skin rashes, or became dehydrated. We drank *shnina*, salted yoghurt, as an antidote to dehydration. Our drinking water was warmish; tap water was too hot to produce a cooling shower. We fed on fruit, vegetables, dairy produce, and fresh fish. Watermelons were brought in by the donkey load or by *guffa*. Although everybody sat indoors or in the shade, it was not enough, for the mortality rate among the old and the very young was high. Everyone was nervous. It was the season of the black aubergine (*babenjaan*). At this time, if someone went out of his mind, you said jokingly: "iyyaam el babenjaan" (it's the *babenjaan* season)—it is forgiven.

Everyone simply had to stop for a nap after lunch or end up giving the gravedigger's business a miniboom. We would have our siesta in the *niim,* a room built lower than the others to keep it cool and a bit damper. Just outside the window, a prolific *'aqool* was sandwiched between two trellises of palm fronds and positioned in such a way as to keep the room dry and cool. The *'aqool* is a desert thornbush that camels feed on, which gives off a refreshing country scent when watered. Every now and then, we would shower it with buckets of water, and as long as it remained wet, it kept us cool, but in the heat of the day the water evaporated in no time and instead the room became stifling. We all aided the cooling process with hand fans. When guests arrived in summer, the first thing you did was present them with hand fans, and two people had to undertake any task such as preparing food or sewing: one to do the job, the other to fan.

It was at this time that the boys of the city either made or were given kites to fly. I don't know how they managed to fly them without a breeze, but they would go up on the roof at daybreak and sundown, and if you looked up, you could see several high in the sky. Some were especially colourful. They even played a kind of kite war.

Tish'a-Bab culminates in a day of fasting, after which the Moshiyah (Messiah) is supposed to arrive and everybody is relieved of a heavy burden.

There was nothing to compare with the bliss I felt when the cooler weather gently crept back with the start of the High Holy Days, some six weeks later in September. We could detect the welcome breezes softly caressing us through the night as they came upriver, without fail, on the first day of Elul, the month of mercy. Next comes Tishri, the month when we celebrate four feasts in quick succession: Rosh Hashanah (New Year), Yom Kippur (the Day of Atonement), Sukkoth (the Feast of Tabernacles), and finally Simhat Torah (the reading of the Torah).

It was a time for rejoicing, and we entered into the preparations eagerly. First, the dressmaker would arrive to take orders. Then the seamstress would come and stay with us for a whole month, kept busy all the time. Her job was to make new pillowcases and bed-sheets for us all. Then came the *neddaaf.* His task was to fluff up fresh cotton for new mattresses and eiderdowns and the cushions and backrests of the *takht* (benches) in the outside areas, to replace the previous year's, which would now be given to charity. We always had everything newly made and gave away the old. Sometimes we would save one or two of the old ones as spares for the many guests who would spend some weeks with us in summer. The *neddaaf* was known to everyone as the *teeteepampa*—an odd name which probably came from the huge bow he brought with him, just like the bows of wood and string small boys made to shoot arrows with. First, he would undo the matted cotton and then proceed to fluff it by twanging the string of the bow, starting on the outer edge of the pile and working through it until it was all fluffy again—and the buzzing sound it made was just like his name: "Tee-tee-pam-pa!" Finally, he would fill the fresh cushion and mattress covers and sew them up.

It was a delicious feeling when, once again, I could sink gently into my soft, springy mattress. But I would ask Nana if I could possibly keep my old eiderdown because it was now softer and lighter and I knew the new one would be hotter from the fluffed-up cotton, and the new cover would be starchy, noisy, and scratchy. Sometimes she would let me. At this time of year, we were still sleeping on the *sat-h* (rooftop) although we usually took a *lebbada* (bed jacket), for at dawn the breeze was cool.

Everything was made new or replaced. It was the time to be lavish and generous, but even a whole bolt of calico, given to the staff for completely new outfits, was not enough to go round. There was Djassem, the gardener, and his wife, Fatoom, who lived at the back of the *qasr;* the guard who slept by the doorway with a gun at his side; and the lad who brought our hot lunch to school to supplement our pickle snacks, as well as my father's to his office. There was also the family who were lodged at the far end of the tennis court: their job was to look after the court and level it, and their two sons acted as ball boys for us. Oh yes, by now we had a tennis court—and a guard.

The household list seemed never ending. There was Zahra, who baked the bread in the *tannoor* and acted as milkmaid, looking after our cows and the dairy and making cheese, sour cream, and butter. She wanted a length of cotton in a dark print. Then there was Hagouli the cook; Farrouh the maid, who did the cleaning and ironing; and the washerwoman . . . and so on and on. To meet these and our many other obligations we often received a boatload of goods from the city. We also hired a *guffa* for the *shakarchi*, or pâtissier, whose cooking pot was too big to fit into a normal boat. He and his assistant would stay two nights to make the *loozina*, a sweet made from quince and covered in chopped almonds and cardamom seed, and the *mann-essama* (also know as *be'be' Qadrasii*—literally, "holy biscuits"). This delicious nougat is supposed to be manna from heaven. The raw material is still collected by villagers in the northeastern corner of Iraq. They put leaves on the ground to collect the overnight dew that forms and crystallises: truly heaven's plenty. The spot is supposed to be where Moses and the Hebrews camped and ate manna, which the Bible describes as having been found "on the face of the wilderness, thin and flaky, like frost on the land" and the taste of it being "like wafers made with honey." Even Marco Polo mentions coming across it on his travels. The *shakarchi* specialised in *mann-essama*. He would melt down the crystallised dew, remove the impurities, and in his enormous cauldron, mix in about two hundred egg whites. Yet more eggs were mixed with the leftover yolks to make *khebz-spania*, a sort of sponge cake, supposedly Spanish bread.

Ibn Brakhel was another sweetmeat man whose arrival, on a different day, was always eagerly anticipated. His speciality was *silaan*, or date syrup. After soaking the dates overnight, he and his helpers squeezed them and poured the resultant muddy-looking juices into about five bags stacked one on top of the other, each bagful filtering through to become a clearer juice. The final result was poured into large, round shallow trays that were then carried to the roof and left in the sun to dry and thicken into a honeylike substance. The problem was that the trays attracted all manner of insect life buzzing around them and often getting stuck, to die a horrible death in the sticky mess. After some days, when the correct density of syrup had been reached, it was carefully "deinsected" and poured into large pottery containers for storage. While the entire process took a whole week, the *silaan* had to last until the following year. It was just so much fun for us children. We loved the messy, sticky chaos, particularly as my aunt always came to stay at this time, bringing with her our cousins, with whom we shared the fun.

The *silaan* would be stored underground, in the *sirdaab* pantry, along with dozens of small jars of sherbet and syrup, each with its brand-new handmade lace cover. We made our own sherbet in various flavours, from rose petals, orange blossom, apricots, peaches, pomegranates, and many other fruits—and almonds. It was more like a cordial, which was diluted as necessary. It, too, was to last all year, for our own consumption as well as for entertaining. We also made jams, preserves, and pickles and stored them in the same place in semiglazed earthenware urns called *bghaanii*. We even made our own tomato paste from piles of tomatoes that we left on the roof to dry out and reduce. All our fruit and vegetables were seasonal: no one used greenhouses. But as well as preserving them, we also strung fruit, vegetables, and herbs and dried them for use in winter. We had garlands of apples, apricots, *baamia* (ladies' fingers), mint . . .

As you can imagine, a *guffa* arrived almost every day. One of them would bring us the two new water urns (*hubb*) that we replaced each year and kept in the recess under the staircase, together with the new drip water filter known as the *naqoota*.

Finally, on the first day of our calendar's seventh month, Tishri (September or October), it was Rosh Hashanah, signalling the start of the ten days of penance—a time to look back at the mistakes made in the year just gone and plan changes to begin a new life. For Rosh Hashanah, rich and poor had to wear something brand new, and of course, the rich could afford more than a single item. Ladies showed off their latest creations, with the well-to-do donning dresses embroidered with gold thread. We girls were given new gold jewellery, more than likely a bangle or two.

The intensity of the preparations left us youngsters breathless with excitement and kept us from sleeping. How could you shut your eyes and miss the glitter of the brand-new golden bracelets made especially for you? They came wrapped in fine fuchsia-coloured paper directly from Yakoub el Saa-yegh, the jeweller (the one who had made the crooked cross). My father brought them home in packets and I couldn't resist the sweet clink they made as I showed them to Nana for her approval. "They are made of pure gold," she told me, "and you must look after them." And although they might have been slightly too big for my little wrists then, the following year they would be just right.

A lavish table was laid with food, prepared without spice or salt, each item with its own significance. Then we began the traditional blessings, to thank God for providing for us and to ask Him to continue to do so. We started with apple jam, requesting Him to grant us a new year as sweet as honey. This was followed by pomegranates so that we might be "as full of *musswoth* [good deeds] as the seeds of the fruit"; chives or horseradish "to wish bitterness on our enemies or those who wish ill of us"; *lubia* beans so that "our merits might increase"; bland courgettes so that "our bad thoughts might be forgiven"; and the new season's dates or figs that we'd refrained from eating until now, so that we could thank God for the past year and hope for yet another year in good health. Last of all came a stewed lamb's head, which we blessed so that "we might always be at the head and not at the tail" of our endeavours.

After the ten days, the High Holy Days reach their peak at Yom Kippur, when the gates of heaven are left wide open and the Almighty is there, ready to listen to any request (for the rest of the year, they are merely left ajar). This, the most important of all our holy days, never falls on a Friday or Sunday, for it would mean working on Saturday. It is the Day of Atonement when we do penance for our sins in the past year and the Almighty decides whether or not we deserve forgiveness. It is the most difficult of all our holy days to observe, for it means fasting completely: no food and no drink must pass our lips for about twenty-six hours, from before sunset one day to nightfall the next—altogether a most solemn and serious occasion.

Like the rest of the community, we started preparing in earnest about two days beforehand, with the arrival of the *shohet,* the ritual slaughterer. That must have been his longest workday every year, as he went from house to house slaughtering everyone's chickens for the pre-Kippur dinner. We children always got in the way, wanting to see everything, but sometimes he was so late coming we had to be wakened. The chickens were all over the place, running around and clucking ever louder as if they knew what was about to happen to them. For each member of the family there was a white bird: a rooster for every male and a hen for every female. And even that was not enough, for we usually had some extra to give away to the servants who helped with the plucking and the cleaning. A pregnant woman merited two hens and a rooster.

Normally, our chickens were lean and usually had brown feathers. Of course, we hadn't even heard of battery hens then. For Yom Kippur, though, white-feathered chickens were much sought after. As nobody knew exactly how to breed white-feathered chickens, lucky was the farmer who found a white one in his brood, for he could charge anything he liked. Few Jews farmed. Although some of our richer families would occasionally purchase a farm in a village, they always had an Arab look after it for them. Once one of them wanted to sell his farm. He had virtually agreed to all the terms with the buyer when he called in his Arab foreman to come and tell the buyer all about the property. "Well, of course, the drought hit us rather hard," said the foreman. "Then the wells dried up. We hardly had a crop, we couldn't feed the animals . . . and then the palm trees blew down." He carried on in this manner, to the disbelief of his master. Obviously the deal was off. "Why did you say that?" the master demanded to know. "That *was* the tax man, wasn't it?" came the innocent reply.

When the *shohet* arrived, he would first examine the chicken to be sure that it was healthy. For the ritual, he then passed it to my father, who held the chicken by the legs. For each one of us, Baba chose the appropriate bird. He circled my hen around my head seven times, reciting a small blessing signifying that, if I had been meant to die in the coming year, let the chicken die in my place, and let me continue to live a good life. After this prayer, the chicken could no longer go free. It was passed from hand to hand, back to the *shohet* waiting downstairs in the kitchen.

The *shohet* had to have studied for at least a year to gain his position. He learned the anatomy of each animal considered fit for consumption so that he could check for any damaged limbs or other abnormalities, as well as being able to judge its overall health. The animal had to be fully healthy; the slightest defect meant it would not be kosher and so would be rejected. It was also vital that it should not suffer when slaughtered: its head had to be turned away at the moment of death, and the *shohet* had to be careful to locate the jugular vein. This was true for all the animals he was called upon to slaughter. The whole business had to be quick, precise,

and humane, and only the jugular could be cut. Should he make a
mistake, the animal was considered unfit.

So now the *shohet* killed my hen with his special sharp knife and
let all the blood drain into a container full of earth. While he let
the bird settle, he covered the blood with some more earth and
recited a blessing, apologising for its death. Then the plucking and
the completion of the koshering process could begin—feathers,
blood, and guts everywhere, what a mess! But that was the way it
had to be. Today the kosher butcher does all that.

The day after the *shohet*'s visit, the eve of Kippur, was spent cooking and eating: it was recommended that we try to eat seven times
during that day, although we had to sit down for supper at around
five in the afternoon so that we took our last bite and last drink by
sunset, around six. The food was bland, with few or no spices or salt
so that you would not be thirsty afterward, just simply cooked with
onion, fresh tomato, and chickpeas, and as usual we ate it with rice.
Many felt sick even before the fast, from overeating in anticipation.
Some food was saved for meals for underage children—girls under
twelve and boys under thirteen—the following day. But it could not
require preparation, for no work and no fires were allowed on Yom
Kippur, the same as for the Shebbath. So the children usually had
some cold chicken, hard-boiled or brown-baked eggs, and *mahallabi*, a sort of rice pudding. After the supper and the last glass of
water, we all rushed to kiss Baba's and Nana's hand, saying "Give
me *mehila*" (forgiveness). They answered "Mahalenu"—"We forgive
each other"—and we expected God also to forgive us for all the sins
collected on the backs of our necks during the year. Then we all
went to *slah* for evening prayers. The whole congregation dressed
in white, but nothing new was allowed. White all over, no leather so
no shoes; instead we wore white espadrilles. Older men dressed in
white *zboon* and jacket, while younger men wore white suits.

Both men and women spend most of the day of Yom Kippur
at prayer in the *slah*. All the men in the congregation wear their
prayer shawls and their black morning-prayer straps. Much of the
morning session is *'amida*—standing—when each worshipper reads
his prayers in complete silence and stillness except for the rustle of
turning pages. It seems to take forever. Children get restless and,
if they fidget enough, you can be sure that at least one man will

show his annoyance by making a noise like "ahem!"—not just to shush the child but also to rebuke the mother for not controlling it. Once, during this most significant part of the ceremony, a noisy fly came to bother my cousin, landing on the end of his nose, making him uncomfortable. He twitched his nose. The fly circled around only to come and land on it once again. He twitched his nose again. The fly, wiser now, moved only a step or two. Deeply irritated, my cousin whispered through clenched teeth: "'I letzakt eb dini?"—"Hey, have you glued yourself to my religion?" In unison those around him went "ahem!" and titters of laughter were heard from the women.

All day, everyone listens to the emotional male voices begging for *mehilah*, forgiveness. Sometimes, the women go home for a rest and a sleep—you could feel your energy slowly being sapped by the heat. Towards the end of the day, the song of *ne-'eela* starts: "God Almighty, give us forgiveness in this hour of distress." Finally, the traditional *shofar* (ram's horn) is blown: at last everyone goes home and we can break our fast when we can count three stars in the sky.

Yom Kippur usually falls in September, and rarely in October. The weather was still terribly hot during the day, although the evenings were cooler. That being so, we could not prepare the table much in advance. As soon as the sun set, a servant sprinkled the floor with water to cool it and wash it, and put out cushions on the benches and chairs and a clean tablecloth on the table that remained in the shade during the day. You had to fill the table with all the food that everybody had fancied during the fast, and more. Anyone who still had energy to spare at the end of this longest of days gave a hand with the preparations. Priority went to the singing samovar, fired by charcoal, with a teapot sitting on top. Over the years we had learned that, for us, the best thing to start with was a hot *stikan tchai*, dark tea served in a small, delicately waisted glass with a lump of sugar, sipped slowly.

For my part, after the tea I usually nibbled a little and felt sleepy. After a short nap, I woke up feeling hungry but more normal. By then the hot *marag* (chicken soup with chickpeas) was ready and we had our meal on the *sat-h-el-nassee,* in the open at the back of the house overlooking the garden.

As soon as we finished breaking the fast, it was a *musswa* (good deed) to start with the *sukka.* Sukkoth—the Feast of Tabernacles—is the festival during which we give thanks to the Lord for sheltering us in the wilderness. To commemorate this, we build a shelter—the *sukka*—decorated with palm fronds and specific fruits. Baba would go downstairs to see to this as soon as he could, because Sukkoth was just five days after Yom Kippur. It is a fun festival in which we all participate, erecting the tabernacle and trying to make it as beautiful and comfortable as possible, for this is a time when friends and relatives visit each other and have meals under the canopy and even sleep there. Certain fruits are de rigueur and their market price soars several times over. For instance, a must is the *ethrog,* a large, knobbly, lemonlike citrus fruit that plays an important part in the Sukkoth ritual in the synagogue, and which must have a bit of a branch still attached. In the market, the price of one *ethrog* would go up to one rupee (about a shilling and sixpence, or three pounds today), and for that amount you could have bought sixty-four lemons. In his excitement during a haggling session, one Arab vendor misguidedly pulled off the attached branch to show his customer that he wouldn't sell this little part of the *ethrog* for even half a rupee—and was astonished when the customer walked off without pursuing the transaction.

The *sukka* would stay up for seven days, by which time all the vegetation decorating it would be dry and sad looking. On the eighth day, blessings would be recited as it was taken down, and the last feast of the High Holy Days would commence with Simhat Torah, "rejoicing in the law"—our Thanksgiving.

Qahwat Moshi

AS WELL AS BEING RABBIS, teachers, civil servants, and manual workers, many of our men were entrepreneurs of one kind or another and went to work six days a week. They would be said to have "gone to the *souq*" for the day. It was a man's world. *Souq* is the generic name for the bazaar or marketplace, and even though none of our men traded in the food market itself, they all had offices, shops, and warehouses around it. The Ottomans had encouraged the growth of overseas trade, particularly with Europe, and this had led to an increased importance of Jews and Christians in the life of the cities. Our most successful men were influential bankers, provincial governors, government officials, managers of farms, craftsmen, dealers in precious metals, professional lawyers, and accountants.

The main business centre was further down Rashid Street, after Shriat el-Nawab, before you came to Kutchet el-Tejjaar (Commercial Street), packed with warehouses known as *khaans*. All the prominent businessmen had their base there, my future husband as well as Baba. One of our most important private bankers, Sion Aboudi, had his large offices, *hejra*, over Baba's *khaan*.

A typical setup would have the ground floor being used as a wholesale warehouse stuffed with boxes and bales of goods, with an office upstairs for the owner or manager and his male secretary (plus, in Baba's case, a messenger). Few bosses could read and write, so the secretary did the correspondence as well as the accounts, while the master received the dealers and negotiated all transactions. Typically, two or more Kurdish men were engaged to move the goods around the warehouse, to deliver to the retailers, and to guard the place day and night.

In the early days, Baba and his brother Shaul represented many agencies, importing textiles from England and India; tea from Ceylon; and coffee, sugar, and gold dust from India. They had the gold melted and worked in Baghdad before exporting it to Antwerp. They also acted as money brokers, merchants, and commission agents. When Uncle Shaul passed away, Baba neglected the money-exchange side and concentrated instead on property. Finding life in Karrada to his liking, this was when he had the synagogue at the *qasr* built and put in the tennis court, as well as buying the extra land alongside us and selling many building plots after having the roads asphalted.

Baba's *khaan* was ideally located, just around the corner from the docks and the *massebgha,* the dye works where fabrics were coloured, on the riverbank. The docks were packed with *guffas* and *sfeenee* waiting to be loaded, unloaded, or repaired. The latter were cargo-carrying dhows with big lateen sails and a cabin below decks in which whole families lived. As the Tigris was too shallow upriver to accommodate seagoing vessels, all goods destined for Baghdad that arrived by ship from abroad first had to be unloaded in Iraq's only major port—Basra, on the Shatt el Arab, where the Tigris and Euphrates meet—and then ferried up to the capital.

At the docks, *hammaal* (porters), usually Kurds, were stationed to carry the cargoes through Customs and Excise and on to the *khaans.* They assembled before dawn to start work after their breakfast of nourishing *paacha*—that stew made from sheep tripe and rejected bones and heads, sold by street vendors who lined up nearby, each with his own huge pot set on an open fire, shouting their wares at the top of their voices. This could be as early as four in the morning in summer, and the *hammaal* continued working all day as long as the daylight lasted. They were capable of carrying enormous loads on their backs.

A porter could carry surprising loads, perhaps fifty gasoline cans at once . . .

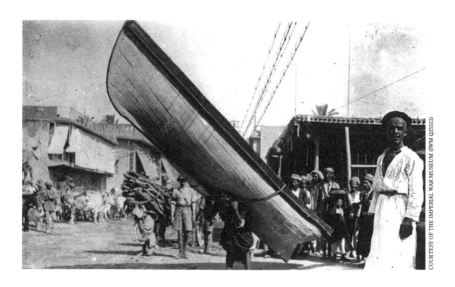

or a boat over three times his height.

A short way upstream was the quay where the water taxis were based, at the end of Shriat el-Nawab, the posh street running at right angles between the river and Rashid Street. Often, at the end of the day, instead of taking the public boat, we children would go home with Baba in a rowing boat, with its *tantah* canvas awning overhead to protect us from the sun. It was easy work for the rower, going gently with the current, but we didn't envy the effort he'd have to put in to row back against the flow. The boat was decked with clean white cushions obviously straight from the laundry, with their hint of laundry blue (a cube of blue that you put in the last rinse to give your whites that extra sparkle). Often we would buy a large fish and attach it to the boat to keep it fresh for our supper.

For all the businessmen, the heartbeat of the *souq* was Qahwat Moshi, the café at the centre of the old city where they congregated as if by appointment to drink their tea or coffee and play endless games of *tawli* (backgammon) and dominoes. Although it was not a club, it might as well have been, as strangers always felt thoroughly uncomfortable among all those noisy regulars who knew each other so well.

All earth-shattering news as well as trivia, jokes, and information were exchanged at Qahwat Moshi. It was a trading post. Any news received by mail or telegram was shared there, to be discussed and argued over and conclusions drawn, since in these early days there was no telephone, few radios, and certainly no TV. Even domestic news and reports from absent friends were transmitted in this manner. The one English newspaper was the *Baghdad Times,* but as it was censored like all the press, it was simply full of advertisements and local gossip.

Qahwat Moshi was where most business deals were transacted. The *souqiyee*—businessmen, both Muslim and Jew—sat dressed in their *'abaayas* or with a jacket over their *zboon,* with only a few wearing a complete European suit. They kept their heads covered, either with a fez, an *'amaama,* a *yashmaagh,* or a *kashiida,* and on their feet they wore *yamanee, kaala* (slippers), or European shoes and sandals. There was never anything to make our community uncomfortable. We got on with the Shi'a as well as the Sunni Muslims much bet-

A riverside café in the 1920s

ter than they did among themselves; we even acted as go-betweens when they quarrelled. Just in normal conversation, voices were always raised, and to an outsider it might have seemed like a place of constant discord. But wrangling like this was how deals were negotiated, both parties having proved themselves tough, usually swearing on the head of their nearest and dearest that this was the tightest deal they had ever struck. The essence of these games was not to give in too easily or there would be no fun in victory.

Strangely, a transaction could fall through if the vendor achieved his full asking price. It verged on the superstitious: something had to be wrong if there was no chitchat. And sometimes bargaining itself was not enough to close a deal. They would stroke their *kahrab sibha*—amber worry beads that gave off a musky scent when rubbed—before making a business decision. To a Muslim, all decisions depended on what his *sibha* told him.

Here's a story I remember Baba telling us, typical of the period. One day, a textile wholesaler friend of his who had been having trouble selling some striped fabric was sitting in his *khaan* when a Muslim approached him and enquired about the cloth, which was of a stripe that was really only fashionable among Muslims. The

Muslim, a retailer, started to chat and after a lot of bargaining finally asked, "But why should I pay you seventy-five rupees a roll
when in Khaan el-Zeroor [a rival warehouse] they are asking only
sixty-eight?"

"Because they are probably making a loss and they need the cash.
I prefer to wait to get my price," said Baba's friend, presuming he
had lost the sale. But later that day, much to his surprise, the man
came back to his warehouse and bought two rolls. A few days later,
back he came again for two more rolls—and kept coming back until the stock was finally exhausted. Curious at this turn of events,
the wholesaler asked him what had happened to change his mind.
"Well, you see my friend," he replied, "every time I consult my *sibha*,
it comes out in your favour, and I am not about to change my luck
by going against what my *sibha* says!"

A man was attached to his *sibha* for life—superstitious if he lost
it and too superstitious to change it. There were no fakes, and in
any case, it was too easy to tell the genuine *kahrab* by the smell, the
feel, the weight, and the magnetism. You could tell a man's status
from the quality of his *sibha* and the way he handled it. If you saw
a man walking around the *souq* with both hands behind his back,
his right hand going through the *sibha* and his wrist resting in his
left hand, you could easily guess that his mind was on his *sibha*. He
would be consulting it for *kheira* (advice) about doubts he had in
some matter, asking God for proper guidance in his choice or di-
lemma. The beads have nothing to do with worries: the actual word
sibha means "in praise of Allah." It is said that they were invented by
Muhammad when he lived in the desert, as a sort of rosary in order
to express admiration and approval of Allah. Muhammad managed
to ascribe ninety-nine qualities to Him in the Qur'an—"great," "all-
powerful," "just," and so on—and thus the original *sibha* had ninety-
nine beads, each named after a virtue.

A man would start consulting the *sibha* by picking a bead at random, taking each successive one and saying alternately, "yes," "no,"
"yes," "no," right through to the end. He would play the beads three
times this way to reach the final decision of yes or no from the final
bead. Our men also carried *sibha*, although in theory they were
only for fun, as it is against our religion to take *kheira*, or be told our
destiny, or participate in any form of "witchcraft." Just the same, we
were all superstitious about most things. For a start, according to

popular belief, you could have a good or a bad day depending on what you first saw on emerging in the morning. So our salute was always "Sabah el khair!"—literally, "Morning of good fortune!" To which the reply was "Sabah el noor!"—"Morning of light!"

We kept our age secret. It was mentioned only once in a boy's lifetime, when he reached his bar mitzvah at thirteen; for a girl, never. There were many reasons, the most important being that we wanted a girl's age to be flexible, depending on circumstances, especially if she came to be married later rather than earlier. So we celebrated our birthdays, uncounted, during the nearest festivities. If, like me, you were born some time around Hanukka—which can fall at any time from late November to late December—you would enjoy a group celebration together with others in your family born around then. Age was not mentioned. We did not like to be told that we "looked young for our age" in case the person paying the compliment was at the same time giving us the evil eye. The reaction to such a compliment was to mumble "bel 'ayn el-raa'a" (literally, "in the evil eye") to counter it. I even knew some women who would dress their baby boys as baby girls because they were so worried some wicked person might envy them their good fortune and put a spell on the infant.

If someone was prone to bad luck, it was always ascribed to the evil eye, and he had better carry a pinch of salt in his pocket, or hang a worn-out shoe or slipper above his front door. To ward off the evil eye instantly, you responded by "a five"—you shoved your hand with an open palm towards the eye—or you spat on the ground and then rubbed it with your shoe, mumbling, "The evil eye is crushed." The truly superstitious even went as far as crushing a fish eye with their shoe until it burst!

If a pregnant woman had a craving, it was important to get what she wanted to her quickly, or else the baby would be born with a birthmark in that colour. And if she scratched herself while waiting, that would be where the mark appeared. Take *kichree*, for example, our tasty vegetarian dish. Just thinking about it proved so appetising that it became a common craving. It would be bad luck indeed if the baby had an orange-coloured mark on its body or, worse, on its face—a disaster for a baby girl. Do you remember the mark Mikhail Gorbachev had on his forehead? I imagine his mother probably craved strawberries while she was pregnant . . .

Another subject we never discussed was our wealth: you never revealed what you were worth. In fact, it was so taboo that even the person concerned never counted his wealth. Instead, he would try to lose count himself, hiding some of his money here and there so that later he would arrive at some forgotten corner and get pleasure from finding it. They called it *baraka* (plenty). And if you hit a lucky streak, you never tinkered with any of the elements that brought you such good fortune. The richest man in Baghdad built himself a mansion across the river so opulent that King Faisal himself took it over until his own palace was completed. Meanwhile, the rich man would not budge from his dingy old office, where he had started years before, and kept doing business there until his death. It had brought him luck, so he would not change his threshold—his *'atba.*

At Qahwat Moshi, the scene was always the same, the men preferring to sit outdoors even during our short winter. The only time Moshi closed, like all our businesses, was late in the morning on a Friday to allow time to prepare for the Shebbath, and all day Saturday and the other Jewish holy days.

It was no wonder that the place was permanently bustling. Moshi kept a slate for all his clients, and his accounts were simple: no matter how often his customers went there, no matter what they had, it would cost them four annas a week (about fivepence then, or eighty pence today) or one rupee a month (equivalent to three pounds sixty now)—pennies! Apart from the noise of all these men talking excitedly, and the rattle and slap of the dice and backgammon counters, there was the jingle of the small china cups chinking around the tray that the waiter, a towel hanging from his belt, balanced on one hand while holding the coffee pot with its straw-thin spout in the other. While sipping the aromatic Turkish coffee strongly flavoured with cardamom, some customers would also puff away noisily at their hubble-bubble pipes, smoking tobacco and sometimes opium. The *nargiila* consists of a large glass decanter half full of water with, above the waterline, a small spout to which is fixed a flexible tube ending in the mouthpiece. On the lid of the decanter is a small tin container full of the smoking material. This is covered in small charcoal embers, and as the smoker inhales, he fans the fire through the holes at the base of the opium container, which causes the water to displace and bubble, the action supposedly purifying the tobacco or opium. Only special opium grown in the east of Iraq and Iran was ever used.

Young boys employed by Moshi ran around doing the fetching, serving, and carrying. They served tea in *stikans,* with sugar lumps broken to size from a loaf of sugar. Some preferred to hold the lump inside their mouth and sip the hot tea through it as it melted, to prolong the pleasure. Tea was never served with milk or lemon.

The customers had wooden or wicker chairs to sit on, as well as several *takht*—Moshi's were solid three-seater wooden benches with back- and armrests—on which they would relax, leaning languidly on the backrests. Well-to-do Muslims often preferred to sit with both legs folded comfortably underneath them, leaving their footwear on the floor. But after lunch, nobody thought anything of it if a whole *takht* was taken up by just one man stretched out comfortably for a nap.

One important habitué of Qahwat Moshi was what you might call an employment agent—a dealer who would go there to pick up the gossip about what domestic servants might be required and by whom. He would then go around the houses from door to door with a troupe of likely candidates, mainly young girls and boys, and you could make your choice right there on the doorstep. When we first moved to the *qasr,* there was so much to be done to keep the household going that an entire team of *domestiques* was required. They were hired on six-month contracts, with renewal either at Pessah or Sukkoth (spring or autumn) and paid monthly, with one month's notice on either side.

Hagouli, our capable cook, was now a family man, so every other night he went all the way into Baghdad to stay with his wife and children in the city. Since there was no kosher butcher in Karrada, he would buy our meat there and bring it back the following morning. Friday night was the start of his weekend. On one of those Fridays, as we were gathered for a chat after dinner, we heard a knock at the door. Young Hassan, the errand boy, came to tell us that a policeman was standing there with Hagouli and wanted to speak to Baba. Curious, I followed my father downstairs—and there we saw a strange sight. Apparently the policeman had encountered Hagouli with a heavy jute sack suspended from his forehead dangling down his back the Arab way. And there was the load, spread out on display for us to see: the whole, giant, white heart of a palm tree (a delicacy); a pile of sugar; about five pounds of rice; and a mass of roasted almonds and pistachios.

"This man," said the policeman with great self-importance, "claims you gave him all these items. Did you or did you not?"

It seems that my formidable father was deeply moved. "Yes, of course!" he said confidently, and thanked the officer for his concern as he accompanied him to the door. Hagouli stayed behind and wanted to kiss Baba's hand.

"What made you take the whole palm-tree heart?" asked Baba.

"The gardener Djassem gave it to me, Your Worship," said Hagouli. "He told me to give it to the children."

"And why didn't you?"

"I thought he meant my own children, Sire!"

We did not sack him for that and he stayed with us for many more years.

Apart from playing backgammon and smoking their pipes, the customers at Qahwat Moshi also enjoyed one other pastime: cracking seeds. Whenever we ate watermelon or pumpkin, we would save all the seeds—*hab*—then rinse, drain, salt, and sun dry them before roasting them on a slow fire until they crackled. The smell of roasting seeds was delicious, and at certain times the aroma seemed to come from every house. Eating them was the best way to idle away the hours. While we children played a game of Ludo, backgammon, or cards, the grown-ups and their guests would sit around gossiping, all the time cracking away at the *hab*.

Hab cracking was in vogue long before cigarettes came on the scene: tobacco became fashionable only with the advent of Hollywood films. At the cinema, during the interval, the vendor would cry, "Hab ya loz!" saying his seeds were as good as almonds, and after the show, the floor would be carpeted with discarded husks. It was the done thing for young men to parade by the river, watched enviously as they chatted with their friends, relaxed, looking and feeling like millionaires while they played with a *sibha* with one hand and cracked *hab* with the other.

It takes years of practice to master the art of *hab* cracking. It is not nearly as easy as it looks. The proper way is to take a good handful, then flip them to your mouth, one seed at a time. Flip carefully, as you must catch each seed swiftly with your lips and not in the mouth itself. Then, with your tongue, you turn the *hab* sideways so that it sits edgewise between your top and bottom front teeth, with the point turned inwards. Be careful not to wet it, lest it resist the cracking. Then crack the *hab*. The mastery is to use just the right amount of pressure, for you then blow the unblemished husks into the air using your tongue. The seed itself should also be left unbroken and stay in your mouth to be eaten. A really advanced *hab* cracker can even organise it so that the unblemished husks are still joined together at the bottom when discarded. All this operation is done in a flash so that all the onlooker sees is flying clouds of husks and the resulting ring on the ground.

I happened to know the champion *hab* cracker of Baghdad well. He was my own Uncle Shaul, brother of Baba, who could crack a good handful in seconds. In fact, in an unofficial competition, he managed as many as fifty in one minute.

My uncle was an unusually big man, both in height and girth. He stood about a head taller than the average crowd and, to my young mind, looked like a herdsman, with the other, shorter people as his flock. He had a proud, erect sort of gait, and because he stood out so much, just about everybody in Baghdad knew who he was. He enjoyed his drink and could demolish half a bottle of *'arak* by himself in one sitting. All the coachmen knew him, for many was the time a coach would almost overturn when he climbed in one side or when they had to take a sharp turn. Eventually, he learned to avoid using the steps and tried to board directly so as not to overbalance. His best friend, Shalom, was another tall man—shorter than my uncle, perhaps, but even fatter. Once Shalom hired a taxi and had great difficulty squeezing himself in. He should have been warned, for when he arrived at his destination there was no way he could prise himself out. The drivers and passersby all gave a hand, pushing and pulling, laughing and swearing until he was free. One evening, as they were walking down Rashid Street together, Uncle Shaul hailed a coach while Shalom lagged behind. Once the fare was agreed, still with no sign of Shalom, the coachman said, "Get in quick, before the horse sees you!" Uncle Shaul replied, "Just a minute, this youngster wants to come with us." The coachman took

one look at the so-called youngster and took off, leaving them standing there as his curses about the load some people expected his poor
horse to carry filled the air. They never tried to board a carriage
together again.

Tales—always beginning "b-iyyaam el Osmali," "in the days of
the Ottomans"—were traded at Qahwat Moshi, which Baba liked to
recount to the family. Many illustrated the fact that justice was dis-
pensed in a most peculiar way during the caliphate, depending entirely on the whim of the *qaadi* (judge) or *agha* (magistrate). He had
an enormously inflated idea of his own wisdom and importance,
even though he had obtained his position through nepotism, and
bribing him was routine. Yet this was the person to whom people
had to turn to settle the most trivial and most serious of arguments,
"rights" having nothing whatever to do with his kind of justice.

A series of typical tales took place outside the *mahkama,* or court
of justice, where the *qaadi* sat before of a mixed bunch of people
who were awaiting trial. First on the list was Fatouma bint Shaukat,
an old woman.

"What is your problem?" demanded the judge imperiously.

"I am a poor widow," replied Fatouma. "My son who lives with
me shows me no respect. Nor does he feed me."

"This is a truly serious offence. He deserves harsh punishment,
so that he should never forget that, in our society, elderly parents
must be shown respect and deference. Where is he?"

Right then, Fatouma's motherly heart gave a lurch. What had
she done? This man might mete out some dreadful punishment to
her beloved only son! She had only wanted the judge to scold him.
Too late! But what could she do now? Looking around, she suddenly caught sight of a likely bystander: a well-dressed, handsome
young man. She had never laid eyes on him before, but she now
turned to the *qaadi* and pointed at the poor fellow: "There he is!
Do you see how he does not even want to greet me?"

The *qaadi* ordered the young man to be brought before him.
"Young man, this is your mother," he boomed. "She is old now, and
as is the custom you must show her respect. Do so in front of me
now. I want to see you bow to her and kiss her hand. I want to hear
you apologise for your unfeeling behaviour."

"Hadrat el-Qaadi," began the young man respectfully, address-
ing the judge as "Your Honour," "she is not my mother."

The *qaadi* was outraged. "How so? You dare to deny her in front of me and lie to *me?*" Turning to the attendant, he said: "Give him a hard whack across his face so that he might recover his memory!" This was considered a shameful thing, to be whacked like that in front of everybody. "And now for your punishment, young man. I want you to get a brand new basket with a cushion and help your dear mother sit in it. Then you will put the basket with your mother in it on top of your head and carry her down the main street so that the whole world can see how much you respect her. And I warn you that, if I have any more trouble from you, I will send you to prison."

The implications of this did not need spelling out, as Ottoman jails were fearful places—dark, dank, and unhygienic, infested with rats and cockroaches. So the poor young man did as he was bidden, and to make sure he carried out his sentence, the court bailiff stood by, watching his every move. As he struggled down the street, bent double, everybody looked at the ridiculous spectacle and roared with laughter—including, as it happened, his own brother who was also passing by. He could not believe his eyes; he thought he had taken leave of his senses.

"Who is that?" he asked in amazement, pointing to Fatouma in the basket.

"This is our mother," replied the young man.

"Don't be stupid. Our mother has been dead for five years," his brother replied.

"You try telling that to the *qaadi*," said the young man, stooping to pick up his burden once more under the ever-present gaze of the bailiff.

Then there was another case: Amina versus Abdullah. A newly married couple, Abed and Amina had been crossing the old bridge when Abdullah, a big burly man, tripped over Amina, who was six months pregnant, and they both fell to the ground. As a result, she suffered a miscarriage. Abed wanted to claim compensation on her behalf. And this was the *qaadi*'s judgement: "You most certainly deserve to be compensated, and so you shall be. I therefore order Amina to go and live with Abdullah. She should not be returned to her husband Abed until she is six months pregnant again. Next!"

Next was the case of Rafik versus Mahmoud. Rafik had just shot down two partridges, and he thought nothing could be finer than to eat them, grilled, after he had spent a relaxing hour or so at the *hammam*. So he gave them to Mahmoud, the kebab man, paying in advance, and went into the bathhouse greatly looking forward to his repast, for he knew that he would be ravenous as usual afterwards. Imagine his consternation, therefore, when he came out, gastric juices working, to find . . . nothing. No appetising partridges. And no Mahmoud.

Days later, Rafik caught up with the kebab man and hauled him up in front of the *qaadi*, who demanded an explanation.

"Hadrat el-Qaadi," began Mahmoud, "please repeat after me: '*Qaader!*'"

"Qaader!" came the automatic response.

Now *Qaader* means "Allah is all powerful," and if he wills it, miracles are possible. If the *qaadi* had refused to say it, he would have been branded immediately as a nonbeliever, and there was no crime worse than that for a man in his position.

Mahmoud explained: "As I salted the birds ready to put them on the fire, I could not believe the miracle my eyes saw, Your Honour. The birds simply rose up and flew away. Say '*Qaader!*' It really was a miracle!"

"Qaader ya Allah, Qaader ya Allah," said the *qaadi*, truly impressed. And poor Rafik had little choice but to join in the chorus.

Case dismissed.

Finally, there was the case of Ismaeel versus Abbas. Ismaeel had had an argument with Abbas, which resulted in Abbas pulling the tail of Ismaeel's donkey so hard that it came away in his hand. Ismaeel went to the *qaadi* with his donkey as proof, hoping for compensation.

"Well?" barked the *qaadi*. "What do you expect me to do?"

Ismaeel suddenly lost his nerve. Having just seen how Rafik had lost his perfectly good cause in the previous case, he feared that he might be facing all manner of religious hocus-pocus and decided to change his tune.

"Sir," he said, "I am a simple man. I am not a believer, but neither am I a nonbeliever. I am from the sect that simply ditches its donkeys and disappears into the crowd." And with that, he left his dumb friend in front of the equally dumbfounded judge—and fled.

Cracking *hab* was one of the few things one could do on a Saturday that was not forbidden. The Lord commanded that it should be a day of rest. But over the ages, as the rabbis and wise men tried to interpret the meaning and lay down some hard-and-fast rules that everyone could understand, it became complicated. The slightest thing that might be called work is not allowed. Obviously, you are not allowed to chop wood, but surprisingly you are not allowed to walk in the garden in case you step on a twig and inadvertently break it. That is *'awon,* a sin. What is a sin? It is doing anything that is *assoor,* forbidden. Similarly, in biblical times when lighting a fire for cooking or a lamp for illumination took a lot of effort, it was *assoor* to do so on the Shebbath; by extension, today the rabbis have decreed that switching on a light or the oven is *'awon.* Touching money on the Shebbath is *assoor,* too—and so on. You get the idea.

When we first moved back to the *qasr* in 1919, we were not allowed to touch the new electric light switches, either on or off, on *lailt el-Shebbath*—the Friday evening (the actual day always starts at sunset and ends at sunset the following evening, not sunrise to sunrise). So we were always looking for a *goy,* a non-Jew, to switch off the light for us after supper, when we were ready to go to bed, although it really was impractical to call someone simply to push a button at around midnight. Somehow, we didn't think of leaving it on. One day, we heard that one of our friends had convinced his father that switching on the light with the end of one of his *qabqaab* (clogs) was not a sin. The father did not raise any objections, but just in case, he would not do it himself. Eventually, most people thought it a good idea and followed his example, and gradually, we children switched on the lights in our bedrooms, always pretending we had forgotten what day it was.

You commit a sin every time you eat *tareif* (nonkosher food), for eating *tareif* is *assoor.* Whenever you sin, it immediately shows up on the back of your neck for the Almighty to see. For example, if you were to eat meat—any meat, even kosher meat—and then follow it with a dairy product such as milk with your coffee before six hours have elapsed, then you have committed an *'awon* and the feared invisible mark appears. This *'awon* might or might not be erased after fasting on Yom Kippur. It all depends on the number of *'awonoth* you have managed to collect during the year, the gravity of them, and how keen you are that they be erased. The opposite of a sin is a *musswa,* a good deed. Unfortunately, though, this does not show up on the back of your neck in the same way, but He gets to know about it and takes it into account. Giving money to the poor is a *musswa,* helping the aged is a *musswa,* and so on.

One Saturday, on her way home after prayers, my grandmother, who considered herself to be pious, saw a valuable coin in the street. As it was forbidden to handle money, she drew a handkerchief from her pocket and picked up the coin without physically touching it. She hid it in a crack in the wall and went back to collect it on Sunday!

If you found something in the street, no one would think of reporting it to the police. If you made an important find and it weighed on your conscience, though, you consulted the rabbi—as in this story of Yussef.

"Rabbi, I found this beautiful cockerel in the street. May I keep it?" asked Yussef.

"No, son," replied the rabbi. "First you must go to the main square and shout out your discovery at least three times to see if anyone has lost it. If no one comes forward, then you may keep it."

So Yussef went to the main square and shouted out loud and clear: "Has anyone lost . . ." then in a low murmur, "a cockerel?" Obviously, no one heard what Yussef had found and he kept the bird.

In Baghdad, we never had any rabbis who were religious in the extreme, as they have, for example, in Jerusalem today. That would have been classed as fanaticism. To our thinking, fanatics like that are themselves breaking the sanctity of the Shebbath with their violence, trying to make the less observant observe the Shebbath their way.

In my grandfather's time, the Jewish community in Baghdad was still behaving the old-fashioned way—like their ancestors, obedient servants of the Rabbanut. To this day, the Rabbanut is made up of a group of rabbis (*hakhamim*) who learn to read the Bible in Hebrew and interpret it for the community. They nominate a leader and call him the *hakham bashi* (chief rabbi), who becomes their representative and spokesman in dealings with the government. The task of every *hakham* (rabbi) is to keep the widely diverse community knitted together, and to enable him to do this, the Rabbanut turned the Ten Commandments into hundreds of commandments in order to repeat, enforce, and emphasise the words of the Bible. Unquestioningly, the community would follow the *hakhams'* interpretations, for the law was a muddle to the majority.

To make sure everybody observed the law, the Rabbanut elaborated on it and gradually tightened it; as a result, it was always crowded at the Rabbanut with people asking for clarification. For example, Moshe Rabenu (Moses) had told us not to cook a lamb with the milk of its mother. In Baghdad, not only did we not cook any dairy product with lamb, we extended the rule to cover beef, veal, and even chicken, although Moses never mentioned these. And then we still had to wait six long hours to be allowed to eat any dairy product after tasting a chicken, let alone a lamb. We all kept two sets of crockery, cutlery, and saucepans: one for meat and one for dairy. And another two sets for Pessah. It became so time consuming and complicated.

Our rabbis would give a *daroosh*—a general sermon—at the end of prayers on Saturday, but it would then be left to the individual to follow his conscience. And the overwhelming majority were observant, each in his fashion, to the best of his own interpretation.

Back at the *qasr,* Baba worried about venturing out into his garden on the Shebbath, due to his early religious schooling. However, his later education at the Alliance was of a more understanding and easygoing nature, and coupled with his own love of gardening, the pull was too much. His learning told him that this particular interpretation, like so many others, had obviously gone too far. Surely God would not have decreed this petty *'awon,* and certainly it did not appear in the Ten Commandments. So, gradually he gave in, and we all came to greatly look forward to the Shebbath, when we would receive our guests who would walk miles to visit us and all enjoyed every bit of it.

Gardening soon became Baba's consuming hobby. He took a passionate interest in it, learning all there was to know, and soon made sure that we grew all sorts of fruits, vegetables, and flowers, including rare species. He would import seeds from India: Pochas Seeds were his suppliers in Poona. Every day, on his return home,

*With Baba
and Nana
in the garden*

he would first inspect the garden, then give his instructions to the gardener and workers to help with the pruning, digging, and planting.

People soon knew that we had an exotic garden, which was behind the house as you looked at it from the river. First, you would pass a large pergola heavy with assorted grapes. It was clever, for it gave us a lot of shade to laze under in the summer, and in the cold months, the vines lost their leaves and we had sunshine. Gardenias were planted nearby that produced a heady perfume as you lazed. Then you came upon a long path known as the *maderban,* wide enough for three people, which went right through the garden, sharply edged on either side by a narrow stream that watered everything. It was part of an intricate system of irrigation channels and sluices that had to be fed, laboriously, by a man who drove two oxen hauling huge buckets up the sloping ground from the river, day in and day out. The oxen were roped together in such a way that, when one was at the top and the man could empty its bucket into the first sluice, the other was at the bottom and his assistant would fill it up. What did we children care! It felt so good to go barefoot in the stream on hot days, with the water right up to our knees when we were little.

All along the *maderban* many different sorts of citrus trees were grown, with the other fruit trees behind them—and by now we had them all: apricots, peaches, plums, cherries, mulberries, figs, pomegranates, apples, pears, and exotic fruits such as the lotus berries I've mentioned—deliciously scented, red and yellow—and bananas, until then unknown in Iraq. We had nut trees: walnuts, almonds, hazelnuts, and a real rarity, a pistachio tree. There were haphazard patches of vegetables—tomatoes, cucumbers, aubergines, courgettes, and so on—and several tenacious plants like mint and pepper, as well as flowers, such as violets and hyacinths, that grew wild. There was no purposeful symmetry anywhere. Flowers and vegetables grew between the fruit trees, which in turn grew between the date palms. It was truly wonderful to wander round and pick fruit of different textures, flavours, and tastes, and as always, the younger generation went for the green, unripe ones, to our cost.

The blossom of the orange trees and petals of some special pink roses Baba planted were carefully collected and then distilled to make *maay qedah* and *maay waghd,* orange-blossom and rose waters. A man would come down the river with an alembic still aboard his *guffa* and set up shop in the open space leading to the garden from the kitchen. Djassem, together with Fatoom and anyone else who cared to join in, would gently shake the orange blossoms onto a sheet to avoid damaging them, then place all the flowers in the still with some water and start to warm the mixture. As it was coming to the boil, the distiller connected a pipe, and the vapour condensed as it passed through and cooled, dripping into a bottle. Same again for the roses. We had plenty of supplies for our cooking (flavourings for desserts and pastries) as well as for our toilette.

The *maderban* ended at the back gate that gave on to the main road where you could now catch a small bus into Baghdad, all the way to Baab el-Mu'Adham. There was no bus stop: you either flagged it down to catch it or if you wanted to alight called out "Yammak!"—a catchall word meaning "Near!" "Next to you!" or, in this case, "Stop right here!"

Alas, the garden soon became too tempting for passing urchins, so in due course we built a high boundary wall, made of mud bricks and topped with broken glass, but even that did not deter the petty thieves from climbing over to see what fruit they could pick. We children were not allowed to wander far into the garden, lest we came across one of them. Once I did encounter a Muslim boy of about ten, my own age, trespassing. Trying to look important and unafraid, I asked him, "What are you doing in here?" "My father was going to hit me and I ran to hide here," he said. "I found those grapes under the tree," he quickly added when he saw that I'd noticed them. He was wearing a rope around his *deshdaasha* like a belt so he could double it up into a large pouch and load up with stolen fruit by putting it inside the gown. As I guided him towards our door so that Djassem could talk to him, suddenly he saw what was in my mind, found an opening, and fled like a monkey up the wall.

Djassem was particularly good at keeping a lookout for any fallen palm trees, quickly breaking open the bulbous part at the top to retrieve the palm heart that we all loved so much (it was crunchy, with a delicate sweetness, and was served like fruit). He was given additional help at peak times for pruning or fruit picking. Baba loved to watch them at work, showing off their expertise shinning up a date palm without the help of a harness or a rope. Baba also much enjoyed chatting to the workmen and hearing their uncomplicated views on life in general.

One of the regular helpers was Abd Ali, and one day I overheard him telling Baba one of those tall tales from Ottoman days— "b-iyyaam el Osmali"—about a wealthy Arab called Tariq. This man was superstitious as well as religious, so he went about reciting his prayers like a mantra, repeating and repeating, "Beware of the diabolic Shaitan (Satan). Do not be taken in by his loathsome ways!" Well, the Shaitan had had enough of all this name-calling and decided it was time to put a stop to it. He had done no harm to Tariq, who was, after all, the richest man in the village, wasn't he? So why was Tariq going around giving him such a bad name?

Musing to himself like this, the Shaitan decided to give Tariq something to think about. He disguised himself as a horse and mingled with the other horses in Tariq's stable, all the while watching Tariq and biding his time. When Tariq found a free moment and knelt down in the stable for a quick prayer, the Shaitan looked around and espied a drainpipe opening just in front of Tariq's face. A golden opportunity! The Shaitan immediately shrank himself and entered the drainpipe right in front of the worshipping man.

When the astonished Tariq rubbed his eyes in disbelief, the Shaitan turned around and wiggled his ears as if to mock him. Tariq started shouting like a madman: "A horse! A horse! There is a horse in the drainpipe!"

Everybody rushed over to see what was going on. There was Tariq, pale and trembling, pointing his finger at the now-empty drain, sweating profusely and swearing by Allah that he had just seen with his own eyes a horse climb into the pipe and wiggle its ears. No amount of persuasion could convince Tariq otherwise. And no amount of protestation by Tariq could persuade the onlookers that a horse could become three inches high and trot into a drainpipe. His wife, his parents, and his children all talked to him, telling him it was inconceivable and couldn't he see how ridiculous he was being. But Tariq was adamant. There really was a tiny horse in the pipe.

So they called a doctor. Same story. The doctor told the family that Tariq had gone temporarily mad. The heat must have gone to his head. There was nothing for it but to put poor Tariq away in the lunatic asylum.

Over the following days, all the relatives and friends took turns visiting him, and it was always the same story. Every day the doctor would see him and ask about the horse in the pipe, and Tariq stood his ground—until, one day, his best friend decided to help him. "Look, Tariq," he gently cajoled, "I agree with you, but you do want to leave this madhouse, don't you?"

"Oh, yes, please, I must get out of here—they are all mad here. Help me get out!"

"Well, as from today, my friend, when the doctor comes to test you, you must disclaim everything, and ask him if he is joking, for how could a horse possibly enter a drainpipe?"

And so it happened, and Tariq was released. As soon as he could, he went to the same spot to pray and give thanks to Allah for his release and to watch out for the Shaitan. As if on cue, the Shaitan was waiting for him in the pipe, mocking and wiggling his ears with impudence. Tariq started to shout hysterically, then quickly thought better of it and gulped and spoke into the pipe: "You devil, Shaitan, you! I know you're in there, but which madman is going to believe me if I tell anyone?"

Love and Marriage

EVEN THE MATCHMAKER did business at Qahwat Moshi, for arranged marriages were still the rule of the day, the choice of a groom or bride being entirely the parents' concern and "romance" the stuff of storybooks and films. With children brought up to kiss their parents' hands as a sign of submission and obedience, it was no wonder that boys were timid and girls shy, disciplined, and dutiful. They had no say in the matter whatever.

The whole business followed an accepted procedure, run by go-betweens. The *dellaal* went the rounds at the cafés, while female *dellaalat* deployed their skills by visiting prospective homes. Matchmaking was conducted no differently from any other business deal, with heavy bargaining and negotiation, so the middleman's role was vital. It was his or her job to ensure that the families were compatible, but there was a limited pool of available candidates—an exclusive clique.

A process of natural selection took place instantly. A Cohen was descended from the high priest of the original Temple, so he required an obedient and compliant bride and could not marry a widow or a divorcée. Next came the Levy, deputy to the Cohen and also much respected. The Shamash were also descended from the original Temple—they had managed its upkeep—but had nothing like the same status, being modest and simple straightforward people. Families were labelled like that, with their own characteristic trait, or genetic code. (I was born an Ishayek, a name that probably evolved from S'haaq, our version of Isaac. We were supposed to be headstrong, argumentative, and proud.) You could easily predict the outcome of relationships between those branded as hot tempered or placid, cheerful or sour, generous or mean, arrogant or simple, clever or dumb. The *dellaal*'s skill was to remind the parents of the virtues or vices of the "matched" family.

Many of our family names had historical origins, with real meanings. I know there is nothing exclusive in this—in English, there are Smiths, Coopers, Weavers, and Taylors. Likewise, we had weavers (Haayek), tailors (Khayat), healers (Hakim), scribes (Sopher), teachers (Muallem), judges (Dayyan), watchmakers (Sa'atchi), and bankers (Saghaaf). But we went one better. We added a little spice by calling attention to a person's physical appearance. Some names were pretty tame—Tweel, for instance, which means tall, or El-Q'sayyer, short. But what do you make of Da'bul, which means short and fat, Shahmoon (very fat), El-A'raj (lame), Kharmush (scarred), Mdallal (pampered), El-Yteem (orphan), or El-Mjanin (crazed)? I once even heard of a family called Daasu-el-Jamal—"stepped on by a camel!" We didn't take it all that seriously, of course, but all the same . . .

Once a girl became marriageable, she was kept indoors, out of sight. The rich families knew among themselves who might be a suitable contender. The class system worked, with everyone conscious of "position" and marrying "correctly." We were comfortable with what was familiar, so intermarriages between cousins, second cousins, and cousins once removed were so frequent that we easily lost track. Such an arrangement offered the bride security and obliged her husband to respect her: she was not a possession. If it was a bad match . . . well, divorces were rare. If the groom misbehaved, his bride could only turn to her father to know her fate; mostly, he would tell her to stick it out, for it would have been unusual for him to take her back into the family home.

The matchmaker discreetly approached the parents, telling them who was available on the market. Then, once a likely candidate was hit upon, the discussion progressed in stages, with four main areas of consideration: social background, wealth, age, and looks. The ground covered was vast: family status, connections, ancestry, immediate relatives; likely inheritance from rich parents and dowry; appearance, character, and age compatibility. Finally, a bonus was reserved for other assets such as educational level, intelligence, skills, and manners.

With fair hair, milky skin, and blue or grey eyes being everyone's idea of beauty in a girl, it was not unusual for the groom's mother, along with her female friends and relatives, to go and inspect the prospective bride at her family home. They could ask the girl to wash her face in front of them to check for makeup. They could also observe the way she walked to make sure she was not lame, and examine her closely for other defects that might not have been immediately apparent. We had a virulent insect whose sting created an infection that could leave a scar, the *ekht,* more like a blemish, which often ended up on the face and could be disfiguring. Sometimes, whole families were marked in this way, giving weight to the theory that it was "in the blood"—the insects had a preference for whom they bit. Luckily for us, this wasn't so in our family.

Next, just like any other business transaction, came the inevitable haggling about the dowry. Technically, it was given to the groom, but the money always belonged to the bride, and in the case of a divorce or his premature death, it had to be returned to her before any other debts were settled. If the groom was rich and old, the bride's father was in a much happier position altogether: not only did he not have to pay a dowry, he could expect a substantial lump sum from the intended. All financial arrangements were written into the *ktebba* (marriage contract), along with any other details such as damages, divorce settlement, and even the bride's right to divorce and claim the money in case of her husband's impotence.

So, as you can see, it was a case of convenience for the parents, and although love did sometimes follow, in the main, couples just became used to each other. It was only much later that a boy and girl could meet by chance, at an event or social club, become friends, and ask for their parents' blessing. For the *dellaal,* of course, matches were always "made in heaven."

The bride's house was the focus of attention in the run-up to the wedding, where the mother had been creating her trousseau with gold thread since her daughter was a child. The announcement of the nuptials was accompanied by a profusion of sugared almonds and *halqoon* (Turkish delight). Then, two or three days before the wedding, all the fingers of the bride and just one of the groom's little fingers were covered with henna for luck at the *henni* party, when the inner circles of both families gathered. A *deqqaaqa* troupe improvised songs complimenting the bride's beauty or praising the father's decency and big-heartedness. They picked out other honourable guests and invented songs about them, too, similarly praising them and flattering them for their generosity—important because the troupe made their living solely from tips. Money was literally thrown to them by guests.

About then, the bridal home received another visitor. Discreetly, this time, for she had come to epilate the bride, leaving her body hairless and as smooth as marble. The *heffafa*'s beautification process was efficient but painful, as her method involved dragging strong thread across the skin. At the groom's home, meanwhile, preparations were well in hand for the wedding party and wedding night to be held there. The matrimonial mattresses and quilts were the centre of attention, with the *teeteepampa* called in to fluff up the cotton filling, ready for the newlyweds' arrival.

After the wedding ceremony in the synagogue, where guests had left their gifts, the celebrations would begin. In olden times, the bride donned thick gold anklets (*hejel*) and had gold tassels (*dhafaayir*) plaited in her hair before making her appearance at the party. It was essential to have a *chaalghi* musical band—I'll tell you about them in a moment—singing lovely songs extolling her virtues and those of her husband and other named members of the family. With their drums and fiddles, the band made a huge rhythmic noise in the courtyard where all the relatives assembled, waiting for the big moment when the happy couple would make their excuses and retire to bed.

The hullabaloo continued after they had gone, the idea of the incessant rhythm being to give the groom confidence and encouragement to perform, although it could have the opposite effect, serving as a reminder that there was an audience. The all-male band played on, its music filling not just the courtyard but the whole neighbourhood, leaving no doubt about exactly what was taking place and precisely where. It halted only when a stained sheet appeared, waved from the *tarma,* as proof of the man's virility and the bride's virginity. The night was called the *lailt el-dakhla*—literally, "the night of entry."

It didn't always go smoothly. Information about the facts of life were well concealed, kept secret from youngsters to make sure that they were all virgins when they married, so what to do on the wedding night remained a well-kept secret right up to the last moment. Then the parents engaged an instructor for the groom and an instructress for the bride and all was revealed. Some grooms became so frustrated with all the waiting that, when the time came, they were impatient and forced their attention on the shy bride; there were stories of torn clothes, broken necklaces, and doctors being called in the middle of the night.

After the consummation, the groom's father tipped the musicians handsomely from his ready bags of coins—and continued to tip them every time they mentioned the names of his other children, which the canny players had memorised well in advance, along with those of the remaining single people present, and wished them good luck in the hope it might soon be their turn. The musicians often came back at sunrise to give a repeat performance.

The ceremonies did not end there. On the first Saturday after the wedding it was customary to have an open house: the "Saturday of the Ladies," or *Sabt el-Nesswan*. Hundreds of women, mostly curious strangers, each covered in a black *'abaaya* and veiled to avoid recognition, would file into the house to peer at the bride dressed in her wedding finery with all her trousseau now on show for everyone to admire.

Not until the 1920s was there a glimmer of emancipation or modernisation to challenge these age-old rituals. Thankfully, by the time my sisters and I were of marriageable age, we escaped the more outrageous aspects of these traditions and were spared these indignities.

When the oldest of us, Regina, became engaged, she was about twenty or twenty-one. Near his office, Baba had spotted a good-looking young man who came from a really impressive background: the family of Eliezer Khedouri, the founder of our school. So Reuben was considered a great catch—handsome, too, and someone who had even studied in London and travelled to Shanghai to see relatives. Evidently, he was going to go far.

One hot evening, we were all on the summer roof and had just finished our dinner with some refreshing watermelon. In summer we always had a lot of watermelon; it was plentiful and thirst quenching. But the added bonus for us children was the fun of squeezing the slippery seeds with two fingers and watching them shoot out. My younger sisters and I—aged about eleven then—were competing furtively, giggling away to see who could shoot a seed furthest and, at the same time, trying not to call attention to ourselves. Unfortunately, my seed misfired and hit the handsome young man right on his forehead. I was appalled but did my best to look innocent. Reuben looked around, Baba and Nana looked around, Regina looked around—so I also looked around, as did my sisters. All was seemingly innocent. Reuben looked at the sky. We all looked at the sky. He asked: "Where could it have come from?" To prove my innocence, I repeated, "Where could it have come from?"

There was some talk of their wedding being held in the *qasr*, but instead it was at the school itself, which they decorated with palm fronds. A lot of people came. We all had to go to Baghdad in *'arabaanas* and I remember how dusty and hot it was and how dusty the bride became. But that wasn't the only disappointment: it turned out that Reuben was not wealthy, Eliezer Khedouri having been only a distant relative. But he was a very kind man, because not only did he live with his older brother and their mother but also his mother's mother-in-law.

Next to be married off, in 1925, was Na'ima. Her fiancé was Sasson Soussa. He was from Hilla, a village some distance from Baghdad, close to ancient Babylon, where his family had always lived and were considered to be the local seigneurs. Sasson's father, Moshi, had passed away only a year earlier, at the age of forty-three, while undergoing heart surgery in Vienna. (Sasson had given up studying to be a doctor in Beirut in order to take care of him and had been at his bedside when he died.) Aged only twenty-two, he was left with huge responsibilities: being the eldest, he had to look after Moshi's many business interests, which were mostly in Hilla, and included trading in agricultural commodities—wheat, rice, and sesame—as well as owning the plantations that produced those crops. In addition, he had the monopoly for generating electricity for the town, and also, in those days before electric fridges, supplying ice. Most important, he had to look after his mother as well as his younger brother and find husbands for his three unmarried sisters.

Sasson married Na'ima in Hilla. I remember the lovely silks that made part of her trousseau, which Baba had been fortunate to obtain, as he was working with a firm that imported luxury goods through their family, who were settled in England. My lasting memory of Sasson is his beautiful handwriting: I loved to watch him write.

Next came Fahima. She was considered the best looking of my siblings, and Jacob Gareh was another handsome young man, though almost twenty years her senior. He came to Baghdad from Palestine, where he lived and had a business, expressly to find a bride whose roots were similar to his own. Fahima must have been only twenty then, like Regina when she married. But by this time, Baba had decided that it would be better to have the wedding at the *qasr*. So all the guests came to us, in hired buses.

Soon after the wedding, Jacob took her back with him to Tel Aviv, which involved crossing the great Syrian Desert by motor coach and was an adventure. However, like the rest of us girls, she had never travelled abroad before. She had a hard time settling down and became homesick, not just for her family but particularly for her clique of girlfriends of whom she was the leader. It was 1931 and Tel Aviv was just a small town, having been founded only twenty-two years earlier. Suddenly, she had to come to terms with an alien lifestyle: instead of a fine house with servants, she was living in a modern apartment and had to fend for herself. Not long after arriving, she sent Baba a telegram: MALADE. VENEZ. ("Sick. Come.")—even today, we still correspond in French. Extremely concerned, Baba took Nana and the baby of the family, Marcelle, and set off for Tel Aviv in response. When Baba had been assured his daughter was all right, he took advantage of the situation by leaving Nana and Marcelle with Fahima and went off on a grand tour of Europe by himself. He visited relatives in Switzerland, Paris, and London, making stops along the way in Prague and other capitals. He must have had a guilty conscience, because he had a whale of a shopping spree in Paris, where he bought fashionable clothes for us all from the Galeries Lafayette, including fur coats, plus a jewellery box with the Eiffel Tower pictured on it, which I still treasure.

Fahima and the Nairn coach en route to Palestine, 1931

Postcard from Prague: Baba seated above the letter P

The promise to me of finishing school in Paris never material-
ised, as I've said. (I don't know why. Was it because Baba was afraid
that, if one went, all his other children would follow?) But one
of my friends made it. She was an only daughter and her parents
were extremely well-to-do, her father being an important advocate.
When she begged to be allowed to study in Paris, the family not
only agreed but went along with her and lived there for a year. You
can just imagine what it was like when she returned with her Parisian wardrobe and her Parisian accent, rolling her *rr*'s the Parisian
way—like a gargle. *Weh hoo weh!* We were all in awe. Almost everything we did and said seemed wrong to her delicate ears now. She
was always trumping us with *"Chez nous à Paris . . .* we do things differently," or *"Chez nous à Paris . . .* we say things differently." In the
end, it wore us down, and we all mimicked her when we wanted to
imply it was an exaggeration. Others, to show off their education,
developed an affectation and would intersperse their conversation with the odd French word, hastily translated into Arabic, thus:
"Non—laa." Or "Au contraire—bel 'aks."

Habits were changing, but her case impressed us for another
reason. Prior to our time, young girls had absolutely no say with regard to their future, and boys were hardly given any greater consideration: they were expected to live in the shadow of their fathers all
their lives, demonstrating their subordination to the world at large
and the staff at work in particular, for of course the scion would be
working with his father. We all followed a pattern set by our parents. It had little to do with our personalities, abilities, or tastes—
the richer the father, the stronger his grip, the more authority over
his children. Take my brother Salman, for example. Baba never
sent him abroad to pursue further studies, even though he did well
at school. This was the norm for all parents at the time and I have
often wondered why. Was it because Baba was afraid it would lead
his son to take up a profession? The professions were considered
to be worthy but not lucrative. Much better to be an entrepreneur.
So Salman later joined my father in the business, and Baba had a
smaller *qasr* built for him adjacent to the master house.

During Baba and Nana's absence in Palestine I had found it difficult, staying behind with my brother and younger sister Daisy, as
I had no job and nothing to do. So, two years later, when Fahima
sent another telegram and Baba and Nana made ready to go back

to Tel Aviv yet again, I begged to be taken with them. They agreed
and took me, along with Daisy.

The route was well established: we went by Nairn coach just as
Fahima had, through the desert to the border at Rutbah, then to
Ramadi in Syria, and from there a taxi took us the rest of the way.
Camels and other beasts of burden had been the means of transportation in olden times, of course; there were hardly any roads
crossing the desert and anyone trying to travel a distance faced all
kinds of possible obstacles, not least sandstorms and Bedouin raids.
The Nairn bus company, begun by two brothers from New Zealand
who had been serving with the British army, was therefore an instant success, and "Nair-renn" became part of our vocabulary. The
service opened possibilities beyond our wildest dreams: compared
with the camel days, it was now a relatively fast trip from Baghdad
to Damascus or Beirut or Haifa, and from there, we could take a
train to Egypt or Turkey, or board a boat to Europe, as Baba did, or
even to America.

We stayed in Palestine for two years, from 1933 to 1934, while
Baba and Nana looked around, considering settling. I had a great
time. It was my first experience of life in a freethinking society. I
could not believe the freedom of it. Daisy and I enrolled for English
lessons, Hebrew lessons, dancing lessons—and we even had a dip in

Postcard from Palestine: Violette and Daisy, 1933

the sea. It was such an adventure, and a measure of the far-reaching changes that were happening in our lives and the emancipation we were experiencing. Back in Baghdad, change had initially been limited to the imitation—at home, at least—of Western fashion. Then women started to remove the veil, and finally the *'abaaya* disappeared and the wearing of Western clothes in public was adopted. This occurred only in the "cosmopolitan" city, however; when we went to the countryside, we still had to honour tradition.

Can you imagine how liberating all this was, to someone brought up respecting the conventions of Baghdad? Before I was born, women had been prohibited from removing their stockings in their homes, even on hot days or in old age. And here we were, only a generation later, in Palestine swimming in the sea in full public view.

The modernisation of Mesopotamia/Iraq had gathered pace during World War I with the arrival of the British and the realisation of the country's vast oil potential. New social clubs—*naadi*—sprang up in Baghdad where our friends enjoyed meeting regularly: the Rashid, the Zawraa, the Rafidain, and the Laura Khedouri. My sisters and I had few opportunities to participate, however, as the *qasr* was so far out of town. So, naturally, in our Palestine years Daisy and I were thrilled to be able to go out in mixed company. Although I had approaches from young men during my sojourn (I particularly remember a Russian philosopher), I rebuffed them, as I was not yet ready to settle down, and anyway it was unthinkable.

Baba did not consider me pretty. He was always worrying about me: "Who is going to want you? Your eyes are far too big . . . Can't you half close them? . . . I've heard of a plastic surgeon who is able to make them smaller . . ." But Baba and Nana were not in a hurry to have me married. They had already seen off half their daughters, and I was turning out to be useful in the home. And while we were in Palestine, I discovered another way to be useful: I found my lifetime hobby when I took a dressmaking course and became fascinated. I even learned to make good, supportive bras. (I am big bosomed so this was a revelation. Until then bras had not been made to enhance bosoms but rather to flatten them by tying them down.)

My wedding came much later. Matches were proposed, and Baba mentioned some to me—one being Reuben's younger brother, the others being either brothers of my school friends or Salman's friends.

In Baghdad, one of my father's best friends was the chief justice. He was a widower and often came to the *qasr* with his children, one of whom was *my* best friend in school. This is how I met (and liked a lot) the justice's second son, who was one year younger than me. But I saw nothing wrong in that, for, after all, Baba and Nana themselves had a similar age difference. I was wondering about this, hoping something might come of it, when one day Baba said he had something to tell me that would be of great importance. My heart beat a little faster.

We were in the garden, and I can still smell the jasmine as I remember his words. He had indeed received a proposition of marriage for me from the chief justice . . . not on behalf of his son, but for himself! I can't remember my reaction, but it was a mark of Baba's thoughtfulness that he did not force his friend onto me as others in his position might have done. The justice was a marvellous "prospect" and a bond with him would have greatly increased our family's already-high social standing. But I certainly had no feelings for him, an old man, and how could I have lived in the same house by his side while having romantic feelings for his son? For me, it was a triangle of disaster, a three-way trap. I could not marry the father and I could not marry the son. And I risked losing my best friend in the bargain. Of course, I could not explain any of this to Baba. He just took my reticence as further evidence that I was a bit "different"—or was it that he was having second thoughts himself and was glad he was not going to lose me after all?

And then, in 1937, a certain Abraham Shashoua approached Baba and asked for my hand on behalf of his brother-in-law Dahoud. First, they bargained. Baba wanted to know what the prospective groom did for a living. It turned out that he worked as a junior partner (very junior, Baba later discovered) at an import wholesaling *khaan*. This was not good. Then he wanted to know about the family background and status—respectable all right, but not of an equal social standing to our own. They discussed the dowry and a sum was agreed. I, meanwhile, was kept in the dark totally until one day Baba sprung it on me that this time I definitely was going to get engaged. I knew nothing of the identity of the man I was to marry. I had no idea what he looked like—not even a photograph. I was just told his name: Dahoud—David.

It had been like that for my sisters, too. My father had just brought their husbands-to-be and the girls had been told, "This is the man you are going to marry"—and that was that. All the more remarkable, therefore, for me to have escaped the chief justice. Many of my school friends were married off to friends of their fathers.

The next thing I knew, an appointment had been made for the groom to come to the *qasr*, along with his parents and many other members of his family, about a dozen in all. My parents and many members of my own family were also present, including Yemma, who was getting deaf and needed everything explained to her, loudly.

It was intimidating to enter a room full of people, one of whom was to be my husband—someone I could not identify among all the strange faces. Even today, I couldn't tell you all the people who were present. Baba had also said, gently, that if I didn't like the look of him I wouldn't have to marry him—but that was inconceivable. Everybody was gathered for an engagement; it was a fait accompli.

I was not introduced. They could see me: I was obvious. But it was not immediately clear to me who was to be my groom. The *qasr* was large, with people all over the place, and voices chattering. If I didn't like the look of him? If only I could get a glimpse of him! Gradually, by process of elimination, I worked out that it was the youngest male stranger in the room, a man of about thirty-five. There was a lengthy discussion, a *meqaddesh* (registrar) recited a *berakha* (blessing) and now we were considered betrothed. David was thrilled with what he saw on that first day—me, the grandeur of the *qasr* and the lifestyle he was marrying into. And I was happy and excited: he was handsome and likeable. The guests had all come a long way for this ceremony, so they sat a while longer while my fiancé invited me to take a walk in our garden, just the two of us. On our return, they all left.

Next day, he came visiting (and forever afterwards told me how he dreaded coming and drinking my parents' weak tea; he liked it strong). He invited me to go to Baghdad with him to have our photograph taken at Arshak's—the best photographer in the city. We discussed future plans: houses, that kind of thing. Suddenly I was really free—I could make my own decisions with my future hus-

The ktebba *wedding
contract, written in
Judeo-Arabic.
Dowry: £2,000.*

band. After a couple of busy months preparing my trousseau and
hunting for a suitable house, we were married in Baab el-Shargi at the
Rashid Club. In recognition, Baba gave Abraham, our go-between,
a beautiful gold watch, which he passed to his eldest son, Maurice,
who must have been about ten at the time. He was an inquisitive
child, who promptly took a screwdriver to it and dismantled it so
perfectly it could never be put back together again. Maurice went
on to be a brilliant engineer.

The contract money for my dowry, written into the *ktebba*, was
two thousand dinars (we had given up rupees by then)—equivalent
to two thousand pounds, a large sum indeed in those days. David's
brother Haron, ten years his senior, made the journey from Europe
to be present. A bachelor, he was impressed with me and wanted
my help finding a bride for himself, which I did: another Violette.
(She was one of three sisters who had grown up in Basra. She later
told me that their neighbour opposite, a Christian woman, was al-

ways pushing the unlikely idea that one of her sons should marry one of the sisters. Violette was particularly wary of the youngest, the short, fat one who went by the name of Tariq—the very Tariq Aziz who became vice premier under Saddam Hussein.) By way of thanks for my introduction, Haron bought me the latest in modernity: a beautiful radiogram.

While David was not on par with Baba scholastically—who was?—he was certainly no fool and had a way with people that was a true talent that others envied. His schooling had been interrupted due to the displacement of his parents during World War I; like many others, they had travelled to Basra because it was the first town to fall to the British. They had been liberated, yet there was still much confusion, and after a while they found that Basra did not suit them and they returned to Baghdad. As soon as David had earned enough money, he bought himself an *'oud*—an instrument like a lute—and took a few lessons. He was soon doing well with his music for he truly had a musical ear and the potential to earn his living as a musician. His personal charm, lovely singing voice—he sang like Abdul Wahab, the heartthrob Arabic crooner—and the accomplished way he played the instrument placed him in high demand in our circle of friends. This earned him popularity and respect.

Two Violettes: the author and Haron's bride

COLLECTION OF VIOLETTE SHAMASH

David's father, Shm'oon, clung to the old ways, still wearing a *zboon, 'abaaya,* and fez right up to the time we were married, when David finally convinced him to modernise and change into a suit. In the evening, he liked to puff away at his *nargiila* with half a bottle of *'arak* beside him. He wasn't too impressed by his son's musical abilities. "Do you want to be a clown? It's about time you stopped this foolishness and put aside your *'oud* and joined the business," he admonished David one day. Stung, David joined the business full-time and relegated his *'oud* to the background.

We all loved music, and the *'oud* was one of the principal instruments played by the *chaalghi* bands that entertained us on the radio, in the coffeehouses, and at all large parties and family gatherings. David explained to me that the other instruments were the *kamanja* (fiddle), *dumbuk* (hand drum), *qanoon* or *santour* (zither), and *daff* (tambourine). The songs sung in the *chaalghi* did not necessarily have a Jewish theme: they were love lyrics of all types and ballads expressing all kinds of emotion.

The 1930s

AS I WAS GROWING UP, Iraq was maturing, too. The defining development came in 1927 when huge quantities of oil were discovered near Kirkuk, and the government granted oil rights to the Iraq Petroleum Company, which the British controlled. Tragically, instead of integrating as a nation, the ethnic differences within the population were beginning to tear it apart. On top of everything, while many Iraqis wanted the British out, our people considered the colonial power a steadying influence and saw no benefit in rocking the boat. A diplomatic way out of the impasse was found with a treaty in 1930 that allowed Iraq independence while still permitting London to exert strong military and political influence, especially regarding foreign policy.

The British mandate expired in 1932. One year later King Faisal died, and our community lost a sympathetic ruler. His inexperienced son Ghazi succeeded him at the age of twenty-one. For our people it was a disaster, but for the Assyrian Christians it was worse: they staged a revolt and were brutally crushed. Ghazi himself showed more interest in playing with expensive toys than in leading a nation responsibly. He ran his own radio station from the palace, from which he himself often read the news, and collected a stable of the latest European and American cars. His broadcasts fright-

Downtown Baghdad

ened us, for they bore the first breeze of anti-Semitic propaganda coming from Nazi Germany.

Three years later, in 1936, with Palestine on the boil, Ghazi signed a friendship treaty with other Arab nations, vowing to kick the British out. But most disquieting for us was the arrogant way he expressed his admiration for Hitler and Mussolini. With Nazism on the rise, there were sporadic attacks against the Jews and their businesses: three Jews were murdered on a Baghdad street, and on Yom Kippur the following year, a Baghdad synagogue was firebombed by an Iraqi nationalist. There was a succession of military coups d'état, all aiming to "save Palestine," in which Ghazi and a secret brotherhood of Iraqi army officers played a prominent role. They belonged to a movement known as the Golden Square, which took its name from the square-and-compasses symbol of Freemasonry and had many adherents among officers who had served in the Ottoman Turkish army.

King Ghazi died violently when his sports car crashed into a concrete lamppost in 1939. The cause of the accident remained a mystery, but many people believed it to have been the work of British Intelligence.

In the 1930s, the total Iraqi population reached two million, with three hundred thousand living in Baghdad, including almost all of the minorities. It was a largely rural economy: people toiled the land for little return and all earnings were spent on the most basic of all necessities—food and clothing. We city dwellers thought that they led a healthy country life, because few ever needed a doctor—though, with hindsight, this was probably because they could not afford one. They ate simply, bulking out the meal with flat pitta-like bread called *semmoon*. A worker often lunched on two of these pittas and a kilo of dates, that nourishing staple, the cheapest and most plentiful fruit around. His appetite would be such that he could have just as easily eaten ten eggs or half a kilo of meat. But although certain foods were plentiful and cheap, few could afford such luxuries as eggs and meat.

We were in daily contact with the Muslims in Baghdad, of course, and had warm feelings towards those we knew or met in the countryside. At the festival of Shavuot (Pentecost) in May, for example, we had a tradition of making a pilgrimage to the village of Al-Kifil, near Hilla, a long way off on dirt roads, to the shrine of Nabi Hesqeil—the prophet Ezekiel—which we revered as a place of miracles. It was looked after year-round by the local Muslim villagers, and they looked forward to our visit because without fail we always took them something. It was an uncomfortable ride, dusty and extremely bumpy. Tyres were not what they are today, and it was several punctures and hours later that one arrived with relief at the village on the banks of the Euphrates. When we went to the shrine, all I saw was a dark room in which the tomb of Nabi Hesqeil was covered in dark rough velvet. I was told to follow the line of pilgrims, round and round, and kiss the shrine and repeat "Bless Baba and Nana" in a whisper. By the end, I was tired and my lips were sore, but I proudly told everyone how wonderful it all was.

My grandmother Yemma used to tell us how much she enjoyed the same journey when she was just sixteen and Baba was not much more than twelve months old, sitting comfortably in front of her on her donkey. How much longer it must have taken them then! All the family travelled—mother-in-law, sisters, brothers, cousins, children. They used to stop at every village on the way and buy a delicious snack of *qeimagh,* a local clotted cream made from buffalo milk, and freshly baked bread. So that they could be sure of eating nothing but properly slaughtered meat, a *shohet* accompanied them all the way. He took care of the ritual dispatch of whatever chicken or baby lamb they might fancy for their dinner, and it was then immediately grilled on a wood fire. They never questioned the friendliness of the local Muslims, a proud people who fully lived up to their reputation for hospitality, honour, and honesty. The party would stay the night in Al-Kifil, but the locals who accommodated them would not take money, as that would have been embarrassing. They preferred instead to be given presents, such as a pair of sandals or a length of calico or printed fabric to make a new dress for a bride-to-be.

The Ishayek dynasty had come from Aleppo in Syria around 1700: I have a family tree tracing our beginnings to that date [see appendix]. Our founder, S'haaq, came to Baghdad as part of the entourage of the *hakham* Sadqa, who it was rumoured had originally come from Salonica—the city that welcomed many of the Jews fleeing from the Spanish Inquisition in the sixteenth century. Most of S'haaq's descendants spelled their surname in a variety of ways; I have seen Schayek, Shaiq, Sehayek, Sehayik, Sehaiq, Sehaik, Ishaiq. A branch of the family that settled in London became known as Sassoon, after my grandfather's given name, Sasson.

Sasson was my mother's father, who died in 1901 in circumstances that were still being talked about when I was a child. Apparently, he had cataracts and had been told that there was a surgeon in Vienna who could remove them, the Austrian capital being the centre of medical knowledge at the time. Travel over such a long distance was a huge undertaking, but he set off with his eldest son Heskel, heading for Port Said, where they boarded a ship bound for Marseilles. From there, they intended to travel to their destination by train.

They were ill prepared for the voyage, failing to realise that the ship would not have any kosher food. This did not deter other Jewish passengers who somehow managed to get by with what they

could—hard-boiled eggs, cheese, bread, and so on. But my grandfather was too proud to be seen giving in. He ate only fruit and
vegetables, took ill, and is said to have died of starvation. The ship
stopped in Algiers, where his body is buried (a monument to his
memory was erected in the cemetery by my cousins in 1952). My
uncle Heskel returned to Baghdad alone but he died only nine
years later, drowned in the Tigris in a swimming accident.

So, Mesopotamia. When I was born, there was no industry, no fruit
exporting, and certainly, as I've said, no battery hens. Cooperatives
had not even been thought of. Green grass was a rarity, a luxurious
sight to be spotted only in the short winter; in summer, the country
landscape was desert and animal husbandry was primitive. Irrigation, as such, was limited to the areas around the rivers.

At home, storage was a problem for anything perishable. Few
fresh eggs were offered for sale, most being saved to hatch a new
generation of chicks which would in turn grow into egg-producing
hens as well as chickens for slaughter. Farmers had to provide their
own transport to Baghdad if they wanted to sell the surplus eggs,
and for the journey to be cost-effective, they had to save them in a
zembiil basket until there were enough to make the trip worthwhile.
The warm *zembiil* acted as an incubator, and the consequences were
predictable. A friend of ours who had the unenviable task of organising fresh provisions for the British military told us how he
despaired of ever finding a source of fresh eggs. According to him,
the cook always broke each of his eggs separately, one by one, in a
bowl for safety's sake: it might be bad or, worse, a chick could pop
out. One day, as he was chatting to the NAAFI [Navy, Army, and
Air Force Institutes] inspector in the place where they kept their
eggs, to his horror he spotted out of the corner of his eye a chick
running around the back of the storeroom. With a sinking heart
he glanced at the inspector—and was relieved to find him highly
amused by the spectacle.

By the 1920s, modern shops had begun to appear, and we even
had that ultimate luxury, the department store. In many Middle
Eastern capitals, Orosdi Back became a household name, with its
funny trademark of an elephant riding a tricycle. We all knew it as

MATSON PHOTOGRAPH COLLECTION, LIBRARY OF CONGRESS

The arcaded storefronts of Rashid Street

Prix Fixe—the only place in Baghdad where there was no bargaining—take it or leave it! Oh, and it had another unique feature: a lift, the first we had ever seen, which for us was its main attraction. The store, owned by European Jews, was famous for its luxury goods. Everybody loved to shop there, particularly for wedding presents and trousseaux. It was the ultimate, the Harrods of its day, always the first with the latest fashions from Europe. We knew we were not going to be cheated there; it was so elegant, worth every penny, selling Bally shoes, cashmere outfits, silk ready-to-wear dresses, beautiful fabrics, the best china, silver cutlery, silk eiderdowns, underwear, and even children's ready-made clothes from Petit Bateau in France. It was like paradise. Even now, sweets and chocolates don't taste as good as those that came from Orosdi Back.

Then, with the 1930s, as the country started to benefit from oil revenues, society advanced at an astonishing pace. We became used to indoor plumbing, electricity, and paved streets with proper lighting. There were buses on Rashid Street, and a few private cars and taxis started circulating. Telephones were installed in the richer homes. Baghdad was expanding, with new housing going up in

Growing up: Violette inside the qasr

COLLECTION OF VIOLETTE SHAMASH

what had become the suburbs, slowly edging their way towards Karrada. Cafés and restaurants sprang up along the riverside. People began to travel more, sometimes as far afield as the United States. I remember how one of our former neighbours from Hennouni, Salim, went to visit his uncle in New York and came back, so impressed with the way the Americans "live in box homes they call apartments." He told his father that when he arrived, he thought his uncle's apartment was the attic, so he asked why they couldn't go inside the actual home. "But we were already inside their home," he said. "There they live in compact homes—all on one level floor."

There were further surprises awaiting him. His uncle had begun his working life selling ladies' stockings; now he was the proud owner of a modern factory that turned them out by the thousand. Salim saw whirring machinery controlled at the touch of a button, this one for knitting the stockings, that one for wrapping them in pairs, another one for boxing them a dozen at a time. All most impressive. When he arrived home, he could hardy stop regaling the family with stories of wonder, of modernity and mass production and how advanced America was. It was about then that Charlie Chaplin's film *Modern Times* came to town.

Soon his uncle sent his son George—Salim's cousin, previously known to us as Nadji—back to Baghdad to seek a wife. A room was booked for the young New Yorker in the most expensive hotel on the Tigris, from where Salim's father collected him to visit his grandparents—a twenty-minute walk through the narrow alleys of the old town. When they arrived at a door with an old shoe nailed to it and a *mezuza* on the right, Salim's father knocked—and like magic, the door opened almost immediately. They entered and passed down an empty, dark, and narrow corridor until they reached a patio—but still there was no sign of anyone. So who had opened the door? George looked around, puzzled. "Oh, that door is automatic," said his uncle nonchalantly. "Don't you have that in America?"

George's mind was already working on how to make a million out of this novelty back in New York. An automatic door opener! What he had failed to notice was the string tied to the latch that passed through the bannister and on up to the first floor where the grandparents sat, keeping guard, anticipating the moment when they had to pull it.

Although the old quarter of Hennouni was no longer a fashionable place to live, we were drawn back to the old city for our daily needs and, in particular, to the streets of the Shorjah market area. And when the men went shopping, they sometimes took the family cook along to carry all the purchases or hired a *hammaal* for the heavy goods.

The Souq el Khubuz was where people bought their bread. It was an extraordinary sight to see all the *tannoor* bread ovens glowing, several to a row, as the bakers flipped the dough expertly, like acrobats spinning plates. The aroma met you well before you got there. Then there was Souq al Safafiir—*safafiir* means "brass and copper"—where we bought all our cookware and metal utensils. The din that came from there was incredible, with all the artisans hammering the metal into shape, making new items, and repairing

LEFT: *A street scene in the market*

BELOW: *The metal market, Souq al Safafir*

old ones. Everyone cooked with copper pans lined with a thin layer
of tin to prevent them from reacting with acidic foods. This would
wear out from time to time, so they had to go back for relining. I
loved seeing the men at work, for although the racket hurt the ears,
the sight of all that gold colour glinting in the sunshine as they
turned the pans by hand was so pretty. When they hung them up, it
was like Aladdin's cave.

Both markets were, in effect, extensions of Souq Hennouni
in the heart of the Jewish neighbourhood, which centred on the
Great Synagogue. It was subdivided into four main areas, for meat,
fish and chicken, plus one particular spot for fruit, vegetables, and
cheese. Oh, those rich smells and the colours of the fresh herbs
and spices, the fruit and vegetables, the sweets such as baklava,
semsemiyee, and *zingoola* (honeyed batter)! In one alley, the butch-
ers' shops stood next to one another. They sold mainly mutton,
lamb, and other parts of the sheep, but little beef. Elsewhere, other
shops sold fish, fresh from the Tigris; *shabboot,* a kind of carp, was
our favourite. In another alley, you could buy chickens, which were
always sold live, to be taken to the *shohet,* who would check for defects before doing the necessary. In yet another alley, vegetable and
fruit vendors sold seasonal produce, and there were also shops that
sold cheeses (the one we consumed most was like feta), as well as
thick, strained *laban,* butter, and *qeimagh.*

Making
tengaayee *jugs*
for cooling water

MATSON PHOTOGRAPH COLLECTION, LIBRARY OF CONGRESS

In those crowded conditions, you had to watch where you put your feet; the chances were that you would sooner or later either step on someone's foot or be stepped upon. The civilised British way of dealing with that would be to say, "Sorry!" (both offender and offended, in unison). Not so with us Baghdadis. " *'Aammia!*" you would shout if you were the victim: "May the treader be rendered blind!" It was the expected reaction, quite normal. On a different level, the worst insult to a Muslim (or to a Jew, for that matter) would be to remind him of his origins or to cast doubt on his parenthood. A phrase such as "kalb ibn kalb" ("dog, son of a dog") or any idiom mentioning his mother could lead to a bloody fight with much punching and head banging and more name-calling— "Scoundrel!" "Parasite!" and so on—bland by today's standards. Passersby and friends would try to pull the fighters apart and defuse the anger, but this would serve only to inflame them and even get the onlookers involved. Someone could get hurt, so, afraid of being roped in on such occasions, Jews and Christians quietly disappeared from the scene.

The cinema became the main source of entertainment—another sign of the changing times—and the best was Rafidain in the heart of Rashid Street. Films were closely followed and played a large part in contemporary life, often influencing our fashion purchases at Orosdi Back. Like children, adults would be entranced and totally involved in the story unfolding before them, believing everything they saw on the screen. It was no surprise when a spectator became so carried away that, in his anxiety to come to the aid of the hero, he would throw a missile, usually an empty bottle, at the villain, and we'd end up with a gaping hole in the screen. Romantic films such as *La Dame aux Camélias* and *Sous les Toits de Paris* were banned to us teenage girls, but I remember how greatly excited we were when it was arranged that the top-grade classes at school could go *en groupe* to see *All Quiet on the Western Front*. I also recall that the most popular film was *Ramona,* with its romantic songs translated into Arabic, but everyone loved Charlie Chaplin and Laurel and Hardy.

All the younger men began emulating their screen heroes, growing mustachios, slicking and brilliantining their hair à la Clark Gable or Humphrey Bogart, or our own singing star Abdul Wahab. The gramophone became widely available, and the singers of Baghdad also exercised a lot of influence with their ironic themes. Every open-air café in Baghdad played one particular song at high volume all day, every day, which became a favourite with David, who continued to sing it all his life. Interpreted by Aziz Ali, it was called "Shobash." According to the song, the bewildered singer's son Shobash had just returned from "London School" with newfangled ideas, totally flouting parental control. The father thought he looked like a crow in his dark European suit, rebelling against the old traditions and behaving in an affected manner.

Comparing him to a crow, *ghraab,* had a deeper meaning, for *ghraab* is an insult, the crow being an ugly and ungainly bird, taken to be a bad omen. It was just one of many strange expressions we had. "Booma!" was another, which we'd say of someone behaving like an idiot (don't ask me why: it means "owl"). Worse, someone you didn't like might be a *wabba*—a plague. If you saw him coming you'd say as an aside: "Dja l'wabba!"—Here comes the plague! But the universal, catchall expletive was "Wudja!" meaning "pain." We used it to express dismay, unpleasant surprise, shock, annoyance, and so on.

At the start of the century, our men were indistinguishable from Muslims, as they all wore the same garb: long-sleeved shirts, pleated trousers with wide waistbands, and voluminous long robes. By the 1930s, both men and women preferred Western clothes, but all men from all religions still kept their heads covered with a fez or *fiina.* There was a more old-fashioned variant in which a *chitayi,* a long band of material, was wound round the crown of the fez. Whatever the headgear, it was important that it should be kept smart. If it was made of felt, it had to be taken regularly to *abul fiussah,* the pressing man—today we'd call him the dry-cleaner, but one specialising in headgear, complete with copper moulds heated by a petrol burner. Our men felt somewhat safer with their heads inconspicuously covered like all the others, in case they were picked on by a Muslim bully.

The *fiina* was made of vivid red felt that was stiffly lined—the stiffer the better, as this was considered to be more elegant, particularly if the hat was worn slightly cocked to one side. It had a large black tassel swinging from the topknot as if it was a fly swat. The un-

COLLECTION OF VIOLETTE SHAMASH

David's father, Shm'oon,
wearing the traditional
sidaara

lined but still well-shaped fez, a red felt cap also with a black tassel, was still in everyday use despite being outlawed in Turkey itself as a symbol of the Ottoman regime. In Iraq, following independence in 1932, King Faisal decreed that it should be replaced by the *sidaara* as the country tried to create its own identity. The new headgear was made of black felt and boat shaped. Many Arab men thought this suggestive and refused to don the new hat, while Jews and Christians remained undecided for a long time. Finally, in the late 1930s, another popular song by Mulla Abboud al-Karkhi decided them all: "Ya helou ya-boul sidaara"—"Hello there, handsome, with the *sidaara*." After that no one could resist wearing one.

But it wasn't all songs and laughter. How can I think of the 1930s without some memory of the Depression? There has always been depression in Baghdad, but when *the* Depression hit the city, it was even worse. I think you understand by now that nothing was ever wasted even in good times, and this was especially true when it came to food. There were many stories that played on this. I liked the one about Ismail, who was riding his donkey between two villages. Hungry and thirsty, he stopped at a shepherd's hut, and after saluting the man politely, said: "I am hungry and thirsty and so is my donkey, but I only have a small coin in my pocket. How can you help me?"

"I will take your coin and give you a watermelon," replied the shepherd. "Eat the watermelon to satisfy your hunger and thirst, feed your donkey with the hard skin, and you can then enjoy yourself cracking the seeds as you ride."

Then Baba loved to tell the story of Abu Naadji, a middle-aged man who had made an art of being thrifty. One day he went to see his friend Abu Shaul, who also enjoyed seeing how little money he needed to live on. They sat on Abu Shaul's patio solving the world's problems, and soon Abu Shaul made a thin tea with the dregs from the last pot. He brought out two *stikans* and, indicating the sugar, said to Abu Naadji, "One or none?" Abu Naadji did not take offence—he enjoyed their bantering rivalry—but he smiled as he conceded a point to Abu Shaul. It was considered the height of bad manners to ask how many of the uneven pieces that had been broken off the sugarloaf you wanted in your tea.

Later, when night began to fall and the host lit a candle hardly thicker than a matchstick, Abu Naadji commented: "We have already seen each other now, so let us not waste the candle. We can talk just as easily in the dark." It was Abu Shaul's turn to concede a point. He blew the candle out.

Some hours passed. Finally all talk was exhausted and it was time for Abu Naadji to go home. Abu Shaul was feeling around for the matches when Abu Naadji said: "Wait a moment. First let me put my trousers on again. It was pointless wearing them out if they could not be seen!"

Wudja! Game, set, and match to Abu Naadji.

All joking aside, there was severe poverty in some quarters. An essay that my friend Daisy wrote at school well illustrates the situation. The subject was "What do you cost your parents?" and this is what she wrote:

Ever since I was born, I have been wearing my elder sister's hand-me-downs when she out-grew them. Now, she wears higher heels on her shoes, so when they wear down sufficiently they are just right for me. As I am eighteen months younger than her, I get all her schoolbooks when she has finished with them. I get her copybooks, too, and I carefully rub out everything she has written with an eraser so that I can have a clean exercise book to use at school. As my parents cannot afford the school fees, we are here at the community's cost.

If I am good, and look after my younger brother, my mother gives me one fils [about a farthing] to buy *gargaree* candy. My mother almost invariably cooks a soup for us so it is always easy to feed an unexpected guest by adding another glass of water, as she does for me, but my father is always served his meal before the gruel is thinned down. In summer we get a wood containerful of yoghurt, *'elba laban,* every day. My mother adds a pinch of salt and a glass of water to it, then stirs it to a creamy mixture and offers the first glass of this to my father. She then adds another pinch of salt and another glass of water and my eldest brother gets the benefit of the second dilution, and so on down the line. By the time my turn comes it is the colour of pallid milk and tastes more like salt water.

We all sleep in the same room, on a thin mattress that we put on the floor, and we roll up our coats and use them as pillows. And we still have room if a guest wants to spend the night. In summer, we sleep on the roof, and then we don't even need a mattress to sleep on, as we use the palm leaf mats that we make. This way we do not wear the mattress down too quickly, and anyway the mats are cooler to sleep on.

Unfortunately, I cannot tell you exactly how many fils my mother has given me so far, as I have not counted the number of times I have been able to look after my younger brother. You see, the work is not regular.

In this way, a clever and cheeky schoolgirl described what poverty could mean, even though her family was not poor then by any means. She married, had four sons, and emigrated to England in 1947 with her boys. Their name is Sa'atchi.

Revolution

ALTHOUGH PROGRESS was breathtakingly rapid and enthralling, I was also deeply involved in adjusting to my new life, my new family, and my new circle of friends. In all the changes happening around me, I was aware of shifting attitudes among the Muslims, but they didn't worry me. As long as I wasn't directly affected, I thought they would blow over, and the worst they would mean to me was that I would have to hide behind an anonymous black *'abaaya* in public. But that also served a useful purpose: it meant that I could blend in and escape men's leers. As a result, I was totally unprepared for the about-face that was waiting around the corner. At that stage in my life, if you had asked me, I would never have dreamed that I would one day flee from my home and country.

The 1930s brought new freedoms. By now all of my generation were young adults, each with a widening circle of friends. We had a lot of cousins, and there were also the friends of our parents who had children of our age. The *qasr* by default became the magnet, and when we had company, it seemed that Zahra could hardly keep up with the baking. She had to work faster and faster, preparing *sembousak* for us by the *zembiil* load.

At first, individuals and families would just drop in, but with more of us now having telephones, we could prearrange an event. Everyone was welcome, and we'd have an impromptu picnic on the island of Jazra, taking the gramophone with us. Any excuse was good enough, and in my carefree days, the fun seemed never ending.

Jazra was so special throughout our lives. It was our private refuge and we went there whenever we could—that is, when the river was low enough to walk across, for it could disappear completely in spring when the Tigris was in flood. One hot summer's day when I was just a child, a party of us including my aunt went there for a picnic. It was an extremely fertile place, and even though nobody cultivated it, vegetables self-seeded there: it was heavenly. We looked forward to picking cucumbers, the little tender ones that are so crunchy that they snap when you bite into them. I looked at my aunt and saw to my surprise that she was bare legged. It had become fashionable to wear flesh-coloured stockings (when you bought them, you asked for *lahmi*, which can mean either "my skin" or "my flesh"). So when I asked my aunt, "Are you wearing stockings?" she replied, "No, this is *lahmi*" and we all laughed because of the double meaning. She was bare legged, definitely.

On another occasion, eight of us girls went to the island, and when we tried to go back, we saw to our horror that the river had suddenly risen and we would have to wade across. We were standing there, wondering what to do, when a young man in a boat appeared and agreed to rescue us. He gallantly put his knee up for us to step on, one by one, to get aboard, and rowed us to the riverbank, where we thanked him profusely. I thought no more about it until a few years later. By then I was married, and David came home one day accompanied by a friend—the man in the boat! I don't know who was the most surprised of the three of us.

With a bit of advance planning, we could organise more ambitious excursions. We were able to charter a bus to take us to Hilla to visit Na'ima's estates. When I look at some of my old photographs now, I see that it was green and shady with many trees, but the earth was so parched after the spring rains that it was crisscrossed with deep cracks. We put watermelons in a running brook to keep them cool, and drank the water from that brook without any thought as

Wearing the 'abaaya *on an excursion in the 1930s (Violette, right)*

to whether or not it was pure—in fact, we never caught a bug from it. In other photos, I see the children on horseback, my girlfriends carrying baskets of fruit they had picked, and all of us wearing the latest fashions.

We also took advantage of the railway that had been started by the Germans under the Ottomans to make Istanbul, and thereby Berlin (via the Orient Express), more accessible to Baghdad. The British finished the line and eventually extended it to Basra. It was a fantastic mode of transport and an exciting adventure, creating new opportunities to the north and south of the city. We sometimes chartered a whole carriage on a train and travelled to the cool Khanakin area in the Kurdish north or visited the Hindiya Barrage, where we looked forward to seeing a host of unusual birds attracted by the water. I remember more trips to the ruins of Babylon, which I had first seen in my childhood, and also to Basra, where the canals with villas and gardens on their banks produced an effect like Venice. It was magical after the confines of our own city.

When King Ghazi was killed in 1939, the monarchy passed to his infant son Faisal II, who was only four years old. His pro-British uncle, Emir Abd al-Ilah, was appointed regent. But at the same time as we inherited a sympathetic ruler, we also acquired a plague: the grand mufti of Jerusalem, Haj Amin al-Husseini, who had been causing havoc in Palestine with a campaign of terrorism against Jewish and British targets. He escaped to Iraq to continue his invective from Baghdad—a sinister development that none of us could ignore.

By then I had been married for two years and my life had totally changed. David and I had invested my dowry in a plot of land in a development area called Bustaan Elkhas, and while our house was being built, we were living nearby with his parents in the new district of Orphaly. Even though David was the youngest of three sons, this duty—that the eldest bring his wife to live with his parents—had fallen to us because the other two were abroad. At times I found it difficult, as I had become pregnant straightaway and was suffering from morning sickness. However, I soon got used to David's family and his three sisters who lived nearby, each married with several children. There was a constant *va et vient* in the house, with family dropping in for a bite or chat. There was hardly any privacy, but this was more than made up for by the different social circle I found myself in—all clubs and music and parties. My first baby, a girl, arrived in August 1938, and we named her Lena. She immediately became the centre of attention.

My new family had a well-established and thriving business in the middle of the commercial centre of Baghdad: Shamash Bros., with E. Joury & Bros. as partners. We had a *khaan,* which meant that the whole building was ours, and just like the *khaans* that I've already described, it was a traditional two-storey warehouse, with storerooms and offices built around a central courtyard with a gate that was wide enough for carriages to pass through. We imported textile piece goods from Italy and Belgium, where David's two brothers, Haron and Ghali, lived. These goods were then sold on a wholesale basis to shopkeepers. David was the partner responsible for clearing them through customs. That was not as simple as it sounds: there was no proper tariff, and his expertise was in haggling over the amount payable. He was very skilled at using a mixture of charm, cajoling, and *bakhsheesh* to get his way.

The building was usually well stocked and busy, with much coming and going. David, his partners, and my father-in-law sat together on the first floor with a clerk and the male secretary receiving customers, with four Kurdish porters employed to do the heavy work. The ground floor was usually stuffed to the brim with rolls of all kinds of fabrics for both men and ladies, as well as upholstery and sheeting fabrics—silk, cotton, woollens—cheap as well as expensive. Apart from Orosdi Back for special occasions, Baghdad had no shops selling ready-to-wear, so everything had to be fashioned the long way round. Today it doesn't bear thinking about: going to the fabric shop to choose a nice length of cloth, taking it to the dressmaker or tailor to have your measurements taken, then choosing a pattern and trimmings, and going back for several fittings before finally having a new outfit. We at least had the dressmaker come to us.

That year, war broke out in Europe. Both of David's brothers managed to escape with their lives and return to us, leaving everything behind. But the Baghdad they came back to was not what they remembered, for already the political climate was changing and local sympathies were swinging dangerously towards the Germans.

Developing Baghdad: roadwork in progress

The house in Orphaly was rented from a prominent Muslim. Because he had agreed to renew our lease, we felt secure and there was no hint that our situation was anything other than stable. Then one day, soon after the renewal, he gave us three days' notice to quit. No warning. No reason. Although we wanted to protest, my father-in-law, Shm'oon, a modest man, strongly advised us against arguing. We all felt jittery because of the war and heard rumours of armed gangs being formed. So when a lorry arrived the next day and a number of crates were unloaded and placed by the doorway blocking our path, we panicked, imagining the cargo to be guns. Where to go? Our new house was nowhere near ready, and the landlord seemed determined to evict us. But that evening, he sent us word that his cousin had a vacant house not far from us, if we were prepared to pay more rent for a smaller home. We quickly agreed and moved the next day.

We had hardly settled in when my brothers-in-law arrived from Europe. First came Haron, who stayed only a short while before he found more suitable accommodation and moved out. Then brother Ghali turned up with his wife, Lilly, and two infant daughters, so that made three babies in the household. Now there was even less privacy and less room to manoeuvre, but Ghali lightened the mood by mimicking Mussolini and making us all laugh. They all counted themselves lucky to be back home, even though it had meant abandoning everything they possessed. Lilly started to take charge without consulting the rest of the family—for example, telling the cook what to make and when to serve the meals, upsetting the schedule that the family was used to. I became fed up with this. I thought about it a long time, then one day, while they were out, I stitched together the arms and legs of their pyjamas as a prank. It was so funny to see them struggle—it was worth the mischief—but Lilly would not speak to me any more.

David was caught in the middle. He needed to show his elder brothers respect, but at the same time he wanted to take my side. Eventually, he asked me to apologise, promising to take me to Basra for a weekend if I did. It was to be our honeymoon, as we had never taken one after the wedding. This was all the encouragement I needed. Of course, I apologised, and we went by train, having left Lena safely with her nurse and grandparents. We stayed at the most luxurious hotel, the Shatt el Arab, and were given a lovely room overlooking the water as well as lots of little presents to take away. We had a wonderful time.

But as the war progressed in Europe, its contagious sickness spread to Baghdad. Backed by money, books, and propaganda from the German Embassy, the mufti stepped up his verbal attacks, stirring unrest and street demonstrations against the British and us. The violent cleric had already expressed his solidarity with Germany and asked the Third Reich to oppose the establishment of a Jewish state in Palestine and supply the Arabs with guns. Unknown to us at the time, they had struck a deal whereby in exchange for Germany's support for Arab nationalism, the mufti and the Golden Square would make sure that Hitler got his hands on all our country's oil for his planned invasion of Russia.

Muslims identifying with Hitler conveniently forgot the fact that the Germans were just as much infidels as the British, and that Muslims were not Aryan (even Hitler had not thought of that). And so the Baghdadi Muslims grew bolder in their aggression against our community. They created antipathy where none had existed before, and every day we heard worrying stories that went unreported in the papers as everything was censored. Soon they were swearing by Almighty Allah to join forces with Hitler and help exterminate the Jews from the face of the earth. They began molesting and attacking individuals and breaking into some of the poorer houses and shops. Our men started coming home early, worried about staying too long in the city.

With the situation deteriorating rapidly, the brothers found that there was not enough business to keep them all busy. One day, Ghali, having watched as other Baghdadis moved to India and made their fortunes, decided to chance his luck in Bombay. He and Lilly tried to park their two daughters with one of his three sisters, with no success, as each already had several children of her own and did not want more responsibility. Ghali managed to get visas for India for all four of them, and they fled there as fast as they could. It was the logical destination: the British Raj was firmly established and we had trading contacts in the city.

Brother Haron's situation was more delicate: by now his bride— the other Violette—was expecting her first baby, so they moved to a larger house in Orphaly and both his parents moved in with them. Our own new home nearby was finished at last, so we also moved.

Life became harder: more intimidation, more discrimination, more harassment. By early 1941, we were debating whether to follow Ghali's example and leave Iraq, but we had a serious problem. Whereas his brothers were too old for military service, David was eligible and therefore unlikely to be granted papers for foreign travel. Being Iraqi subjects, all men of military age were supposed to show patriotism and join the army to fight the so-called British oppressors.

The Muslims saw the continuing British influence on Iraq only as meddling by infidels, overlooking all the benefits that they had brought the country. The pro-British prime minister Nuri al-Sa'id had been struggling to keep the lid on the cauldron but had little success, and now mobs started chanting in the streets: "Rommel, qaddem khatwaatak, ya Rommel"—"Rommel, hasten your footsteps towards us, O Rommel." It became so bad that, if a Muslim had a grudge against a Jew, or if he simply owed him money, he used the mobs to settle the score once and for all. The increasingly dangerous Golden Square copied the Nazis. They set up a mass movement for young Iraqis just like the Hitler Youth—Al-Futuwwa—with their own uniforms. They also formed an elite troop of fighters known as Kataa'ib a-Shabaab (Youth Regiments). What we didn't know was that the Golden Square was waiting for the signal from the mufti that the "national revolution" had begun.

The government was in turmoil. Regimes toppled regularly. They could not agree on what was best for the country—and in this period of uncertainty we now had our own crisis. David had never travelled out of Iraq but was increasingly determined to make the move to India. We talked about it endlessly. Apart from the general disquiet, he wanted to get out of the shadow of his brothers and set up on his own. As for me, having spent two years in Palestine as a young woman where I had enjoyed such a liberating and instructive time, I really looked forward to the prospect of being independent. David took courage from my travel experience and my languages, and so we determined to do it—but first we needed to get over the conscription problem and overcome another barrier, too. Both my parents and my in-laws raised strong objections to our planned departure. To leave our home with two infants—by then I was pregnant again, with the baby expected in May—and go into the unknown? "You can't speak the language, you will soon run out of money and come back penniless," they said to David, and I trembled, worried that my husband would listen to them and change his mind.

How could they not see the danger we were in? The awful chanting in the streets was getting louder, the harangues on the radio more vicious. Nothing mattered to me any more. All I wanted was to get out. Two thoughts were uppermost: we had to dispose of our house and property and, crucially, we had to get those travel documents.

The relatives on both sides of the family continued their objections over the following months. Nevertheless, David approached the authorities to ask them for passports and exit visas. A functionary took one look at him and, because there were no official birth certificates, declared him to be of military age. David with his usual sense of humour said to the functionary: "In that case, mark me down as even younger, and I will go back to school!" The functionary then gamely agreed with David that, if he could produce papers showing that he was too old for army duty, he would respect them.

David, who had been born in 1905, had great difficulty in convincing the authorities that he was older than his looks, and for a long time the rumour was that he would soon be conscripted. But, by and by, and with a lot of calling on old friendships, he did manage to obtain passports for us by procuring a "birth certificate" from the president of the Jewish community showing him to have been "born in Baghdad in the year 1900." He had aged five years overnight, but it was worth it!

I was heavily pregnant, we were feeling increasingly uneasy about David's situation, and the atmosphere was terribly tense when the phone rang early one morning, the bell sounding especially shrill at that unusual hour. I leapt to pick up the phone. My heart sank as I heard an official-sounding voice saying to me in a Muslim dialect: "Is that the residence of Dahoud Shamash? He must report to the police station at once with regard to army recruitment!" David— oh! My worst fear. But then, quick as a flash, I replied: "Abu Nessim, this is not at all funny. Try another joke. You need more practice to fool me." You see, I'd recognised the voice of David's brother-in-law, someone who came from a long line of teachers and therefore, to follow tradition, should have been extremely correct about everything—etiquette, manners, and language. Even his family name, Muallem, meant "teacher." But his wife, Rosa, one of David's sisters,

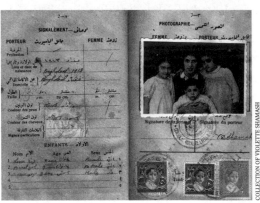

TOP.
*David's passport,
showing falsified
date of birth*

BOTTOM.
*Violette's 1947
passport, with
Lena, Mira,
and son Simon*

was such a lot of fun, a charming, happy-go-lucky girl, that some
of this had rubbed off on him. He had developed an advanced
sense of humour and we were always playing tricks on each other.
However, this one was a bit too close for comfort, and Abu Nessim
laughed it off as a failed attempt.

"Please don't try it again. You gave me the fright of my life," I said.
"If you do, I'll be bound to get my own back."

"Do by all means," he said as we laughed and chatted about other
matters.

I plotted and schemed, and later that afternoon phoned them
to invite them over for a game of rummy. Abu Nessim answered the
phone. "Hello, Victorine," he said, mistaking my identity. "I always
recognise your nice voice. How are you? How is Moshi?"

I thought, *Well, he's asked for it.* If I sounded like Victorine, a well-
known party giver, this was too good an opportunity to miss.

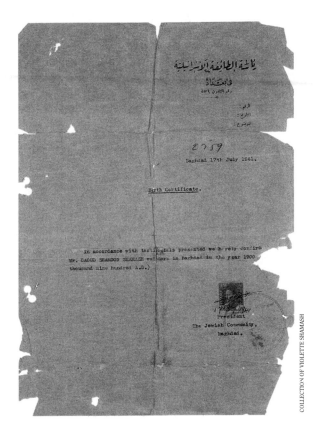

COLLECTION OF VIOLETTE SHAMASH

David's "birth certificate"

"My brother and I are giving a party tonight and want you and your family to attend," I said. "Moshi has booked Saleh-le-Kuwaity [the best *chaalghi* group in Baghdad]. Can you come?"

"Of course!" replied Abu Nessim with alacrity. Nobody ever turned down such an opportunity. Moshi was a young bachelor with an important job with Customs and Excise; his mother was always trying to find a Joan Crawford look-alike to wed him off to. David and he were great friends.

I decided to wait a while and then make my way to their home—we did not live far away and it was quite normal to drop in on each other for a chat or a game of backgammon or a singing session with David playing the *'oud* and singing Abdul Wahab songs. I took baby Lena's hand and set off to see the result of my prank.

When we arrived, I found the whole house upside-down, with people scurrying everywhere. Abu Nessim was shouting orders:

"Where is the hot water to shave my beard?" (It was his second shave of the day.) "Hurry up, hurry up!" he yelled at *abul ooti,* the man who did the ironing. "I want my white shirt at once!" Then came a shout from upstairs: "Mummy, which dress shall I wear?" "The red one!" Rosa told her daughter Habawi. Then Abu Nessim started shaving in the courtyard where I was sitting and spotted me.

"What's going on?" I asked innocently.

"We're all going to Victorine and Moshi's party. There's going to be *chaalghi* tonight. Didn't he invite you? Victorine called us earlier today."

"No, we haven't been invited."

"That's odd," said Abu Nessim as he carried on shaving.

How on earth was I going to get out of this one? It was getting embarrassing. He still hadn't guessed.

"Might I use your phone?"

"Of course—you know you don't have to ask."

The phone was right there and I called David at work. I said, "David, I am in big trouble. *Weh hoo weh!* What have I done? Please come to Rosa's as quick as you can." Everybody could hear me as I was almost shouting down the line to be sure of being heard. They were all curious, naturally, to know the nature of my trouble because of my delicate state and they were concerned that something could be wrong.

"Why, what happened?" said David.

"I can't tell you over the phone. Just come!" I could see Abu Nessim's ears flapping. "Please, please come! Oh, all right then, I'll tell you from the beginning. It's about a trick I played on Abu Nessim and I don't know how to get out of it . . . Please come now, David. I am covered in embarrassment. I have done a terrible thing!"

Abu Nessim's face, as the truth dawned, was a picture. Half-shaved, he hesitated, not knowing whether to continue or stop. Then, laughing, he banged down the soap and brush and said, "That will save me having to shave in the morning!" He was a good sport, and when David joined us, the day was saved. Fortunately everyone could see the funny side, and our laughter became a wonderful excuse to recount all of our well-remembered tales about Abu Nessim and other hilarious situations that he and members of his family had found themselves in. They still make me chuckle.

When he and Rosa were first married, they had many heated arguments. He always ended up the loser, for all she had to do was run home to her parents, who lived just two doors away. He would go and fetch her back because he loved her and did not mean to upset her. But they always enjoyed telling anybody who would listen all about their tempestuous arguments.

One hot summer's day, he had come home from work to find the children's shoes and slippers scattered all over the place while they played barefoot in the water. Not wanting to point it out to Rosa and start another argument, he angrily gathered all the footwear and took it to the first-floor bedroom. He then fetched a hammer and nails and nailed each shoe and slipper to the wall, as you would hang pictures.

Abu Nessim had six brothers, one of whom, Dahoud, was a doctor. One day Dahoud warned Abu Nessim that his children looked skinny and that they needed to drink milk. So Abu Nessim ordered two litres of milk to be brought home. He had it warmed and brought it to the children, but no amount of cajolery could persuade them to drink it. He tried to convince Rosa that she should set an example, but when she also refused, exasperated, he drank it all! Soon, they had to call Dahoud back to attend to Abu Nessim, who was sick with diarrhoea.

All of Abu Nessim's brothers were sticklers for correctness, and you could count on them for some surprising behaviour. One of them regularly took his morning coffee at a café on the riverbank where you could sit, play backgammon, and watch the water flowing past. It was a pleasing way to spend a quiet moment—until urchins started pestering you, wanting to shine your shoes. Abu Nessim's brother had barely sat down when a child approached and made as if to shine his shoe. He was told to go away. He came back five minutes later and tried to grab the shoe again. "Imshe!" cried the brother: "Clear off!" And the boy disappeared—only to return yet again moments later. Exasperated, Abu Nessim's brother jumped up, took off his shoes, and flung them in the river.

We laughed so much and had a great time, staying late. It was only towards the end that we started discussing the seriousness of the situation that was facing us. For all our gaiety, the evening ended on a worrying note.

Curfew

ON APRIL 1, 1941, the Golden Square colonels struck. Their front man, the rabidly pro-Nazi lawyer Rashid Ali al-Gaylani—a former captain in the Ottoman Turkish army who had briefly been in power before being ousted at the start of the year—organised a "government of national defence." Its first action caused us real concern: it tore up the Anglo-Iraqi Treaty of 1930 and opened negotiations for a military alliance with Hitler.

Although we heard vague stories, the truth didn't come out until much later: the regent had been tipped off on the eve of the coup and managed to escape. He had fled the royal Palace of Roses and had been smuggled out of Baghdad lying under a carpet in a car owned by the American Legation, to be taken to the Royal Air Force base at Habbaniya in the desert fifty-five miles west of us. From there the British had flown him to Basra and the protection of the Royal Navy. Six-year-old King Faisal II was left behind, and Rashid Ali named a new regent to look after him. What happened next was the beginning of something terrible. For us, the Jews of Baghdad, it was to bring about our ultimate exile, a trauma that saw the oldest community in the Diaspora virtually liquidated at a stroke.

The black month of Rashid Ali started in May. It was all curfew and blackout. We moved into each other's homes, families grouping together for safety, and word spread that it would be wise to bury any valuables. Everyone, including us, withdrew their savings from the bank. David immediately put all our cash and jewellery in a tin box and secretly buried it in our back garden, careful to choose a spot that he could remember. Regina, her husband and seven children sought refuge in the *qasr* with Baba and Nana. Na'ima and her family, who had been staying in their Baghdad home, planned to leave the city and seek safety in the countryside at Hilla, but before doing so buried her valuables and several property deeds. David's own sister Na'ima, her husband Abraham (who had been our matchmaker), and their three children moved from Karrada to be with Rosa and Abu Nessim.

David and I didn't know which way to turn. Nazi-style attacks had begun, with bands of Muslims roaming the Jewish areas, persecuting us, pillaging, killing, raping, setting fire, looting, smashing the "singing boxes" (radios) to kill the devil inside who sang Jewish songs. And me with a new baby about to join the hullabaloo at any moment.

The word went round that the British were on their way back to protect their interests, and on May 6 we saw RAF planes overhead— but no bombs fell. That same day, I heard later (because of my pregnancy, I wasn't told everything at the time), Muslim hoodlums carrying cudgels and guns broke into the Meir Elias Jewish hospital with the intention of wrecking it on the pretext that two British pilots were hiding there and another British citizen was also inside, signalling to the bombers and directing them to their targets. Within minutes, the hospital turned into a battlefield, with shooting and screams being heard everywhere. As the patients scrambled to find hiding places, the mob seized doctors, nursing staff, and administrators. They shot the pharmacist dead. The hospital was paralysed and attempts were made to grab authority from our community and hand the hospital over to the Red Crescent.

The next day, May 7, there was a *brit mila* (circumcision) ceremony in the house of Jacob Shalom in Shorjah Street. According to Abraham Twena, who told the story, a number of youths forced open the door and entered, knives in hand, murdered a young boy, and seriously wounded his brother. On the same day, again according to Mr. Twena, they planned to murder the railway stationmasters. Fearing for their lives, the Jewish staff wanted to flee to their homes but could not: in this emergency, their desertion would have been considered sabotage—the penalty: death.

We thought one of the British bombers must have been shot down, as we heard about a plane being captured and then paraded through the streets on the back of a lorry, together with its hand-cuffed pilot. The hordes followed it, chanting and jeering. We shivered and trembled in our homes, listening to the radio turned down low, not knowing what to believe, not daring to go out. It later transpired that the pilot was German, shot down by mistake.

With just the three of us, and our staff, our big house became a liability. We were exposed. Where could we hide in case of attack? How could we get a midwife to come in a blackout and curfew?

I stubbornly insisted that I had to have some of my family around me to give me moral support and assist me just in case. Everyone was apprehensive in that reign of terror. Who could we ask to leave their house and come and stay with us? David persuaded my sister Na'ima and her husband Sasson ("Sass") that it was safer for them to stay in the city than to travel to the countryside, where an influential Muslim friend had offered them refuge. David talked them into unpacking, and we all agreed it would be safer if we moved in with them and their five children. Na'ima had had misgivings about making the journey anyway—and so they said good-bye to the family they had intended to travel with, who now went off alone: Sass's sister, his brother-in-law Menashi Khalastchi, and *their* five children.

Na'ima was marvellous as we literally invaded her home. Apart from myself, David, and Lena, she also had to put up Lena's nanny and Farridja, a twenty-five-year-old nursemaid hired to look after the new arrival and me. We also had a new young cook, Shemtov, who prepared meals for all of us. As Na'ima had been intending to leave Baghdad, she had no staff left except Ismaa'il, a Muslim, whom we used to send out to get food.

Only a few days after we moved in at Na'ima's, our misgivings about travel were proven tragically correct. There was ghastly news about Menashi. He had been killed—not, as it turned out, by the mob but worse: at the instigation of his own business partner, a Muslim sheikh who took advantage of the lawless situation to gain control. Menashi's widow returned to Baghdad with her children, in a terrible state. There, but for the grace of God . . .

Regarded highly in our society, Menashi had been a grain trader and gentleman farmer, much loved and respected. He had been a good friend to all, and he and his family had lived in the same street as Na'ima. All our community was shocked and saddened, but Sass just couldn't take it and cried inconsolably like a child. Both he and David mourned Menashi and went for the *shiva* (mourning) every day. Sass spent most of the coming days comforting his sister as best he could. What a tragedy, to add to our horror.

Na'ima suggested that we have the midwife, Mess'ouda, come every evening and stay until morning in case the "happy event" surprised us in the middle of the night. She was the midwife of choice for all the ladies in our circle and had delivered Lena, so we were happy to pay her double rates. For a whole fortnight, she came before sunset and left after breakfast. Every day she brought reports from her rounds about what was happening in our community—even one of her own daughters had been attacked and robbed. She was fond of David, who loved telling stories, and we spent the hours listening to them both. We could not go out even if we had wanted to, so there was nothing to do but pass the time telling stories, reminiscing about the good times when the communities had respected each other, discussing the latest news from the war front that we had read in the paper, and wondering how much was true. We were afraid to use the telephone, as all calls had to go through an operator. In any case, the number of people we could call was limited, for there weren't that many phones in Baghdad—our numbers had just three digits—and it was obvious they were all being monitored.

One night Mess'ouda brought back disturbing news. Some people we knew had found themselves in urgent need of cash and had dug up the treasure they had buried—only to discover that the banknotes had been soaked to a pulp. Imagine our consternation. Early next morning, David went back to our house with our Kurdish guard for security, but once he and the guard arrived, the last thing David wanted was to have the guard witness what he was up to. He sent him to fetch some milk for us all, and somehow he also freed himself of the other two Kurds we had left behind to guard the property. Now all he had to do was find the spot. He remembered it was near the garden tap, because the earth had been softer and easier to dig—but where exactly? Several holes later, in a sweat, he found the box at last. Pleased with himself, he brought it back home and when we opened it we took out the jewels and the cash. His mother's pearl necklace was ruined, damaged beyond repair with black stains. The banknotes were dripping wet, but thankfully we were just in time to save them, spreading them in the room and leaving them to dry.

We could not depend on the radio for news, knowing that everything coming from Iraqi sources was untrustworthy, with ranting speeches directed against us. We tuned instead to Radio Ankara, broadcasting in Arabic, which seemed a less biased source. For eighteen hours a day on Iraqi radio there was nothing but martial music, tirades, and news of "victories" everywhere. And then, on May 9, the mufti declared a *jihad* and invited every "able-bodied Muslim to take part in the war against the greatest foe of Islam." There was Nazi propaganda throughout the day as well as readings from the Qur'an, anti-British news, and calls for the population to revolt against foreign domination and follow the lead of Rashid Ali. Darkest of all was the threat contained in a government announcement, repeated frequently, that warned the public not to "spend their ammunition in vain" in the joy they were experiencing over the victory—we could only assume this meant there had been firing in the air. It continued: "We wish peace to prevail in every place, and after the victory over the British, revenge shall be taken on the internal enemy, and we shall hand him over to your hands for destruction."

It was not difficult to guess who this internal enemy was, or why this instruction was being given.

There were few doubts in our minds how perilous our position was, with the city's policing now in the hands of the Al-Futuwwa mobs. Every night Mess'ouda brought us news and sad stories of what was happening in the east of Baghdad, in the poor quarter, where the only defence Jews had was to prepare quantities of boiling water, bricks, and gravel and stand guard on their roofs, ready to drop them on the attackers if and when the mob tried to break in. It was medieval, primitive, desperate—and this was World War II. Much of Europe was under Nazi domination, while closer to home, British forces were suffering defeats in the Western Desert and Palestine was in chaos (this much we did understand from our newspapers). Every now and then our conversations were interrupted by the wail of the siren telling us to take shelter. What shelter? And why was it always a false alarm? I still haven't worked that out: was it to intimidate us even more?

Once, we were all trooping down to the semi-basement, the *niim*, when my two-year-old, Lena, who had slipped in ahead of us, found a box of spare lightbulbs that Na'ima kept there. She picked one up and smashed it to the floor: bang! We all jumped out of our skins. Everyone panicked. David wanted us all to evacuate immediately. And then Lena ran out of the *niim* and all became clear. She was always running around and getting up to some mischief.

The radio broadcasts began to work. A Jewish woman whose gold-coloured button had inadvertently appeared through her black *'abaaya* was detained for signalling to the British. A Jewish student holding an English book was accused of spying. A French music teacher was arrested and accused of carrying a radio transmitter in his violin case. Schools were forced to close, and businesses came to a halt as banks were ordered not to pay out any money. Collections were taken for the army and the wounded. A group of Kataa'ib a-Shabaab, the ultra-Nazi Youth Regiments, demanded that the Jewish community hand over the Rachel Shahmoon school for their use, as well as the cash register, and administration office. (Police later found detailed maps of the Jewish quarter in the Kataa'ib safe and a list of its members with aliases after their names.) The Jewish I'daadiah secondary school was also seized. The government appropriated "our" Shamash school for a Red Crescent depot, and perversely, members of our community were appointed to operate the storehouse where merchandise was received and sent to the army.

There were no fewer than twelve of us, that evening of May 15, sitting together in the darkness and overwhelming heat and listening to more distressing tales, when the baby gave notice of its imminent arrival. It had been an unusually hot day for the time of year, with temperatures in the shade up to 111 degrees Fahrenheit. We had blacked out the windows of our room on the ground floor with rugs and curtains in the hope that we would not be noticed—a forlorn gesture. The candle we had lit and put on the floor gave only minimal light. So when, two hours later, my new daughter entered the world and gave her first cry, there was a sense of theatre: quite a scene but for our fear of imminent attack.

"She's a beauty!" exclaimed Mess'ouda. "Born in darkness, gives brightness to the room. Bless her and may she bring us good luck now that we most need it."

All the children, aged two to thirteen, were excited. When all the family heaved a sigh of relief with me for having rid myself of my burden, I was amused to see them crowding round, fascinated by every little move she made. "What was she wearing when she arrived?" they asked. "How did she come? Who brought her?" Mess'ouda's lovely blessing made us all forget our difficulties for a moment and glow with pleasure despite the circumstances. "What's her name?" the children asked, and without hesitation Mess'ouda replied, "Amal," which is Arabic for "hope."

I didn't say anything—she had already told me that all the girls born that month had been called Amal. Secretly I knew that I would later change that name to Mira.

Farhud

WE WERE DESPERATELY short of news in those dark days of 1941. After a month of blackouts, curfews, and hiding, we were literally in the dark. We heard more planes flying overhead, and later there were rumours of battles in the desert as the British army advanced on Baghdad. We did not dare hope that the British could defeat the might of Iraq, but like a miracle, God delivered us and we heard that Rashid Ali and the mufti, our twin tormentors, had run away. Then we understood that the British were at the gates of the city and had come to rescue us. But although the Rashid Ali clique had gone, one fanatic, Yunis al-Sab'awi, stayed behind to create more problems for us. We knew him as the leader of the Nazi youth organisations that had been attacking us—he had even translated *Mein Kampf* into Arabic—and now suddenly he was on the radio, declaring himself the military governor of Baghdad.

How close we came to annihilation I learned only years later from Na'ima's son-in-law, Meir Sasson. Just when we were beginning to believe that our ordeal was over, at ten o'clock on the morning of Friday, May 30, al-Sab'awi summoned Meir's father, the chief rabbi, Hakham Sasson Kadoori. The message our leader heard came as a shock: the Jews were to go to their homes and not go out again after noon. They should cook enough food for three days, prepare one suitcase per family, and stand by to be taken to detention camps for their own safety.

What else could it mean but that he planned to slaughter us all?

Hakham Kadoori desperately conferred with the elders of the community. To whom could they turn? One by one, they finally agreed that there was only one man capable of sufficient humanitarian compassion: the city's mayor, Arshad 'Umari. The rabbi requested an urgent audience, and despite the city's turmoil it was granted. Hakham Kadoori immediately made a gesture so surprising and dramatic that it took 'Umari aback. The *hakham* swept off his turban and flung it to the floor—baring his head in the presence of a Muslim, the ultimate display of desperation—to show his intense grief. 'Umari, a superstitious man with fear in his heart, picked up the turban, asking, "Tell me what the matter is." Then Hakham Kadoori explained, begging 'Umari: "Don't let them do this terrible thing!" The mayor handed back the turban. "Please, put it back on and go home," he said. "Tell your people not to worry. I shall take care of everything."

The noon deadline approached.

On the hour of twelve precisely, the broadcasting station in Baghdad had been ordered by al-Sab'awi to call on the masses to rise up against the Jews and massacre us. But the broadcast was never made. We later heard that the mayor had seized power at the last minute. Al-Sab'awi had been relieved of his post and was allowed to slip away and flee to Iran, having been given one hundred dinars, his monthly salary. That evening the radio announced that the entire government had fled, and a security committee had taken the responsibility to enter an agreement with the British that would not harm the state's honour or dignity. A miracle.

We had stayed at Na'ima's for all of May. Then, finally reassured that the danger had passed, we decided to move back to our own home on Saturday, May 31, the eve of Shavuot, despite her pleas for us to stay longer so that I might convalesce. An *'arabaana* took us all, including my new baby and the nursemaid, and I remember the fuss Na'ima's children all made, wanting us to stay, as we trotted away down the road.

I felt very good. After a month of fearing for our lives, it was marvellous to be back on my feet, savouring the fresh air and the freedom, when only such a short time ago it had seemed that we were doomed. On entering our home, we became emotional and said a prayer of thanksgiving, "Barukh mehiyai hametim": a blessing on him who resurrects the dead. The British were back and the month of Rashid Ali was over.

We were wrong. There was worse, much worse, to follow.

Shavuot is a happy day, a celebration of the time when Moses received the Torah on Mount Sinai, having spent forty days on the mountaintop listening closely to the Almighty dictating the Ten Commandments. These he carefully engraved on two tablets, and as he came down from the mountain, he handed them to Yehoshua Ben Nun, who in turn passed them to the *nebi'im* (prophets). It was they, together, who deciphered and elaborated on them to give us our present-day Torah.

The whole month leading to Shavuot should have been all joy and picnics. Normally, on the eve of the holiday, prayers are said in homes all over the city until the early hours, with all the family and relatives assembled. All night as the vigil continues, small glasses of Turkish coffee are served by the women, and by daybreak there is *kaahi* ready for breakfast: crisp, sweet, deep-fried puff pastry dusted with icing sugar to be eaten piping hot. Only then can everyone return to their homes or continue their devotions in the synagogues. We call it 'Iid el-Ziyaaghah, the Feast of Pilgrimages, an occasion to travel to the shrines of the prophets of Babylon, through whose patronage and kindly guidance we might be shown favouritism and good luck.

Every household should have been busy baking *mekhbooz*, lovely sweet and savoury delicacies to take with them on their travels as *zewwada*, or "provisions for the journey." There was more *kaahi* and all the derivatives of baklava, plus other favourites such as *be'aabe'-ib-dehen*, a kind of shortbread, and *melfouf*, fat cigars of puff pastry rolled around chopped almonds with sugar and cardamom.

With dry, warm weather guaranteed and even a foretaste of the heat of summer to come—it would soon be blistering—these two sacred days of festivities around the end of May came at a perfect time in Baghdad, and children born in May were considered lucky because everyone seemed to be celebrating their birthday.

Our community started coming together again. We had become used to hearing distant gunfire and the planes overhead on their missions. But now a tense silence prevailed in the city, and here and there we could see policemen with guns drawn. Much to our relief, the radio that Saturday evening reverted to playing Arab songs instead of the previous diatribes, and at five-thirty in the afternoon an announcer declared that an armistice had been signed and order was being restored. Half an hour later, another bulletin broke the news that the regent would arrive at the airport at ten o'clock the following morning, to be welcomed by the people.

As we gathered for the evening prayers, warnings were given in the synagogues that we should not appear happy on the streets, and when we went out, we should stay in our own neighbourhoods. The prayers were said, the sweetmeats passed around, the *zewwada* carefully prepared in anticipation of the next day's excursions, though obviously, there was no question of visiting the shrines. But there was danger in the air, a palpable feeling that something was not quite right. There was still no sign of a British soldier. Where were they?

The following morning, our family stayed at home rather than going out for a walk. We knew several people who were planning to walk to the Karkh district, to welcome the regent from the airport, to make up for the disappointment of not being able to go further. It was a nice day, and the thought had crossed our minds to go along too, but in the afternoon, when Haron's wife asked us round to celebrate the festival with them, I jumped at their invitation instead. After all, it had been a whole month since we had all begun our confinement at home in such uncomfortable conditions. I knew I could safely leave little Amal—I mean, Mira—with the expert nursemaid we had found for her, and besides, Haron, Violette, and their firstborn child Simon, who was six months old, didn't live far away. I had every confidence in Farridja, the nursemaid, so I left her in charge and we took Lena with us, resplendent in the red and gold *'abaaya* she insisted on wearing, which her grandpa had given her. We were blissfully unaware of events about to unfold.

We had assumed the British were back in control and were all looking forward to some law and order being restored to our lives. But just as we arrived at Haron and Violette's, we were startled to hear the crackle and banging of fireworks. Fireworks? While we were still puzzling it out, the telephone rang and Haron grabbed it.

"Who is it? Ali? . . . *Salamaat!* Yes, we are *salamaat* [safe] . . ."

It was Ali, the porter from our office, where David worked with Haron. As the conversation continued, the expression on his face left us anxious and silent. I could not hear what else was being said. My mouth went dry and my ears blocked as my mind flew to my baby at home with Farridja the nursemaid; Malka, who looked after Lena; the cook, Shemtov, who was only a teenager; and the two Kurds we employed as watchmen.

"We're OK," said Ali. "How about you? The mob has been round but we managed to deter them."

It was the first we knew that something dreadful was happening, the start of the two days of *farhud,* or "violent dispossession." The word is so horrible, it has no direct English translation. The best I can come up with is "the breakdown of law and order, where life and property are in peril." A pogrom.

We should have known better. For days before he fled, dressed as a woman, the scheming mufti had been broadcasting more of his vicious venom on the radio, blaming the Jews for the plight the country found itself in, and radicalising the gullible. What he said was crazy: we were all spies; we had been signalling with mirrors to British bombers flying over the city; we had intercepted phone calls and telegraph traffic and passed the information to the British Embassy. In the prevailing atmosphere, the Muslim majority was prepared to believe anything—and to further inflame their anger we had heard a broadcast in Arabic by an Iraqi radio announcer, Yunis Bahri, on the German station Berlin, who reported that Jews from Palestine had been fighting alongside the British against Iraqi soldiers near the city of Fallujah.

Baghdad was soon beyond anyone's control.

At the same time, many of our community who, like our friends, had wanted to welcome the regent had gravitated to the other side of the river, and as the occasion was a feast day, it was natural for everyone to be dressed in their best clothes. What a mistake. Defeated groups of Iraqi soldiers were trudging back into town in the opposite direction, following the signing of an armistice. They were dejected and totally without command, though fully armed. They knew nothing of our Shavuot. As far as they were concerned, the day was a Sunday, and therefore not a Jewish holy day. There could only be one explanation for the Jews to be so smartly dressed, loitering in the streets as they did. They had to have been celebrating the return of the regent under the armed protection of the hated British, and therefore rejoicing in the country's defeat and reoccupation by the infidels.

All this we learned later.

At three in the afternoon that Sunday, June 1, a group of Jews was crossing Al-Khurr Bridge on their way back from the Karkh on the right bank when they encountered some demobilised soldiers and remnants of the Kataa'ib a-Shabaab. First came blows, then an attack with knives. One Jew was murdered and sixteen wounded in full view of Iraqi military police, who did nothing. The *jinni* was out of the bottle.

The phone call from Ali had left us all in shock. What to do? In my anxiety, I forced myself to think clearly and not to faint. After a quick discussion, the decision was made that we should stay where we were, but David should go and fetch the baby. Safety in numbers (again!) we hoped. But no sooner had he opened the front door than a private car stopped on the other side of the street. David approached the driver. It was getting dark, and although we were no longer under curfew, the street was completely deserted, not even a cat in sight. The driver started babbling, begging, talking nonstop.

In his worry, David had not even noticed the young man's terrified face, all covered in blood, or the bloodstains on his car. The driver then told him of the chaos that had reigned that afternoon downtown. The mob had gone on the rampage, breaking, pillaging, setting places alight, knifing, and killing. He himself had been transporting wounded, he said, as he had a car. He was utterly exhausted and disgusted by what he had seen. One youth whose stomach had been slashed calmly collected his spilt entrails and held his guts together for God knows how long until he was miraculously rescued. David then heard the victim's name and realised in horror that he was a distant relative. After the driver advised David to get back inside and find another way to our home, he returned and recounted the sorry tale.

From eyewitness accounts, friends' stories and reports in our community's archives, I have now pieced together the events that followed.

After the first attack, the tinderbox ignited. Spurred on by the sight of both the army and the police taking part in the fighting, civilians, passersby, and anyone with a grudge all joined the fracas. Violence spread quickly on the left bank to the Al-Rusafa and Abou Siffain districts as well as to Ras el-Tchol, where Muslims and Jews lived side by side. Now we were being killed openly in the streets. Looting by the Bedouins and the remnants of the army and police turned into a full-scale pogrom. The ransacking of these destitute neighbourhoods began, with large lorries moving furniture and other household goods from one side of the city to the other.

Women were raped. Infants were killed in front of their terrified parents before they, too, felt the knife or bullet. Jewish shops were looted a second time and then torched. Jewish drivers were dragged from their cars and passengers pulled from buses and roughed up or killed. Homes were broken into, the mob often torturing and mutilating those they found as a diversion from killing before looting the property and setting it ablaze. Targeting homes where they knew pretty Jewish girls lived, soldiers beat up guards employed by the householders. The menfolk mobilised to help save their daughters by throwing the girls over the back balconies into the waiting arms of friends and neighbours, or the girls themselves escaped to the neighbours over the roof boundaries, since almost all Jewish houses in the city were terraced and shared partition walls, if not communicating doors. Other children, similarly, were saved when their parents took them to their rooftops and flung them across the void to the outstretched arms of terrified friends.

A synagogue was invaded, set ablaze, and its Torahs destroyed in classic Nazi fashion. One man survived the carnage by hiding in a hole he dug to save his life. He later told everyone how he saw Iraqi soldiers pull small children away from their parents and rip the arms off young girls to steal their bracelets. He also saw pregnant women being raped and their stomachs cut open. Another survivor was a thirteen-year-old boy who looked out from the curtained window of his home and saw men dragging two Jewish girls down the street by their hair. He saw Muslims attacking Jewish men with axes

The flat rooftops of the Old City. Many escaped from roof to roof.

and hammers, and heavy smoke rising from businesses and homes that had been set ablaze.

Our first witness to all this was the driver who had advised David to get back inside and find another way to bring our baby to safety. Safety? What safety? We were trapped! There was no way we dared go out, even though our area was calm. There was only the telephone, which still worked. I took a sip of water and, keeping the panic from my voice, called the nursemaid on the phone: "Farridja," I began, "David's parents want to see the baby."

"I can bring her over," she offered quickly. "I'll be with you shortly. I'll walk her over in the pram."

"No, listen carefully, and do exactly as I ask. Get Walii [one of the Kurds] to hail an *'arabaana* from the main road and bring it right up to the door."

"Oh, you don't need a carriage," she argued. "You're only round the corner. I'll be with you in a minute."

Now I was getting desperate. "Oh, Farridja," I said, "it's nearly time for her feed, and they want me to stay the night to celebrate Shavuot. So please do exactly as I ask or I'll worry. Bring Malka with you and let her carry the nappies and baby's clothes as well as a nightdress for me. Let Walii come with you and sit beside the coach driver. Promise me not to carry anything but the baby! Malka must help you."

All the time, I wanted to shout my panic. It took all my strength to convince Farridja calmly and patiently, being careful not even to hint at what was really happening lest her own panic communicate itself to the rest. It was imperative that they all came to us, too: Malka was only eighteen and it would not have been right to leave her alone at home with young Shemtov and the Kurds.

After what seemed like a lifetime, Farridja and Malka arrived safely with the baby, totally unaware of the threat to their lives. We did not tell the girls about our anxiety, as there seemed no point, but they immediately sensed the menace all around and realised how critical the situation was.

We were tense. It was hot and already the season for sleeping on the roof. But no one moved towards the stairs. Instead we made preparations as if for a siege. We barricaded ourselves in by moving heavy furniture against the front door. We blacked out the windows with carpets and rugs, making a stifling atmosphere in all that heat. We were still frightened to use the phone for fear of eavesdroppers. Then we all went down to the *niim*, and tried to keep the lights out, but it was difficult because Violette's baby Simon hated the dark and kept crying—a sure way to attract attention. Lena, too, hated the dark, so we turned on the radio with the volume down, hoping that the weak light from the dial would pacify them. It was the most horrific nightmare, a city without police, a paradise for thieves and murderers. All night long we could hear the distressing sound of women screaming and calling the names of their loved ones who were being murdered. We were all sitting in the dark waiting—for what? For our turn, for a solution? Trying to think of some safer place to hide? Wondering what to do if . . . ?

That night my baby had her feed and then went to sleep like an angel, while we spent the worst night of our lives. Meanwhile, in Karrada, fourteen members of my family—Baba; Nana; Salman; Daisy; Marcelle; Regina; her husband, Reuben; and their seven children— were joined by the staff (Djassem, Fatoom, Hagouli, and Zahra) preparing for the *qasr* to be stormed. Their existing defences against attack were minimal, and desperate measures were under discussion—for instance, Salman was all for burning the house down if the mob came, an unrealistic idea that Baba immediately forbade. Instead, they barricaded the door and locked it with the big key. The children were told to go to the *niim* and stay quiet. Baba and Salman put on *deshdaashas*, Arab style. Clara, my niece, remembers watching as the mob came closer. First, they went to the old Khazam house next door, and she stared in horror as they looted the deserted property. What they could not carry away or did not want they dumped into the river—even the crockery and cutlery. The mob then moved on to the *qasr*, banging on the front door loudly and throwing their weight against it. We thanked God that they had nothing like a battering ram or they could have been inside in seconds. Baba propelled Djassem forward, who roared at the intruders in his most authoritative voice, ordering them to go away and leave them alone, as this was a house of Muslims. Luckily they believed him.

Another young family from Karrada, the Yedids, sought refuge in Battaween, where the wife's parents lived, and joined the rest of the family there for safety. They later told us how all night long they had watched from the roof as the sounds of victims' agony filled the air and the rampaging mob closed in. The Yedids and their relatives barricaded themselves in the house to give themselves time to escape over the rooftops if the mob were to break in. They buried their valuables in the kitchen in a hollow area under the floor, and slept fully clothed, ready for the worst. Their story was typical.

And still, there was no sign of the British as Baghdad burned. Day broke, and now it was Monday, June 2. A frantic rapping upstairs startled us. Our menfolk went to investigate, timidly approaching the front door where the noise was coming from. Haron recognised the voice outside: it was their Muslim neighbour, a former mayor of Basra and a friend of Violette's family. What a relief! He had come to fetch us and take us to safety at his house, just down the road near the Egyptian consulate. He said it was still dangerous out, but we should come quickly and join the other Jewish families sheltering in his *niim*. As we scuttled out, just after dawn, we caught sight of our own Muslim next-door neighbour, the noble-hearted Abdel Razzaaq Hilmi, who insisted that our part of the family should go with him, to the safety of his home. So we split up. Haron, Violette, and their baby Simon were in a *niim* with twenty-six people, but we were to find that our generous benefactor had about 150 sheltering in his.

As we headed for it, an angry crowd gathered. Mr. Hilmi had two revolvers that he waved in the air to protect us and he began shouting at the mob, swearing that such behaviour was shameful. (We later heard other stories of Muslim families standing up to the hooligans threatening their Jewish neighbours. In one place, fifty thugs found themselves confronted by a sixty-five-year-old *mukhtar*— sheriff—who resolutely refused to let them pass.) Mr. Hilmi was busy all morning on the telephone, doing his best to find out what was happening and exert what influence he could. Even though she was overwhelmed, Mrs. Hilmi kept asking if I needed anything for my baby, as Mira was the centre of attraction. Such was their natural hospitality: these were acts of kindness none of us has ever forgotten. Lives were in jeopardy but Muslim-Jewish friendships prevailed.

What a day that was. At eight in the morning, the attackers started flowing in, group by group, well organised by police who by now had removed their badges to avoid recognition. Hordes of Bedouin tribesmen who had caught wind of the disorders came to join the maniacal onslaught, alongside slum dwellers. All night long, it seems, Kataa'ib a-Shabaab elements and soldiers who had fled the battle-field were organising themselves for the same moment, but this time they met strong opposition. Our community's defences were now better prepared. On the rooftops we had heavy stones, pitch, boiling oil, and rags from which to create weapons, and a commander and aides had been appointed to give orders. Many were saved by escaping from roof to roof, as before. At the Yedid family home in Battaween, they watched aghast while the mob started on their street.

Above all, it was the rioters' greed that saved lives. Many of those who had instructions only to kill began to search the homes they had broken into, looking for items of value. And while the commanders were starting to raid the houses, the rabble turned to Rashid Street to plunder the shops lest others get there first. The looting lasted for four hours in the main streets and until two o'clock in the Jewish quarters. Only when it was feared that the rioters, in their zeal, were planning to move into Muslim neighbourhoods did Iraqi troops enter and seize positions. They opened fire with machine

guns and swept the streets clear of people. By some miracle, just as
the rioters were approaching the Yedids' house, soldiers on horseback finally arrived and chased the mob away.

That second day passed uneventfully for us, thank God. By one
o'clock in the afternoon, the shooting around us had stopped. Food
became a critical problem for all of us sheltering in the Hilmis'
house, but at least Shemtov was able to climb the fence to our house
next door, go to our kitchen, and bring us everything he'd cooked
and everything else he could find, which we gave to the children.
We emerged when we heard a truce had been called, but it was still
unsafe. Looters were running through the streets, with lorries carrying away their plunder.

Calm was not restored until five o'clock that evening, when it was
announced on the radio that the regent had appointed as prime
minister Jamil Madfai—a man known for his humanity, with no hatred for our people. A dusk-to-dawn curfew was declared and scores
of violators were shot dead on sight. Within an hour, the streets
were silent and empty. The only evidence of the horror of the previous twenty-six hours was the loot that the rioters had dropped while
running for their lives, and the blackened buildings. The Yedids'
grandson David Kehela now remembers how, shortly afterwards,
there was token retribution when four rioters were hanged—each
at a different gate of the city.

Not until much later was the full extent of the devastation revealed. There have been various accounts, with the number killed
ranging from 110 to as many as 700, the injured from 240 to 2,000.*
Also listed in the official records among the victims were large
numbers of non-Jews, including rioters, security men, and Muslims
who came to the defence of their Jewish neighbours. Reflecting
the friendship that had existed between our communities, as in our
case, hundreds of normal, nonmilitant Iraqis had opened their
homes and fed and protected their Jewish friends, sometimes at

*Different accounts give a wide range of figures. However, there seems to be
consensus of a figure of 187 dead and 240 injured, the victims including Muslims as well as Jews. Jewish community officials said 586 shops and stores had
been broken into; the total value of goods, valuables, and money looted was
271,402 dinars (or more than $19 million today). The number of homes at-
tacked came to 911, involving a total of 3,395 families and 12,311 inhabitants;
their total material loss was 383,878 dinars (more than $27 million today).

the cost of their own lives. Others who survived had not been near
the mob scenes and had slept right through, totally unaware of the
catastrophe.

The brutality and terror of those two days of Shavuot would be forever seared on our collective consciousness, and I shudder even
now as I write these lines. For the victims who survived, nothing was
ever recovered. There were no accusations or claims, no arrests or
prosecutions, no investigation and no compensation. It was take it
or leave it. That is the moment that confirmed our decision. David
and I would definitely leave it, *coûte que coûte*—at whatever cost.

The next morning David cabled his brother Ghali in Bombay
to ask him to apply for entry visas for us for India—just two words:
OBTAIN VISA. We started liquidating, and gave David's sister Na'ima
whatever she wanted of our furniture, for her home in Karrada
had been stripped bare after the mob had broken in. She was the
one who had left with all her family at the beginning of the month
to take refuge with her sister Rosa and Abu Nessim. When they
first heard that trouble was brewing, Na'ima and her husband had
phoned their Muslim neighbour and asked him to keep an eye on
their property, especially their brand-new Persian carpets, which
they had carefully wrapped and stored in their *niim*. He was someone they knew they could trust, as he would go round every Saturday morning to partake of Saturday eggs, which he liked. When the
trouble was over and they returned home, hoping for the best, they
were appalled. The mob had broken in, killing and trampling the
body of the Kurdish guard who had refused to admit them. Nothing was left, not even a broom; what the rioters could not take, they
had destroyed—the bath, the ceiling fans, even the toilet and the
taps, so flooding the house. Naturally, the carpets had gone.

But worse than their material loss, what hurt them most was the
way their friendly neighbour had broken their trust and betrayed
them. They could see their carpets in his house.

First Flight

IT WAS SIX O'CLOCK in the morning on a cold November day on Baghdad's airstrip. I shivered, pale and anxious with nervous anticipation, emotions totally drained and tears utterly dry. We could hardly believe it was happening and could hear our hearts thumping *good-bye . . . good-bye.* None of the family had accompanied us to the airfield for fear of attracting attention, as we were still concerned that David's exemption from call-up might be revoked. Who knew? Anything might happen and we could be called back. Only Shemtov, our faithful cook, came with us to help with the two infants. Our good-byes to our families and friends had been said in private.

Already our community seemed to be disintegrating. Regina and her family had decided to sell up too and were leaving overland for Palestine one week after us. And David's father continued to be critical of our decision, chastising him for sending an expensive cable to Ghali instead of posting a letter. As it turned out, those who did send letters got nowhere, for it was too late: no more visas were issued and they were trapped. The only escape route open for them was across the border to Iran disguised as Arab villagers.

Regina and her family were staying at the *qasr* prior to their departure, so we spent the whole day at my parents' to say good-bye to everyone. Na'ima and her children had also come, and we had a hectic and enjoyable day, which passed in a dizzy whirl. The emotional part had been at the end: tears of joy that we had escaped the carnage of the Farhud, and completely different tears at the thought of being separated. God only knew when or how we would ever meet again. I was going to be the first of my family to take to the air, just like a bird, or just like Sinbad and the roc in the *Arabian Nights,* as Nana imagined. In the end, she had become resigned to the fact that she could not dissuade us.

Five months had passed since the terrible events of Shavuot. Baghdad was seemingly back to normal—it was as though the Farhud was just a nightmare to be forgotten—and with the British in control, a doubt entered our minds: were we doing the right thing? Once out, there would probably be no turning back. Were we right to leave our homeland, family, friends—everything that we were familiar with? Our people, probably the oldest surviving community of Jews in the world, had lived in Mesopotamia continuously since the days of the Old Testament. They were the ones who had stayed behind in Babylon when the others had marched back into Israel. Were my in-laws right, and we were being shortsighted? Was Baba right in saying we had no future in India?

We were not well travelled, David and I. Neither of us had ever flown before—few people had in those days—and it seemed extraordinary that a British airline should still be flying despite the war. The only trip abroad I had ever had was the time spent in Palestine with Baba and Nana. David had travelled even less. What could we look forward to in a strange land like India? When and where would we ever see our families again? The audacity of it all and the heavy responsibility seemed enormous to David and me. We had always done things the conventional way, neither of us being the oldest, the youngest, or the head of the family. We had always done what was expected of us, never stepping out of line.

Even as we settled Mira's cot in the centre of the aircraft and took our seats, we were still worried. I tried to look normal, but it was only when we reached Bahrain for refuelling that we were able to breathe freely and slowly relax. We had got away. After all the difficulties and anxieties of the last few weeks and months, *we had got away.* We had really managed to trick the authorities into believing that David was older than he looked and not of military age. It had taken a lot of time, bribes, and help from friends in high places.

Being Jewish, how could he possibly fight for Arab causes after the Farhud and the baiting of previous months? We had survived weeks of lengthy and tearful farewell parties when all our friends and relatives continued to try to dissuade us, telling us, "It's not too late"—but here we were on the way to a new life. By coincidence it was our fourth wedding anniversary.

And so we started rolling like a rolling stone, wandering like the proverbial wandering Jews. Indeed, it was an adventurous step for a couple with two babies to undertake at any time—but with the world at war?

At the stopover in Bahrain, we discovered that one of our fellow passengers, a gentleman by the name of R. Rushtie, had lived opposite us in Baghdad and knew my husband well. He turned out to be good company for the rest of the journey. He was making the move without being able to speak a word of English, and it boosted our morale to see someone even more unprepared than we were.

After Bahrain, our first stop in India was at Jodhpur, on what happened to be Poppy Day. We had never heard of that before, let

COLLECTION OF VIOLETTE SHAMASH

Safe in India, with Lena and Mira, a year after leaving Baghdad

alone knew what a real poppy looked like. We were given a button-hole of a poppy that we accepted without question. A British army officer greeted my three-year-old, Lena, with the words: "I do envy you. I am sixty years old and have never flown in an aeroplane. You are so tiny!" Then he turned to me and said: "What did it feel like to be flying in the air? Were you scared?" I wished I could tell him what was in my heart. Perhaps I should have felt scared, but after all we had been through, the only shock to the system was the apparent normality of it all. We just felt uplifted, relaxed, and free—so much so that we immediately decided to stay on and recuperate before taking the train to Bombay. But India is another story.

Last Flight

AFTER WE LEFT Baghdad, the fortunes of our community followed a downward path of persecution and deprivation that has left a bitter chapter in our communal history. Suffice it to say, nearly everyone wanted to get out: over the next decade a mass exodus took place, thanks largely to an airlift—the Aliya—that brought 120,000 Jews from Iraq to Israel between 1950 and 1952, with one suitcase each, compelled to abandon everything they owned. By then, every single Jewish community in Iraq's provinces had been eradicated. From a population of over 130,000 Jews throughout the country at the time of the Farhud, only 6,000 remained in Baghdad. Among them was my sister Na'ima—who would be the last member of my family to say good-bye and so bring down the curtain on our Babylon years.

Na'ima's farewell was extraordinary, even in those extraordinary times. Years of political turbulence led to yet another army coup, which brought an end to the monarchy and the slaughter of young King Faisal and the former regent Abd al-Ilah. That took place in 1958, the same year that my old school, the Laura Khedouri Alliance, was destroyed by a mob. There was a ban on foreign travel, and by 1963, all Jews were made to carry yellow identity cards.

Three years later, Na'ima found herself in detention in the main prison of Baghdad.

All their lives, Na'ima and Sasson had been used to a wonderful standard of living, with all the latest luxuries. But now, aged sixty-one and a widow for the previous nine years, Na'ima was totally alone. She was a grandmother eight times over, and her five children had already left Baghdad: my niece Doris and nephew Frankie were in Tel Aviv; my three nephews Maurice, Danny, and Freddie had gone to the United States. Almost all the community had left, too, and our numbers had dwindled to fewer than three thousand. All of Na'ima's children had begged her to join them, but she had held on, hoping to leave with her affairs liquidated and in tidy order when the situation, and particularly the virulent mood against the Jews, had settled. But far from settling, it just seemed to get worse. Suddenly, she found herself trapped: it was no longer possible to obtain an exit visa. She was stuck.

There was one way out. Some Jews were still managing to cross the border into Iran. The escapees would get themselves to Khanakin, on the border about eighty miles north of Baghdad, and have a guide walk them through to the other side. Khanakin was a Kurdish village and the Kurds were generally helpful to us. Iran then was still ruled by the shah, it had diplomatic relations with Israel, and a large Iraqi-Jewish community had settled in Tehran, including our niece Clara (Regina's daughter) and her family.

Despite everything that had happened in Iraq, Na'ima was still a woman of substance, retaining a good deal of property in the country as well as businesses that she continued to manage after Sass's death from a heart attack in 1957. These included properties in Khanakin, where there happened to be an unfinished business deal between her husband's estate and a man with whom the sale of a property had been agreed. He now offered to pay Na'ima if she would agree to go there and register it in his name. To make the proposition more attractive he said that, if she was interested, he had the means to smuggle her out of the country and into Iran. As Na'ima had heard of several who had arrived safely in Iran this way she decided to risk it, although she knew some people had been caught and returned to Baghdad. She told the man that if he could really organise her departure, she would come and sign over the property and forget the payment.

Na'ima had been hoarding whatever cash she could, as well as buying jewellery, in anticipation of such a day. She put all these savings—the jewellery, banknotes, and a stash of gold coins—into a belt that she tied around her waist. She travelled by car, fully aware of the dangers: not only did she not have an exit permit, but it was strictly forbidden to take anything of value out of the country. Once in Khanakin, having dealt with the bureaucracy of registering the property in the man's name, she was ready for her journey to Iran and freedom. But now came a hiccup: he said it would take a few more hours to organise.

This was an unwelcome surprise, but she was entirely in his hands. They agreed that she would spend the night at her own farm, where the family's retainer made her welcome and prepared a bedroom for her. A loud knock awoke her early the next morning. Still jumpy, she had the presence of mind to hide the belt with her valuables before opening the door. But her worst fears were confirmed: it was the police. The buyer had denounced her.

The police said their superintendent wanted her for questioning and took her in. At the police station, she maintained that she was in Khanakin on business to look after her properties. But the police went back to the farm, searched her room, found the telltale money belt and jumped to the obvious conclusion. The superintendent said that the matter was beyond his competence: he was sending her to Baghdad for the case to be considered by a judge. She had to spend the night in custody.

Movingly, the son of her retainer came to the police station to plead Na'ima's cause, saying what a good woman she was, who had never done them any wrong, and how her late husband had been good to them. He even offered to be jailed in her place, to no avail.

The following day she was sent to Baghdad in a police car. She told the superintendent that she was worried about her safety alone in one car with his men, so he kindly arranged for a second one as escort, in which they took the money belt.

Now the road from Khanakin to Baghdad is a long one, and during the journey she chatted nicely to her policemen and begged them to let her to make just one phone call. They stopped the car and she managed to put a call through to Baghdad, directly to the chief of police who was a good friend of her son Maurice. She recounted what had happened and where she was headed—and as soon as she arrived in Baghdad, he came to visit her in jail, weeping at seeing her that way. He asked the prison governor to look after her and treat her well and assured her that, with his help, she would be out within twenty-four hours. Then off he hurried to see the minister in charge.

At the ministry, he apparently received a big welcome and was offered coffee. "Before we take coffee, I have an urgent request," said her son's friend, and went on to explain the situation, saying that Na'ima had only ever seen one of her eight grandchildren.

"What?" came the outraged reply. "Surely you haven't come to me to intercede on behalf of a *Jewish* woman?"

In the end, the only effect that the chief of police had was a bad one: the minister immediately wrote to the prison saying that Na'ima was to pay a five thousand dinar fine in cash to the "Treasurer of the Nation"—a sum equal to sixty-three thousand pounds today.

The female prison superintendent, Sett Sabiha, came to her and told her the news. "Things have just become worse for you," she said.

Altogether Na'ima was incarcerated without trial for more than two years, in the middle of which the 1967 Six-Day War erupted, marking another downturn in the fortunes of the remaining Jews of Iraq. They were watched by the secret police wherever they went, at home and at work. Their property was expropriated and bank accounts frozen; they were dismissed from public posts. Businesses were shut, trading permits were cancelled, and telephones were disconnected and banned. Jews were placed under house arrest for long periods and flung into common jails with no contact with their families, as in Na'ima's case. Beatings and torture went on to elicit confessions of spying for Israel. Some died in custody. Thank God, she was spared that.

Na'ima was grieved and saddened and fell ill. Sett Sabiha called the prison doctor. They both turned out to be sympathetic Muslims, and over a period of time, the three made friends and started to trust one another. The superintendent and the doctor risked a lot for this friendship: with their help, Na'ima was able to smuggle out a few letters. She wrote to Maurice to let him know her predicament. She wrote to me—I was in London with my family by this time—describing her situation and begging me to help. I read the letter again and again with a lump in my throat. I do not normally bother my dear God with special requests; but now, in real desperation, I whispered my Shima Yisrael, our most important prayer, and sought the Lord's guidance to secure her release soon. But now, what to do? Which way to turn?

It was a scary time. Baghdad was in political turmoil yet again. The Arabs were oppressing the minorities at every turn, particularly the Kurds. Riots again erupted in Baghdad and Rashid Street was like a slaughterhouse. Persecution reached its peak at the end of 1968 with the "discovery of a Zionist spy ring" composed of Jewish businessmen. And on January 27, 1969, eight Jews were among those hanged in Liberation Square at the start of a series of show trials. Saddam Hussein, the country's newly appointed vice president, urged Baghdad Radio listeners to "come and enjoy the feast," and hundreds of thousands of Iraqis paraded and danced past the scaffolds where the bodies swung, each with a sign saying JEW attached to them. The mob chanted "Death to Israel!" and "Death to all traitors!" and desecrated the bodies as they were left to hang all day in the sun.

Such was the situation when my dearest sister Na'ima was in detention, at their mercy. She was very brave and we all admired her courage.

The barbarous public hangings shocked the world, and eventually our family managed to mobilise help. Na'ima's sons in New York approached prominent figures and U.S. senators. They hired important lawyers and advisers. They paid a lot of money. In Israel, her daughter Doris alerted a minister in the government who happened to be Baghdadi. During negotiations with his Jordanian counterpart, while stressing that Jews were still persecuted in the Arab world, he mentioned Na'ima's case. The Jordanian minister was horrified and promised to look into it.

Mass rallies took place across the globe, and in London the community organised a demonstration by torchlight in which, naturally, all my family—including David, myself, Lena, Mira, and my third child, Simon—and my friends participated. The procession was joined by many sympathisers. A few, including Mira, sat an all-night vigil in front of the Iraqi Embassy. A rabbi came and read Qaddish, prayers for the dead, and blew the *shofar*. It caused consternation among the workers at the embassy, for it is a bad omen for a Muslim to be forced to listen to Jewish prayers and, more especially, to hear the ram's horn, which is sounded in times of distress such as Yom Kippur. It was reported on all the TV channels and in the newspapers. Afterwards, we all went to join in the mourning prayers at the London family home of one of the hanged men. But the Iraqis did not relent.

In life, I have often found that my instinct guides me better than my brain, and so my feet took me to the Gardenia Club—the London rendezvous for Iraqi Jews—where I poured out my troubles to anyone who would listen. Finally, our president Naim Dangoor suggested that I get in touch with Amnesty International. I had never heard of them; the organisation was still in its infancy. But it proved to be an inspiration.

I visited their offices several times. In due course, a really kind man, Sir Osmond Williams, took up my cause. In an interview with him, he warned me that he was not a lawyer, Amnesty was a charitable organisation dealing with human rights, and results could not be guaranteed. "But," he continued, "supposing I were to go and see the Iraqi ambassador myself—what should I tell him?"

"Tell him that both my parents are still alive and they are worried about my sister. Tell him that she will soon be a great-grandmother herself. Tell him that she is over seventy years old"—of course, I knew I was exaggerating her age—"and remind him that all her property, money and jewels, everything, has been confiscated. Surely she has paid enough. She has now been in detention without trial for two years."

I choked on those words with tears in my eyes, and I could see the compassion in his. After all this time, I hardly dared hope that we had found the key.

Back in Baghdad, Na'ima's case had still not been heard in court, no judge had been appointed, and Na'ima was being held indefinitely. But the enquiries about her from abroad that had been piling up—from various international authorities, among them the lawyers and senators, the Jordanian minister, and Amnesty International—must have had an effect, for one day Sett Sabiha came to her and told her that there was good news at last: she was to be freed.

All her assets had been frozen: her farms, properties, businesses, bank accounts. If she wanted to be liberated, she would have to go to the Treasury and sign a document agreeing to their confiscation, so "voluntarily" giving the Iraqi government all that she had once possessed. She had no choice in the matter.

They sent a cattle truck to transport her. It was one of those big open-backed lorries into which she was expected to climb and stand in the back and hold on to the sides. There was absolutely no way she could possibly climb such a height. She told the driver: "With all the money I am about to 'donate,' couldn't they even send a car for me? I can't possibly climb that."

He replied: "Lady, I agree with you. But if you don't get up there, I will get into a lot of trouble. I will probably lose my job! Please help me. I will go on all fours, and if you stand on my back, perhaps you can make it."

Na'ima felt sorry for him. She removed her shoes and did as he bade. It was an awful ride: the wind whistled in her ears and the truck shook her bones as she held on for dear life. Even now, nearly forty years later, she tells me she still suffers the consequences of that journey, with ear- and backaches. But such was the price of freedom.

Apparently, Na'ima asked if she could go to her home and pack. Permission refused. She asked if she could visit her husband's grave one last time. Permission refused. She was taken to the airport, given some pocket money, and put on a flight to Tehran, and thence Tel Aviv and eventually New York. Only in the departure lounge did Na'ima think that it was safe to ask the question that had been on her lips ever since her prison friend had told her that she was going to be freed: why? The official accompanying her admitted that she had simply become an embarrassment.

In London, we learned that our prayers had been answered. I received a telegram from Amnesty in Paris saying that she had been freed and was at that moment in Iran. I immediately rang New York and broke the wonderful news to Maurice. Then I called Nana and Baba and Na'ima's children in Israel and everybody rejoiced and gave thanks to God.

Na'ima had been the last of our family to leave Iraq.

Good-bye, Baghdad.

Farewell, Babylon.

Adieu, Eden.

Postscript: January 2006

TWENTY YEARS AGO when I first started making a few jottings of my most cherished memories in preparation for this book, I scribbled the following note: "All that I am telling you about does not exist any more. It was *my* Baghdad, *my* native land where I grew up. Now it has been replaced almost altogether. Ninety per cent of it has been erased like chalk on a blackboard and a new story is written."

How much is left today? The new millennium continues to write a troubling story, with different developments filling the headlines and TV screens daily. Dhaak el-Sob—"the other bank" of the Tigris—where once tents, shacks, and palm trees had been the only shapes to grace the skyline, long ago became an important part of the city centre, housing many government ministries and other key buildings. Presidential palaces and the famous army parade ground where Saddam Hussein took the salute were located in the Karkh—key targets for the missiles that rained down in 1991 and 2003. Two Gulf Wars later, the Americans are uncomfortably installed there in their Green Zone and have managed to brand themselves as the new occupiers. Even the Arabs are killing each other, with the various factions tearing themselves apart. Where will it end? How will it end?

Baba and Nana always intended to return to Baghdad one day and so never sold the *qasr.* It was confiscated and later demolished in the creation of modern Baghdad. The Babylon Oberoi Hotel was built in its place, while the whole of the Karrada peninsula became the campus of the University of Baghdad. Gone is our island of Jazra where we used to go for picnics. Gone the neighbourhoods where our friends used to live. Gone, too, the mulberry tree at Beit el-Naqiib, the house of our important neighbour, the Sunni leader, on the right overlooking the river, where an old blind donkey harnessed to a treadmill went round and round all day to draw water for his master's orchard. There is a modern bridge now where the house used to be, and water is piped everywhere, although supplies are constantly being interrupted by unrest and sabotage.

I was sad to leave the city. My generation witnessed Baghdad's blossoming from a primitive past. We saw it growing, improving, and progressing so rapidly, as never before since time began. We always shared its moments of sadness and happiness and we took part, a great part, in pushing it to advance into civilisation, bringing a better life and comfort to the benefit of all.

It was where the Muslims and us lived side by side until relationships began to sour and we were attacked without provocation during the time of Rashid Ali. We couldn't comprehend their anger towards us. We were the good advisers, allowed to earn our place irrespective of creed or religion, the good and obedient servants of a society that accommodated the idea of Jewish members of Parliament and even elected a Jewish chief justice, the highest-ranking law officer in the land. The government never interfered with our religion and respected our way of life that was different from, yet in so many ways similar to, their own. No greater tribute is needed than the fact that at one time everything closed on Saturdays—our Shebbath—instead of Fridays as one might have expected.

We were treated as equals and accepted on our own merit until the poison of Nazism and Arab nationalism entered the bloodstream. The evil spread like a contagious disease. Maybe they turned on us, these Arab brothers, instead of fighting among themselves; we were, after all, the easiest of targets for their troubles and highly visible, for we had never seen any reason to hide. But although the country rejected us, we know our neighbours were not devils at heart. Many were good to us. They themselves felt embarrassed to see us pack up and go because, only a day earlier, we had been good friends. Too late. Once uprooted from Baghdad, we scattered all over the world like feathers from a pillow, never to be reunited.

After we left Baghdad, we started our wandering, looking for a new home to put down roots before finally settling in London. We quickly took to our new adopted home. On the one hand, many of our community had settled here and we soon started the Gardenia Club, a social place where we could meet, play a game of cards or backgammon, gossip, talk about the old days, sing some old songs, and have a traditional dinner. On the other hand, London provided an anonymity that had been unimaginable before. My accent was obviously not native English, so when non-Iraqi bridge partners would ask me where I came from, it was awkward trying to give a straight, quick answer. In those days, most people didn't even know where Iraq was, and if they did, they would assume I was a Muslim. So what could I say? I would have to launch into an explanation that was complicated, and to begin with, I did. The response to this was astonishing to me: "Oh, you're a foreigner," they would simplify, as if that explained everything. Well, one day, in reply to the question: "Where are you from?" I just answered: "I am a foreigner"—and surprisingly, my inquisitor was satisfied with that.

After several years in London, most of our community who remembered and missed the old Baghdad succumbed to old age, like me. Fewer and fewer of us were going to the Gardenia Club, and our children were not showing much interest in it. They had now integrated and found other things to occupy their time. They had children of their own who could not even speak our Arabic, so they found our social headquarters irrelevant. The Gardenia Club closed and the property was sold. One by one, all remaining links to our old life are vanishing.

I have sought to tell you, my children and my grandchildren, who you really are, what your background is, because I realise that, like the Gardenia Club, all will soon be forgotten. My mission has been to inform, to enlighten, and not to pass judgement.

Our Baghdad, *my* Baghdad, is gone forever. I just wonder if the new builders found the treasure that Baba placed in the foundations of the *qasr*, on the right-hand side under the *mezuza* for good luck at the front door. He told us about it in great secrecy: it was an amphora of gold coins with a letter in ancient Hebrew that he himself had buried at night after the masons had gone home, walling it in with bricks in the morning.

Epilogue

VIOLETTE AND DAVID spent two and a half years in Bombay, summering in Poona, bringing up Lena and Mira, and leading a happy social life with business doing well. But before long, Violette's health began to deteriorate; for no apparent reason, she started to experience asthma attacks. These, coupled with a decision by Baba and Nana finally to move to Palestine, led the family to change direction once more and head for the Holy Land themselves. In 1944, they embarked on a passenger liner, part of a twenty-ship convoy destined for the Middle East with full Royal Navy escort. Violette recalled how, on the three-week passage, sailors strung nets in the vessel's superstructure to catch migratory birds—"sparrows," she called them—which the ship's cook served for dinner. (Lena thought they were delicious; Mira hated the very idea.) After a short quarantine in Port Said, they sailed on to Haifa and so began another odyssey.

Palestine in 1944 was no paradise. Gone forever was the pampered life of yesteryear. World War II was a large factor in everyday life, and the years leading to independence from Britain in 1948 were tumultuous, marked by bombings and attacks against British authority. One incident in particular will never be erased from family memory: in February 1948, they were living close to Ben Yehuda

Street in Jerusalem when a massive bomb exploded at the *Palestine Post* building, blowing out the windows of their rented apartment. Fifty-six Jews were killed and many more maimed in that attack.

The Ben Yehuda bomb proved a turning point. They had moved house several times, taking the few sticks of furniture they had brought along from India, in the hope that Violette's asthma would improve at each new location. But each time it was the same. (By now, they were five, as Violette had given birth to a longed-for son in Tel Aviv three years earlier. They named him Simon, after his paternal grandfather Shm'oon.) So, with violence on the rise and her health deteriorating once more, the family decided to move yet again—to Cyprus this time. Weeks later, the Middle East erupted in all-out war when Israel declared independence and immediately found itself under attack from its Arab neighbors. It was Mira's seventh birthday.

Any notion that British-run Cyprus might offer a quiet haven was quickly dashed, for soon the island found itself in the grip of the EOKA (National Organisation of Cypriot Fighters) guerilla campaign, whose aim was union with Greece. Clashes between Greek and Turkish Cypriots and attacks against British forces became commonplace as they settled into their new life in Nicosia, which is where, miraculously, Violette found that her asthma had been cured. Doctors could offer no explanation; everyone was puzzled. Then, mentally retracing their steps, they noted that the one difference this time was that they had left their old furniture behind—including the cotton mattress that they had been toting around since Bombay. It had been made to measure in their own home, so they could supervise the Indian *teeteepampa*. Finally, they realized that Violette had been suffering from an allergy, the cause of which she had been sleeping on all those years.

The family moved to London in 1964, where David died ten years later. Violette lived on alone, in the same London apartment, closely watching the continuing saga of Iraq via satellite television and staying in daily touch by phone with her surviving sisters in the United States and Israel: Na'ima, Fahima, and Daisy. Finally, on March 21, 2006, in her ninety-fourth year, in failing health but supported by the loving children, grandchildren, and great-grandchildren to whom this book is dedicated, she passed away.

Na'ima died at Fort Lee, New Jersey, one month later—eight weeks short of her hundredth birthday—leaving five children. Eight months later, in December 2006, Daisy died in Tel Aviv, aged eighty-six, leaving two children. Marcelle died in April 2005 in Tel Aviv, aged eighty-four; she is survived by two children, who live in Brazil. And Regina also died in Tel Aviv, in 1997, aged ninety-four, survived by six children.

Fahima, the last surviving sister, died in October 2008, aged ninety-seven, having lived in the same apartment for more than seventy years since arriving in Tel Aviv by coach from Baghdad. She is survived by five children.

Salman died in February 2005, aged ninety-seven, in Bnei Brak, Israel. While Violette was living in Bombay, she met a pretty girl from the community, yet another Violette, and arranged a match for her brother. Soon afterward, they moved to Israel, where he became deeply religious, and all his family followed suit. He is survived by five children.

Baba and Nana first lived in Tel Aviv before joining Violette and David in Nicosia for a number of years. In due course, they returned to Israel and built a house in Bnei Brak. They occupied the upstairs while Salman and his family lived below. Each lived into their nineties: Nana died in 1973 and Baba in 1975.

David's father, Shm'oon, died in 1945 in Baghdad. Five years later, his mother, Habiba, joined his brother Haron and his family in Milan, Italy, but she died shortly afterward. His three sisters all emigrated to Israel and have since passed away. David's brother Ghali, an admirer of Gandhi, joined an ashram in India where he died in mysterious circumstances in 1955. Haron passed away in Milan in 1987, aged eighty-seven. He is survived by his wife, Violette, and two children.

Rashid Ali and Grand Mufti al-Husseini escaped to Tehran in disguise and eventually arrived in Berlin, where they spent the rest of the war. Neither man recovered his influence. Afterward, Rashid Ali lived in exile in Saudi Arabia and Egypt until he returned to Baghdad after the overthrow of the royal family in 1958. In December of the same year, he was implicated in a plot to overthrow President Abd al-Karim Qassem and was jailed and sentenced to death. However, in 1961, he was granted a special amnesty and soon afterward settled in Beirut, where he died four years later. The mufti went on to recruit Muslims in Yugoslavia to fight for the Germans, without great success, even though his soldiers were crueler to the Jews than the SS or Gestapo. He was finally arrested in France but escaped to Cairo in 1946, where he remained a guest of King Farouk. He died in Lebanon in 1974.

In April 2005, fire ravaged the old Shorjah market area, causing more than $1 billion in damages and wiping out the last vestige of old Baghdad. This item of news made no headlines. Overgrown now, the Baghdad Jewish cemetery lies on the eastern edge of the capital, adjacent to a sprawling slum of more than two million Shi'a Muslims.

Thousands of Iraqi Jews found safe haven around the globe where they make their homes today, notably in Israel, the United States, Canada, Australia, and Britain. In Baghdad, meanwhile, only about a dozen are left, including the last rabbi. On Yom Kippur 2006, he, too, announced that he was leaving.

AFTERWORD

Diplomacy is to do and say
The nastiest thing in the nicest way.

—ISAAC GOLDBERG, 1927

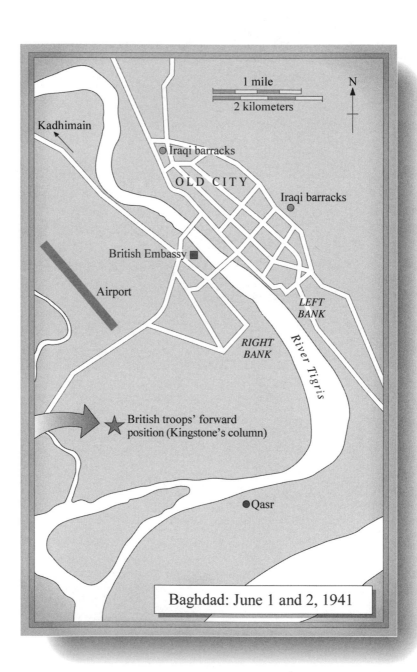

Baghdad: June 1 and 2, 1941

Inside Story: Behind the Farhud

TONY ROCCA

VIOLETTE'S GRAPHIC ACCOUNT of the events inside Baghdad in May and early June 1941 leaves her question "Where were the British?" unanswered. The enemy had been defeated. Why, then, were the British troops not ordered in to stop the bloodbath once the Farhud began?

Before I started to edit Violette's story with Mira, I knew nothing of the Farhud and did not realize that, for the previous sixty-seven years, the same question had puzzled the community at large as well as historians. To satisfy my curiosity, I started my research, believing a simple answer could be found. I was wrong. What I discovered was a tangle of diplomatic and military mistakes, a fiasco in which arrogance played a principal role and the final, fatal decision was left to one man.

Under orders to drive out Rashid Ali and occupy Baghdad, Britain's soldiers crossed six hundred miles of desert to accomplish a stunning achievement against considerable odds. But three miles from their objective, their orders suddenly changed. They were forced to halt. Although victory was theirs, for they had created a stranglehold on the city and the tyrant had fled, the triumph was deliberately muffled. They were obliged to camp on the right bank of the Tigris, outside the city gates, while the left bank erupted in violence, and they were powerless to act, tired and frustrated in their bivouac beneath the eucalyptus and palm trees.

The events of June 1 and 2 had apocalyptic implications for the descendants of Abraham: nothing short of the termination of 2,600 years of Jewish settlement in the land of Babylon. The story of one of the oldest communities in the world was ending as it had begun, in terror, anguish, and mass exodus. The Farhud al-Yahud—the looting of the Jews (as it subsequently came to be known)—was the beginning of that end.

To answer the question, Why? we need to turn back the clock to World War I and later, to the days of the British mandate and the shaky start that Iraq had after being created by the British at the Cairo Conference of 1921.

The Ambassador

To borrow and adapt Violette's opening remark: the last century was a few years into its teens when the British created a secret service unit to coordinate undercover activities throughout the Middle East. As her father and his friends were crossing the border into Persia in 1916 to escape persecution from the Turkish army, it established itself in Cairo, a thousand miles away, in the palmy luxury of the Savoy Hotel, the British army headquarters where ceiling fans whirred above rattan chairs and waiters in flowing robes scuttled attentively to serve staff officers thimbles of coffee and tea in tiny glasses. Two members of this military elite were to become extremely well known by the 1920s: the legendary Gertrude Bell and the flamboyant T. E. Lawrence (better known as Lawrence of Arabia).

The so-called Arab Bureau could have been made for Lawrence and Bell, whose books on the region made them famous. They called themselves the "Intrusives," dedicated (Lawrence wrote) to breaking into the centers of power to "foster the new Arabic world." Less well known was the identity of their bureau chief: a person whose name is curiously absent when the credits finally roll at the end of the saga of imperial Iraq. Lieutenant Colonel Kinahan Cornwallis was the leading Arabist of the day, an Oxford Blue, runner, boxer, and marksman. He could not have been happier than to shelter behind the extrovert facade that his two subalterns presented, which deflected interest and permitted him to remain in the shadows—either from modesty or from a deliberate desire to escape attention. Beyond diplomatic circles, Cornwallis of Arabia (a sobriquet well merited though never applied) managed to remain in comparative obscurity over the following three decades, a simple servant of the Crown despite the honors piled upon him. This was astonishing in view of the recognition he deserved for the huge influence he wielded on the Iraqi stage and for the fateful role he played when the curtain came down on the Jews of Babylon.

Cornwallis led the bureau for four years from 1916 to 1920, during which period it conceived the pivotal act that brought Britain victory in the desert: the idea of persuading the Arabs to rise against their pro-German Ottoman rulers by promising them national independence.

To engineer what history knows as the Arab Revolt, Lawrence found a leader among the Hashemite family of Mecca: Prince Faisal ibn-Hussain, the one man capable of persuading ten thousand tribesmen to forget their feuds and ride, united, into Damascus. As a reward, Faisal was put on the throne of Syria, from where he expected to rule a united Arabia. But the Arabs never achieved their independence. Unknown to Lawrence and the bureau, Britain and France had struck a secret deal to keep the captured Ottoman lands for themselves when the war ended. Adding further complexity, with the 1917 Balfour Declaration, Britain pledged to provide a Jewish homeland in Palestine—now a "twice-promised" land. When the French arrived in Syria to take up their mandate in 1919, King Faisal's short rule was ended.

His years directing the bureau earned Cornwallis huge credit in military and diplomatic circles as well as high honors: he was awarded the Distinguished Service Order in 1917 and was made a Commander of the British Empire two years later. But in 1920 and 1921 came the serious uprisings by Arabs and Kurds that should have proved to the British that the indigenous population really did want self-rule. London brutally quashed the rebellion using mustard gas—despite the revulsion felt after its effects in World War I—on the orders of Winston Churchill, then secretary of state

Faisal's coronation, with Cornwallis, Sir Percy Cox, and British commander in chief Sir Aylmer Haldane

for war and air, who famously proclaimed: "I do not understand this squeamishness . . . I am strongly in favour of using poisoned gas against uncivilised tribes." (The old British Lee-Enfield .303 rifle that Saddam Hussein used to enjoy firing into the air was captured during this so-called Great Revolution, hence its significance.)

Britain decided thereafter that Mesopotamia should be a kingdom known as Iraq, ruled by a complaisant monarch, and Faisal was the obvious choice. Following the Cairo Conference of 1921 and a somewhat dubious referendum (a 96 percent vote in favor of a monarchy), Colonel Cornwallis, as he had become, was personally charged by Britain's Foreign Secretary Lord Curzon to offer him the job.

Cornwallis was just the man. Before World War I, he had served for eight years in the Sudan Civil Service; in the war he had met the royal family when he was posted briefly to Jeddah; and when it ended, he was sent to Syria as political officer, which brought him into contact with Faisal and the two became close friends. However, having been manipulated by the British with their broken promise of Arabian independence, Faisal was not easily persuaded. It took the combined skills of Cornwallis, Lawrence, and Bell ("the uncrowned queen of Iraq"), who plotted to promote Arab self-rule, to get Faisal to agree to pick up the new crown—no matter that he had never set foot in the country nor could claim any connection with it—and placed his brother Abdallah on the throne in neighboring Transjordan. The reluctant Faisal finally acquiesced on one condition: that Cornwallis accompany him on his journey from Jeddah to his new kingdom in June 1921 and there remain by his side. The band played "God Save the King" at Faisal's coronation two months later, a strictly British affair with all due pomp and circumstance of the imperial age, held in the carpeted courtyard of the old Turkish offices in Baghdad, at six o'clock one morning—out of the fearsome heat of the day but also out of the glare of the public eye.

And so was set in motion the wheel of history that led ultimately in Iraq to the rise of the Ba'ath Party and Saddam Hussein, fifteen military coups between 1936 and 1968, the overthrow of the monarchy in 1958, two Gulf Wars, and the entanglement of both the United States and Great Britain with repercussions that continue today. Many of the region's most intractable political problems stem directly from the policies pursued by the British during this era.

Once the business of the monarch had been settled, the next step on the road to democracy was the election of a constituent assembly that would ratify the treaty legitimizing Britain's presence and draft a constitution. But there remained strong opposition, mostly from the Shi'a and their religious leaders. The British high commissioner Sir Percy Cox soon took care of that on his assumption of formal authority in August 1922, when the king fell ill. He ordered the arrest and deportation of the leaders, suppression of their parties and press, and an aerial bombardment of their tribes. One year later, Cornwallis canvassed all of Britain's district officers and Iraq's provincial governors to determine the names of pro-British candidates whom they felt would vote for the treaty. And finally, on February 8, 1924, after considering the names, Cornwallis sent each provincial inspector and governor a list of proposed candidates for the hundred-member assembly. Of the ninety-eight listed, seventy-four were elected, leaving no doubt that the existing Iraqi government—and, behind it, the British—had interfered with the process.

Sir Kinahan Cornwallis, "the British Empire's plenipotentiary"

Both physically (at six feet four) and metaphorically, Cornwallis towered over the construction of the new state. "Tall, rugged and imperturbable," as the *Times* described him, he was, in effect, the British Empire's plenipotentiary in the years of the mandate when Iraq was finding its feet, when oil had already become recognized as the one important resource that Britain needed to fuel its own industrialized economy. (An oil deal was signed, ensuring that Iraq received only token royalties from any future revenues.) Officially, his position was that of adviser to the Ministry of the Interior. This seemingly humble title belied the fact that it was certainly the key post in the country, offering great power and influence, as the ministry controlled all administration, the civil service, and the police. In addition to this, he also acted as the king's personal adviser for fourteen years, during which Britain was responsible for the ultimate security of Iraq and for preparing and developing its institutions for the day of its independence. The British plan was that the king should appear to be striving for that independence, which would be granted with strings attached to ensure that Britain kept a firm domination over the country's oil resources.

When Iraq finally gained its sovereignty in 1932, it came on condition that the Iraqi government support British foreign policy in the region, protect British oil rights, and allow the Royal Air Force to retain bases in the center at Habbaniya and in the south at Shaibah, near Basra, thus safeguarding Britain's strategic interests. These prerequisites were essentially created by Cornwallis, who stayed on in the role of Interior Ministry adviser even after independence. Yet throughout this time, he managed to escape the glare of publicity. It was only in his obituary, many years later, that *Times* readers became aware that "Cornwallis was the clearing house of policy" and had been "cast in the great proconsular mould, and on the rare occasions when it seemed necessary could assume the proconsular manner. But he was always easy of access, simple, humorous, and abounding in common sense."

During the first half of the mandate, Cornwallis—he was knighted later, in 1929—worked hand in glove with Bell, who had been made oriental secretary to High Commissioner Cox. The two enjoyed an affectionate relationship despite her being his elder by fourteen years. With a common background in the murky world of espionage, they were thrown together intimately in Faisal's entourage, sharing a love of the king, dogs, shooting, and other country pastimes, and understanding one another's lonely lives. He was in the early stages of being divorced; she was still mourning the man she loved who had died at Gallipoli. As they grew closer, he offered her a job as chief of intelligence in the Ministry of the Interior, but she declined out of loyalty to the high commissioner.

It is hard to overstate the pair's influence. Bell's prodigious stash of letters—she was a prolific writer, and these have now passed into the public domain—give a personal insight into the fledgling kingdom's early years, when the diplomatic social round played a great part in nation-building, and the fabric of governance was stitched together over games of bridge, vingt-et-un, and mah-jongg; swimming in the Tigris; and taking tea with the king, whose position was largely symbolic. She and her "dear friend Ken" were often thrown together at evening and weekend social functions and were also frequent guests of Faisal at polo matches and on shooting trips for duck, snipe, partridge, and quail.

Bell lovingly recalls her walks through Violette's Karrada district and mentions its exquisite gardens with their "ripe oranges hanging from the trees and the green barley springing under golden mulberry bushes." There, years earlier, she had visited Violette's family's neighbor, the Naqiib, the Sunni holy man who became crucial to the future of Iraq as prime minister in 1921. With his home on the riverbank next to Baba's *qasr*—in 1922, it was where he signed into law the treaty underpinning Britain's presence—one might wonder how many times she passed the family residence, or even if she accompanied the king when he later called on the *qasr* with the intention of buying it.

We learn from Violette that Faisal was a champion of the minority communities, greatly respected for his egalitarian views, and it was Bell who encouraged him to be proactive in this direction, arranging his visits to the Great Synagogue and Alliance schools to stress the impartiality with which he treated all his subjects, even hailing the Jews as "the moving spirit of Iraq."

The public perception was that the newly minted monarchy had brought stability to the new country, a view anxiously fostered by Britain, which was running Iraq as India lite—an extension of the Indian Raj with its rupees and annas, Indian soldiers, and evidently expecting a long tenure, even a place for the Indian post office. What is not generally known is how much the king wobbled in the early years and had to be propped up by his courtiers. Desperately wanting to be seen as the friend both of the British and of the Arab nationalists, he frequently threatened to abdicate and only Cornwallis's and Bell's persuasive powers prevented him from doing so—just as they had persuaded him to accept the monarchy in the first place. Invited to spend some time with the king at the royal farm near the Persian border in October 1924, Bell wrote how he "opened his heart and told me how lonely he was and how he looked forward to coming up to this estate as a means of escaping from the dull round of palace and office which was all that Baghdad offered him." A week later, there were "fearful alarums and excursions over Mecca." The king had "violent hysterics" and formally abdicated in favor of his son Ghazi. But the abdication was in private, to High Commissioner Cox, who advised him to bide his time—reminding Bell of a period in 1922 "when Ken Cornwallis had Faisal's abdication lying about in a drawer for a month."

She evidently thought the world of Cornwallis, her almost constant dinner companion and confidant whose divorce (from another Gertrude) was made final in 1925. "He has such a big position here and is such an important trusted person, and he has the devotion of his friends, of whom I am the chief," she wrote to her father on November 24, 1924. "I do love and admire his salient, his almost aggressive integrity and I prize more than I can say the trust and affection he gives me in such full measure." In another letter to her sister Molly, she described her efforts to convince him that she could make him happy, writing of her love for him as that of a mother and sister, combined with "that other love." But according to Bell's recent biographer Georgina Howell, Bell mistook brotherly familiarity for something else, and when it was obvious that he did not reciprocate her feelings, she was badly hurt. The acutely uncomfortable Cornwallis stonily rejected her advances and began to avoid her. Later, they patched it up, but two days before her fifty-eighth birthday in 1926 she was found dead, apparently from an overdose of sleeping pills.

The day before she died, she wrote to Cornwallis, then forty-three, asking him to take care of her dog Tundra should anything happen to her. (It was her second pet in Baghdad; the first puppy, Peter, had been from Cornwallis's spaniel bitch, Sally. Both had died of distemper within twenty-four hours of each other, bringing the two kingmakers even closer.) Strangely, the "imperturbable" Cornwallis did nothing, and her family never forgave him. In *Daughter of the Desert,* Howell quotes a letter that T. E. Lawrence sent Bell's father on hearing of her apparent suicide, in which he wrote: "I think she was very happy in her death, for her political work—one of the biggest things a woman has ever had to do—was as finished as mine." Presciently, he added: "That Irak state is a fine monument; even if it only lasts a few more years, as I often fear and sometimes hope. It seems such a very doubtful benefit—government—to give a people who have long done without."

For all Britain's attempts to forge a stable Iraq, over the following years the country began to unravel. Almost immediately after independence, Iraqi troops and Kurdish tribesmen carried out massacres against Christian Assyrians, whom the British had employed as a police force. The British tried to put the best face on the situation and blocked a League of Nations inquiry into the violence. But they were not optimistic about Iraq's future. And Cornwallis, once so sanguine and upbeat, made a prophetic pronouncement:

> My own prediction is that they will all fly at each other's throats and that there will be a bad slump in the administration which will continue until someone strong enough to dominate the country emerges or, alternatively, until we have to step in and intervene.

Faisal, too, was heard to speak despairingly of his kingdom just before he died:

> In Iraq there is still—and I say this with a heart full of sorrow— no Iraqi people but unimaginable masses of human beings, devoid of any patriotic ideal, imbued with religious traditions and absurdities, connected by no common tie, giving ear to evil, prone to anarchy, and perpetually ready to rise against any government whatsoever.

The year was 1933.

After the death of King Faisal, the country was virtually ruled by a group of colonels who saw themselves as the future liberators of an oppressed Iraq. (One of the Golden Square accomplices, Khayrallah al-Tulfah, was the uncle who raised Saddam Hussein. His book, whose title freely translates as *Against Iran and the Jews,* became the "voice of the national revolution.") The Iraqi army—trained and equipped by the British—became a breeding ground of resentment against Britain's lingering colonial presence, a presence that had been ensured by the Anglo-Iraqi Treaty of 1930, prior to independence, binding Iraq to a twenty-five-year military alliance. With local civilian politicians being seen as British puppets and British policies in Palestine causing deep discontent, the ground lay open for the Golden Square to breathe fire into the nationalist aspirations being fanned by pro-Nazi propaganda broadcast by Faisal's son Ghazi, the new king. The series of coups d'état that followed—and Ghazi's mysterious death in a car crash—were to result in Rashid Ali's rise to power and, finally, war with Britain.

By April 1941, when Rashid Ali broke the Anglo-Iraqi Treaty and made overtures to Berlin, the British Empire was suffering one of its darkest hours. World War II was twenty months old and hardly anything was going Churchill's way. The Germans had swept across Europe and southward as far as Greece before racing across North Africa to threaten Tobruk and the main British base in Egypt. The Vichy French government, ruling under the auspices of the Germans, was occupying Syria and Lebanon and constituted a threat to British-ruled Palestine from the north; meanwhile the final Allied push to defeat the Italians in East Africa was reaching its climax. Back home, England was being pummeled in the eighth month of relentless Blitz.

The last thing Britain needed in the Middle East was an additional string of problems, but the danger Rashid Ali posed could not be ignored. Uppermost in everyone's mind was the matter of oil: although Iraq supplied Britain with only 5 percent of its domestic needs, the entire British Mediterranean fleet was totally dependent upon it, sent down six hundred miles of pipeline from Mosul to be refined in Palestine at Haifa. In the words of *Time* magazine, it was "the carotid artery of the British Empire." At the same time, Hitler was casting covetous eyes, determined to get his hands on it to fuel the Reich's imminent invasion of the Soviet Union. In exchange, he promised the Iraqis financial and military aid to rid their country of the hated British.

An Axis grip on Iraq posed a triple threat. It would deprive Britain of the crude oil on which its defense of the Mediterranean depended; sever its vital air link and land bridge between Egypt and India and, therefore, the empire; and encourage insurrection in Egypt and Palestine. Given the political volatility of the region and the dramatic shift of focus the war had taken toward the eastern Mediterranean, Churchill found himself compelled, as he characteristically put it, to "make sure" of Iraq. At all costs, Britain's oil rights had to be protected.

Citing Rashid Ali's violation of the 1930 treaty, the British landed Anglo-Indian troops at Basra on April 19 and a second convoy arrived ten days later. Infuriated by this move, Rashid Ali decided a show of force was necessary. At the start of May—"the black month of Rashid Ali"—he ordered the Iraqi army to surround the RAF's desert outpost at Habbaniya, fifty-five miles west of the capital on the banks of the Euphrates, to which a total of 230 British women and children had been evacuated from the capital for safety. What happened next was a hard-fought military operation in which Churchill became so frustrated that he came close to sacking his Middle East commander, General Sir Archibald ("Archie") Wavell, the commander in chief in Cairo, who had argued—along with Cornwallis and the Foreign Office—for appeasement.

The action became known to the British as the Thirty Days' War and, like the Farhud, was largely eclipsed by weightier events in the world conflict—a sideshow. But while military and civilian minds were focused elsewhere, the RAF fought a remarkable battle. It was a classic story of the kind of adventure that appears to belong entirely to a different age: a mixture of Victorian derring-do and stiff upper lips and the kind of soldiering in which each man's individual effort played a vital part to secure collective victory.

The huge Habbaniya base housed a flying school for one thousand cadet airmen supported by nine thousand civilians, many of them British dependents. It relied for protection on a solitary wire along a seven-mile perimeter and six companies of Assyrians recruited into military units, or levies. Being a nonoperational airfield, its offensive resources consisted of seventy-four very old aircraft, mainly trainers unequipped for battle, with just nine obsolete biplane fighters designed for combat in a previous era and thirty-nine pilots who knew how to fly them. Suddenly, staring down at them from a 150-foot plateau was a menacing force of one thousand Iraqi soldiers backed by armor, artillery, and modern aircraft.

In five days of siege, the makeshift British air force, with its motley fleet of antiques hastily rigged to carry bombs, valiantly flew 647 sorties. They dropped more than 3,000 bombs and fired 116,000 rounds of ammunition. Within fourteen hours of the start of the battle, a quarter of the pilots had been lost and twenty-two of the sixty-four aircraft that had begun the day had been shot down. The Associated Press reported: "War flamed fiercely in a graveyard of empires, an area crowded with memories of vanished Babylonian, Assyrian, Chaldean, Persian, Greek, Roman, Saracen and Turk power."

As Violette was giving birth to Mira, the air war in Iraq was still raging. Hurricane fighters and Blenheim bombers were flown in from Egypt, Wellingtons flew over Baghdad, and the Luftwaffe was about to join the fray. For the first and only time in the war, Churchill had directly overruled a commander in chief in the field—"He gives me the impression of being tired out," he wrote of Wavell in his war diaries—and on his own orders, a British army force, initially six thousand strong and flanked by the Arab Legion of Major John Glubb ("Glubb Pasha"), prepared to cross 550 miles of baking desert from Palestine to raise the siege of the beleaguered cantonment.

In Habbaniya, Churchill thundered, people were "hanging on by their eyelids." There was only one problem: it took so long to muster transport for the invasion, the force only began its expedition on May 11, five days after the RAF had defeated the hostile army by itself.

In Cairo, General Wavell had been adamant from the start that forceful British action in Iraq could send the whole Arab world up in flames. Any intervention at that moment would be ill advised, he told Churchill, with the appearance of British troops serving only to spur on Iraqi nationalism—views that were shared in London at the Foreign Office, though not by the chiefs of staff. Wavell had a particular reason for urging negotiation with Rashid Ali: his hands were already full, planning his troops' evacuation from Greece, preparing for a German assault on Crete (predicted in code intercepts), finalizing plans for an attack on Italian forces in East Africa, planning a preemptive attack on the Vichy French in Syria, and most pressingly, squaring up to Erwin Rommel's damaging Afrika Korps offensive. His resources were completely inadequate, he told Churchill, and for his own part, he had no spare men to lend to the Iraq theater. So when Churchill's direct order came, the scratch force that the reluctant commander mounted for the assault on Baghdad was hardly off to a good start. In addition, Wavell found himself saddled with responsibility for the Indian troops that had landed at Basra, which brought him into conflict with General Sir Claude Auchinleck, the commander in chief in India who had robustly argued in favor of intervention, saying that any appearance of weakness would be fatal.

The tension being generated between London, Cairo, and Delhi only worsened when rioting broke out in Basra and looters ransacked the city. It was a terrible portent, a day and night of looting that went unchecked while British forces stood by, under orders not to intervene. Directives issued by Wavell on May 8 and copied to the force crossing the desert laid the ground rules for both sets of troops: they must avoid conflict at all cost; Iraqis must be made to understand that Britain did not intend to occupy the country, set up an administration, interfere with their own authority, or infringe their independence—what sounds like a familiar refrain today. How one might reconcile the notion that they were not infringing Iraqi independence while sending an invasion force to effect regime change was not stated.

The next day, May 9, Churchill signaled Wavell:

> Having joined Habbaniya forces you should exploit the situation to the utmost, not hesitating to try to break into Baghdad *even with quite small forces.* (Emphasis added.)

By any measure, the so-called Habforce—a motorized column, with no tanks or heavy armor and lacking antiaircraft guns—was ill prepared for the task ahead: a grueling journey across sandy terrain in blazing sunshine with daily temperatures reaching 118 degrees Fahrenheit. Thrown together from the remnants of whatever troops Wavell could find in Egypt and Palestine, Habforce was ill trained and poorly equipped. It was based on a division of the Household Cavalry Regiment (the Life Guards and Royal Horse Guards "Blues") that, until then, had been serving in Palestine purely as a police force. It included buses pulled in from the streets of Haifa and Jerusalem, civilian trucks, and any other spare vehicle that could be found. The Guards had only just converted from horses to wheeled transport and were demoralized by the indignity of losing their mounted status, which had come with orders to shoot many of their animals. Few of the cavalrymen knew how to drive, but the Morris army trucks they were issued posed a special challenge, as they had solid rubber tires and appeared to be leftovers from World War I. The armored cars accompanying them were also relics from Lawrence's day. Nevertheless, the force crossed the border into Iraq at the frontier fort of Rutbah—the old Nairn coach staging post—and captured the stronghold on the first day of its eastward march.

For all its initial success, Habforce had made slow progress to reach the frontier. Its commander, Major General George Clark, soon realized that, with time running out for the relief of Habbaniya, it was too slow and unwieldy for the long march: the 285 miles that still lay between the column and the garrison. To succeed, he would have to send a "flying column" ahead, and he ordered Brigadier Joe Kingstone to lead it, giving it the code name Kingcol.

Kingcol left Rutbah and began plodding eastward at its maximum speed of fifteen miles per hour with the Arab Legion in the lead: a straggling column of two thousand men in five hundred vehicles strung out over the desert for twenty or thirty miles with raw, yellow dust funneling out behind them. It was a diverse force. Mixed in with the Household Cavalry were two companies of the Essex Regiment, a battery of Royal Artillery troops and 250 Bedouin of the Desert Patrol swathed in garish robes—"Glubb's Girls," the troops jokingly called them—who raced about in their lightweight Ford trucks, proudly known as scout cars, mounted with 1914-vintage Lewis guns and equally decrepit Hotchkiss guns.

Ahead of them, the Iraqis deployed forty thousand troops in four divisions: two holding the area between Habbaniya and Baghdad, one guarding the Kirkuk oil fields in the north, and one holding back the Indian forces to the south. They also faced appalling heat: when the thermometer reached its daily peak, metal became incandescent and radiators boiled. "The heat felled us like pole-axed cattle," one soldier wrote. Water was strictly rationed, only to be drunk at halts, by order of an officer. Some of it, carried all the way from Egypt, was hardly drinkable: it was either black or purple and had to be given ten minutes to settle, when only the top part could be sipped.

Despite foundering in soft sand, bedding down to their axles, and being attacked by Iraqi bombers as well as German Messerschmitts making their first appearance on the battlefield, Kingcol reached Habbaniya on May 18, by which time the oil situation that obsessed Churchill had turned ugly. Iraqi troops had moved to occupy all refineries and pumping stations, and British minds were concentrated on how to prevent the oil falling into German hands in the event of defeat. Commandos with a specific knowledge of desert warfare and the ability to work independently were needed for a clandestine operation to sabotage the system. In their desperation to find just the right group, the hard-pressed British turned to the unlikeliest of quarters: they called in the Irgun, the armed Jewish underground movement that it had been fighting in Palestine.

The Irgun had only just been tamed. Its leaders had been rounded up and jailed, only to be freed later when the organization pledged its readiness to cooperate in the war effort. Now came the test: would they undertake the mission to destroy the oil refineries and pipelines? David Raziel, the group's head, agreed on one condition: that he could also kidnap the grand mufti and bring him back to Palestine. It was an offer the British could scarcely refuse: the mufti was wanted on a multitude of counts of murder, terrorism, and anti-British atrocities.

On the morning of May 17, Raziel and three colleagues boarded an RAF transport in Palestine for a flight to Habbaniya. On landing, they were told that London had postponed the mission: destruc-

*The grand mufti,
four years on,
reviewing SS troops
in Bosnia (Nazi
magazine cover)*

COURTESY OF THE SCRIBE

tion of the oil supplies should be delayed until the last minute, as rebuilding the pipelines would take years and place an enormous strain on British fuel requirements for the rest of the war. The unit was given new orders: to gather intelligence in preparation for the capture of Fallujah as part of the final drive to oust Rashid Ali and take Baghdad.

The Irgun unit set out, accompanied by a British officer, and soon reached a river they needed to cross. As the one boat available had room for only two passengers, Raziel ordered his friends Yaakov Meridor and Yaakov Sika-Aharoni to proceed while he made his way back to their vehicle with the fourth member of the team, Yaakov Harazi, and the British officer. Suddenly, from nowhere, a German plane swooped down and bombed the area, scoring a direct hit on the car, which killed Raziel and the officer instantly. The driver of the car was injured, while Harazi, who had managed to jump clear, was unscathed. The mission was aborted.

From Habbaniya, Kingcol pushed on to Baghdad, greatly depleted after fierce fighting around Fallujah. Now down to 1,450 troops, Kingstone decided to make a two-pronged attack on the capital and split his force: one column of 700 men would traverse the desert and approach Baghdad from the north; another, 750 strong, which he would lead, would aim at the heart of the capital directly to the east. Factor in the advance of the Indian brigade from the south, and the Iraqis would get the impression that Baghdad would soon be surrounded.

Kingstone's force was tiny: the Iraqi army had at least twenty thousand troops in the Baghdad area, a whole division, with a further force at Ramadi on the Euphrates behind him. But morale was high, and the desert crossing was already being celebrated as one of the greatest marches in history, the first time since Alexander the Great that an army had successfully made it from the shores of the Mediterranean to the banks of the Euphrates—an exercise the Germans had deemed impossible. (The total distance from Haifa to Baghdad is 624 miles.) But as they started to close on the City of Caliphs, only the force's most senior commanders knew the full extent of the psychological blow they had struck. Thanks to a formidable piece of good fortune that fell into their laps, they had managed to create the impression that a vastly superior army was on the march and was sweeping toward the city, backed by heavy armor.

The event that was to prove the tipping point to victory occurred just fifteen miles from Baghdad, after Kingstone's own column overcame Iraqi forces dug in along defensive lines bordering canals and fields flooded by the Euphrates, then in full spate. There it came upon the fort of Khaan Nuqta, where the Iraqis surrendered in such haste that they evacuated their stronghold without neutralizing their telephone switchboard. With the aid of an interpreter, the British were able to monitor all the Iraqis' conversations for several hours and gain a complete picture of the forces ahead of them. Pressing their advantage, they then deliberately planted false intelligence to the effect that a powerful tank attack was on its way. It was a complete bluff: there were no tanks. All they had were six armored cars with their high conning towers, all of World War I vintage.

The mere idea of tanks seemed to terrify the enemy. Before the line went dead, the eavesdroppers intercepted another report, delivered in a great state of agitation, confirming that the British had at least fifty tanks, of which fifteen were already across the flood defenses. Furthering the impression that a great attack was in the offing, about this time the Arab Legion captured the deputy mayor of Baghdad and then released him with the rumor that they were part of a sixty-thousand-strong Allied advance.

Wavell was energized, and on May 24 fired off a "Personal, Most Secret" order to Habforce commander General Clark. It reaffirmed his two essential tasks:

(a) to occupy Baghdad with Habforce at earliest possible date,
(b) to open up communications between Basra and Habbaniya as soon as possible.

(Iraqi sabotage of their communications and the annual flooding of the twin rivers were impeding the Indian troops' northward advance from Basra.) In addition, Habforce was to:

(c) advance on Baghdad as early as possible by whichever route or routes you consider practicable. Situation requires bold action.

Just six days later, on May 30, Kingstone's men arrived on the city's outskirts, three miles short of the center. And stopped. Their orders had been changed.

The Embassy

As the Nazification of Iraq spread in the 1930s, Sir Kinahan Cornwallis's position as adviser to the Ministry of the Interior became increasingly uncomfortable and finally untenable. In 1935, two years after the death of his friend King Faisal, the end came when Rashid Ali was appointed minister and promptly sacked him. The veteran diplomat quietly withdrew and returned to London, though not before receiving a leaving present from King Ghazi as a special mark of the royal family's appreciation for his long and faithful service: the first-class honor of the Order of Rafidain (Order of the Two Rivers). Apart from his knighthood, the recognition he received in London had already been marked by his appointment as Companion of the Order of St. Michael and St. George in 1926 and his elevation to Knight Commander of the Order in 1933.

The outbreak of World War II found the repatriated proconsul, now remarried, on the staff of the Political Intelligence Depart-

COURTESY OF THE IMPERIAL WAR MUSEUM (IWM E3448)

Inside the embassy compound during the Thirty Days' War

ment of the Foreign Office, a secret unit specializing in counter-propaganda based in a small red brick house code named Foxgrove on the Woburn Estate in Bedfordshire. It seems that his espionage skills were much in demand, for in the following year, 1940, the rural obscurity he was enjoying was interrupted when he became an early recruit to the Special Operations Executive, Churchill's so-called Secret Army. Most famously, this was formed to conduct covert operations, particularly in France and the rest of occupied Europe. Less known is the fact that it was also active in the Middle East, Far East, and Africa.

Following such a profound exposure to the Arab world, it would be surprising if Cornwallis had not found England difficult to come to terms with and hankered after a return to his beloved Iraq. Happily for him, he was not kept waiting long. Britain's then ambassador in Baghdad, Sir Basil Newton, was a comparative new boy: he had only recently been posted from Prague after the Czech crisis of 1938 and certainly lacked the wealth of experience that Cornwallis could draw on in handling what was becoming a very tricky situation. The author Dame Freya Stark, who was working at the British Embassy in Baghdad, had a particularly low opinion of Newton, who "knew nothing of the East, and of the mixture of delicacy and firmness there required." The Foreign Office concurred, and Cornwallis landed in Iraq as his replacement shortly before Rashid Ali struck.

Stark, explorer, adventurer, and the doyenne of Middle East travel writers, had joined the *Baghdad Times* in the early 1930s and spent the duration of World War II in the Middle East, working for the Foreign Office and Ministry of Information ("My task was propaganda," she freely admitted in her autobiography, *Dust in the Lion's Paw*, some twenty years later). She moved from Cairo to Baghdad in March 1941, then found herself trapped in the city, and in several of her books her colorful testimony gives vivid insight into the events surrounding the Farhud. She believed "that if Sir Kinahan had been sent out six months earlier, the whole catastrophe might have been averted. As it was, we were already in that smooth race of water that precedes the waterfall."

Having been the power behind Faisal's throne, the empire builder was returning to familiar territory as formal representative of King George VI and his government. The arrival of the kingmaker, armed with full diplomatic power, created a great sense of security among the British community. In her 1945 book *East Is West*, Stark added:

"Among us, he held quiet authority which no one dreamt of gain-saying, made up of wisdom and kindness and courage." But if she was expecting dynamic action from her champion, she must have been disappointed. In *Seven Pillars of Wisdom*, T. E. Lawrence had immortalized Cornwallis as "a man rude to look upon, but apparently forged from one of those incredible metals with a melting point of thousands of degrees. So he could remain for months hotter than other men's white-heat, and yet look cold and hard." But the metal turned out to be surprisingly malleable. He argued fiercely against any kind of British military intervention, reasoning—like Wavell—that armed invasion was risky and provocative and that both sides should accept an offer of Turkish mediation.

Cornwallis hardly had time to have his butler unpack his bags before he found himself imprisoned with no room to maneuver. German broadcasts monitored in London reported him being chased back into the embassy by a crowd of Iraqis who objected, they said, to his "distributing British propaganda leaflets." Unlikely—but for four weeks during the Thirty Days' War, the embassy was trapped in the eye of the hurricane, surrounded by a cordon of Iraqi police, as much under siege as Habbaniya, with not even a vintage biplane for protection.

The evacuation order for British civilians had concerned only women and children, for whom it was hoped flights from the base—a long-established stopover en route between Cairo and Karachi for aircraft of Imperial Airways (British Overseas Airways Corporation, BOAC, from 1939)—could be arranged. The remainder of the British colony, a total of 350 men and women, including Freya Stark, now sought refuge within the embassy's white walls alongside the Tigris and camped out wherever they could.

Stark's honeyed pen reminds us in the literary style of the day how beautiful was the Baghdad of Violette's early life. "Here the Tigris, still flooded with Armenian snows, opaque and yellowish through the day, mauve in sunrise or sunset, filled its bed like some great animal whose scales of small triangular ripples, each with tiny crest, pressed on, one behind the other, like the armies of nations, to meet eternity," she wrote in *East Is West*...

> Across this expanse, which gave an illusion of freedom, lay
> the city surveyed by minarets, with domes now painted brown
> against our bombers and fine riverside houses where the rich

Jewish merchants, who own three-quarters of the wealth of
Baghdad, now lived in fear; and black mouths of streets ending
in gnawed steps, where pointed boats were moored—a rather
dilapidated Canaletto painting, whose varnish is yellowed with
dust and time.

The embassy lay on the right bank of the river, within two acres
of walled garden. Stark describes its velvet lawns being edged with
snapdragon, hibiscus, buddleia, pomegranate, flowering verbena,
and a cluster of palm trees and cypresses smelling aromatically in
the sun. Now, though, the green sward was favored as a place to sleep
rough. Its western side, where a gravel drive came from its great
gates, was fortified by all the colony's motorcars looped into a bar-
ricade with barbed wire. To the south and north it was overlooked
by houses with machine guns on their flat roofs. "Their cross-fire
spat out against our aeroplanes, which twice dived down with messages from Habbaniya, and we were glad that no third descent was
attempted for we felt sure the Iraqi gunner had now got the airmen's
range," she wrote. The planes delivered little weighted packets sewn
up in calico with two long streamers of red, blue, and yellow. By this
time, Cornwallis was being held virtually incommunicado at the embassy, as Rashid Ali had forbidden him and other diplomats from
contacting their governments by diplomatic code. He was obliged

The riverfront, looking north to the Old City from the right bank, near the embassy

to transmit any message to London "in clear," using guarded language. The airdrops were the only way the embassy could receive incoming messages. "We have a big V on the lawn in white sheets to tell the air that we are lost to news."

The besieged expatriates were allowed to bed down anywhere they could find space on its lawns and flat rooftops, as long as they kept a respectful distance from the ambassadorial residence, a white colonial house with green shutters and creepers. The main building, known as Khadim Pasha's Palace, was centered on an inner courtyard with a beautiful marble fountain. Built around 1875, the palace was a magnificent edifice, but it had always been in danger of sliding into the Tigris, and floods were a perpetual risk. Now it faced a far more sinister threat. If any bombs dropped on the city, Rashid Ali coolly informed the unfortunate envoy, the embassy would be stormed and British throats slit.

At the start, forced to ration themselves and live off the embassy's meager resources, the expatriate colony went hungry. But little by little, British phlegm prevailed, and as a way was found for daily needs to be supplied from the outside on a cash-and-bakhsheesh basis, a stiff-upper-lip spirit developed. With the days becoming warmer, morale was boosted by a supply of lettuce and ice and apricots as well as face powder, cosmetics, and Kotex for the women and tins of Brylcreem for the men. However, when the days turned into weeks and someone recalled how the British Residency in Lucknow had been besieged for five months during the Indian Mutiny of 1857, spirits plunged again. Nevertheless, an attitude of determined endurance prevailed. Promptly at six each evening, a bar was opened on the lawn under the palm trees. The day's news bulletins from the BBC were read out (bizarrely—and for no explicable reason—in rhyme). And Ambassador Cornwallis strolled out for a game of clock golf on the closely mown grass. The indomitable British, jaunty even in extremis.

All Baghdadis were unaware of the great drama being played out in the desert, oblivious to the advances being made by the British army in its march on the city. From the balcony of the embassy, however, Stark noted a shift in mood. Huddled with her fellow expats but privileged to have diplomatic seniority as an attaché, she wrote in *East Is West* that she was able to

> watch the passage of [Iraqi] troops in trucks camouflaged with
> palm fronds and the return of the Red Crescent ambulances
> with wounded and judge of what was happening in the battle
> by the traffic on the bridge. Or we could see the crowds from
> the upper town, incited by speeches of the Mufti and their own
> radio, advancing with banners and drums and dancing figures
> silhouetted against the sky, towards our gates. They rarely
> came so far, and only once sent a few shots into our garden,
> for no rhetoric was able to stir this into a popular war.

In fact, the end was rapidly approaching. The city was awash with wild rumors about the vastly superior strength of the approaching, armored British force. Intensive British air activity furthered the impression that the city was about to be cut off and surrounded. The German ambassador, Fritz Grobba, who had done much to fuel the fires of hatred, sent an alarmed message to Berlin on May 28 reporting the enemy closing in with "more than a hundred tanks." Demoralized by the lack of main Axis support and totally unaware that they were victims of a gigantic hoax, Rashid Ali and the grand mufti also panicked and fled to Iran—cloaked in *'abaayas*—together with nearly all of their cohorts ("A total of forty, a figure of significant interest to anyone familiar with the story of Ali Baba," some Foreign Office wag observed). News spread that they had kidnapped the boy-king, Faisal, and taken him with them as possible hostage for future bargaining with Britain, but this was not so; he was found safe in Baghdad, playing in the gardens of the Palace of Roses alongside the Tigris under the supervision of his gray-haired English nanny.

An inch-by-inch account of the advance across the desert and the troops' later disillusionment by the banks of the Tigris has been provided by Kingcol's intelligence officer, Captain Somerset de Chair. A Churchill protégé and Conservative Member of Parliament for South West Norfolk, he wrote a war diary of the entire campaign that formed the basis for a book, *The Golden Carpet*, first published

Somerset de Chair: "We waited as the shooting began . . ."

COURTESY OF THE IMPERIAL WAR MUSEUM (IWM E3447)

in a leather-bound edition of five hundred copies only two years after the event by the Golden Cockerel Press, with special permission of the War Office (and republished for the general public in 1945 by Faber & Faber).

Kingstone's northern column, guided by Glubb's legionnaires, managed to reach the Mosul–Baghdad road on May 27, but instead of grabbing the opportunity to enter Baghdad immediately—an advance from the north being totally unexpected—decided to camp six miles from the city. The next morning, with an Iraqi infantry force putting up strong resistance, the column made slow progress, only to be stopped by stiff opposition in the Kadhimain district.

Kingstone's own column was luckier but was stopped by perplexing new orders. According to de Chair (who was instrumental in the affair of the Khaan Nuqta telephone switchboard), the victorious troops, knowing by then that Rashid Ali had fled, were bewildered to be told that they would not press home their advantage. Instead, they were instructed to set up brigade headquarters in the Washash area opposite Karrada (and the *qasr*) and await new orders. To the men's surprise, on that evening of May 30, a number of civilian cars arrived from Habbaniya, where the royal court of Regent Abd al-Ilah had been hastily reestablished in the rest house built for Imperial Airways passengers by its lake. The visitors included the son of the pro-British deposed prime minister Nuri al-Sa'id, the ex–prime minister Ali Jawdat, and an Iraqi major, who was aide-de-camp to the regent. "Shepherding this flock," wrote de Chair, "was a lean

English sportsman in grey flannel trousers and brown suede shoes from the Foreign Office." He was Gerald de Gaury, the British-appointed chargé d'affaires to the regent.

That night, armed with a large white sheet on a pole, a British delegation eventually met the two Iraqi army officers who were to sign the surrender of Baghdad. (One, Captain Ghazi Daghestani, turned out to be an old chum of de Gaury and spoke perfect English, having spent three years in London.) In the faint predawn light by the banks of the river, de Chair now became gradually aware of a growing British military presence, as nearly all of Britain's top brass in Iraq moved in for the moment. He and a fellow officer, Major Ian Spence, were ordered into Daghestani's car together with de Gaury, with instructions to take a message to Ambassador Cornwallis from Habforce commander Clark. Blindfolded, they passed through the Iraqi lines and finally came to the embassy. It was just after dawn on Saturday, May 31.

To the astonishment of the embassy inmates, the trio entered the building, made their way to the residence, and climbed the stairs to the ambassador's bedroom. "Sir Kinahan Cornwallis lay in bed with a blue cummerbund round his middle. He sat up in bed like one accustomed to focusing his mind on important and unexpected affairs at all hours of the night," wrote de Chair. "Ian clicked his heels, saluted, and handed him the message form 'With General Clark's compliments.'"

Leaving His Excellency to dress, they went out on to the roof of the embassy, where men and women were sleeping everywhere. As they began to wake up and the situation became clear, a cheer went round. In the garden, more people were asleep. The surprise visitors were given a cup of tea as others crowded eagerly around them. "Oh, we have been waiting a long time for this," said one buxom Englishwoman, unable to hold back her tears.

Resplendent now in full imperial kit of white drill suit and white topee, the lanky ambassador joined de Chair's group for the return journey through enemy lines. "There were more people about now, all the colourful pageantry of an eastern city—*tarbushes, keffiyehs,* turbans, robes of every colour; donkeys, mules; and many more soldiers," wrote de Chair. "They looked up at us out of their dark brown eyes as we passed and spat." Once more, they were blindfolded as they passed through the lines.

The Iraqi delegation asked Cornwallis for an armistice and, according to Freya Stark in *Dust in the Lion's Paw,* begged "that the constitution of Iraq may not be taken from them." Cornwallis then "made a wonderful speech in Arabic telling them that as he and King Faisal made the constitution, it is in safe hands." On Britain's behalf, Cornwallis signed a magnanimous armistice on the basis that the war had been a political contest against Rashid Ali rather than a war against the Iraqi people (a refrain that sounds hauntingly familiar today). Remarkably, the Iraqi army was allowed to keep all its weapons and equipment and return to its peacetime garrisons, with its soldiers left free to enter the capital as long as they confined themselves to the river's left bank—the east side containing the old city, the souks, Rashid Street, the commercial center, and the quarters that Violette has described where most of the Jews lived. Thus, key areas were left to the mercies of a defeated, but fully armed, regime. Their barracks flanked the old quarters to the northwest and southeast. There was no provision for stationing British troops anywhere in the capital or its vicinity. The bridges were left unguarded.

The ambassador and Daghestani drove back into the city with a copy of the armistice, and that night, the eve of the Jewish festival of Shavuot, they learned that the Iraqis had accepted it.

De Chair and the men of Kingcol did not know that there had been an unexpected and dramatic shift in the British position. Despite Churchill's May 9 instruction to "break into Baghdad even with quite small forces," and Wavell's unequivocal order of May 25 to "occupy" Baghdad, Clark had been following one clear-cut order that Wavell had originally issued on May 12 concerning the task facing Habforce. This stated: "It is not intended that your force should cross the R. Tigris as it is important that a small force should not get involved in street fighting in disadvantageous conditions." Instead,

It is considered that your operation should be designed to effect the following:
(a) Reach the British Embassy.
(b) Control the bridges over R. Tigris at Baghdad.

Churchill had already been compelled to delegate many important decisions to his generals and diplomats in the field, granting
them great discretion in the handling of the course of the war. But
unknown to the soldiers now poised to enter the city for the final
moment of glory, when Wavell had reluctantly accepted this un-
wanted campaign he had inserted a delegation clause of his own. The
day before he sent his "Task of Habforce" order, he had instructed
General Clark that, as soon as contact with Cornwallis was reestablished, the ambassador was to be responsible for all policy connected with Iraq "and directives will then be issued to the missions
with his approval." Thus, for the final stage, the kingmaker, an avid
bridge player, held all the cards: diplomatic, political, and military.

Despite the brilliance of the Habforce-Kingcol operation, Cornwallis—like the general—still believed that the Iraqis would resent
firm action and that British interests would be best served if the
Thirty Days' War could be glossed over. A light touch was required. A
fiction should be established: Britain had not clashed with the Iraqi
army and had troops present solely to reinstate the legitimate Iraqi
government. The regent would be reinstated but must not be seen
to return "supported on arrival by British bayonets." Wavell himself
had just contradicted his original order to the troops (the need for
"bold action"—underlined—to "occupy Baghdad"). Now, for fear of
provoking new clashes, Cornwallis countermanded Wavell's other
order. Troops would not be sent to control the bridges.

*Ambassador
Cornwallis and
Major General
Clark in
Baghdad, 1941*

COURTESY OF THE IMPERIAL WAR MUSEUM (IWM E3461)

From the very outset of the crisis, Cornwallis had displayed peculiar passivity and had appeared particularly compliant in face of Iraqi demands. When the regent had been safely tucked away on an old British river gunboat, HMS *Cockchafer*, in the Shatt el Arab, the Rashid Ali regime had complained that it considered his presence a provocation. The newly arrived ambassador had agreed, the Foreign Office had acquiesced, and obligingly the regent had been removed to Jerusalem and later to Amman. Inevitably, the move had been seen as a sign of weakness that emboldened the Golden Square and its supporters.

The swift and total collapse of the regime does not appear to have led Cornwallis to change any of his views. In the immediate vacuum of Rashid Ali's departure, he took another step that he thought would lessen the tension. To further prevent Britain's military presence being seen as an occupation, he ordered the northern column of Kingcol to get out of Kadhimain immediately and turn back to Habbaniya—on June 1, the very day that the Farhud erupted.

Cornwallis made one more move to ensure that British troops would be kept at arm's length. Again on June 1, the day after signing the armistice, he telegraphed the commander of the Indian army force that was moving up to Baghdad from Basra that the "Iraqi authorities" were expressing concern about their advance and wanted it suspended until a new government was formed. Accordingly, they were stopped.

That left Kingstone's own column, camped eight miles from the city center under the palms and eucalyptus trees west of the Tigris—still a remote area in those days—with instructions to bide its time and await the return of the regent.

For the British, victory was sweet. Wavell later reported to Churchill:

> Although there was practically the whole of a division of the
> Iraqi army in Baghdad and a further force at Ramadi, Rashid
> Ali and his supporters had lost heart and fled. The Mayor of
> Baghdad sent out a white flag and asked for terms of capitu-
> lation. After discussion with the Ambassador, who had been
> confined to the Embassy for the past four weeks, satisfactory
> terms were arranged. The Regent of Iraq and some of his

*Kingcol's men,
at ease in their
bivouac*

COURTESY OF THE IMPERIAL WAR MUSEUM (IWM E3468)

ministers, who had escaped to Transjordan at the time of
Rashid Ali's *coup d'état,* returned to Baghdad on 1st June and
formed a legitimate Government.

We may consider ourselves exceedingly fortunate to have
liquidated what might have been a very serious commitment
with such small forces and with little trouble.

Daghestani himself provided a footnote to this brief page of history. Questioned by a British war correspondent after the fall of
Baghdad as to why the Iraqi army had given way on the central
front, he replied: "What else could we do? You had fifty tanks there
and we had only two old anti-tank guns."

How could he have known that the tanks had been as illusory as
the images in the magic lantern of Violette's youth? "Shoof 'indak
Ya salaam!" ("Look here, what a wonder!")

The Thirty Days' War was over, but the Farhud was about to begin.
With Baghdad now an open city, the Committee for Internal Security—Cornwallis's "Iraqi authorities"—was hastily convened in a bid
to fill the power vacuum, yet it soon became clear how hopelessly

inadequate it was. Bitterly, de Chair reported: "We waited and, as darkness settled like a mantle over the domes and minarets across the river, the shooting began." His immediate superior officer, Brigadier Kingstone, was at that moment the guest of Cornwallis in the embassy on the river's right bank. "We did not hear it," de Chair continued,

> but to the Brigadier's ears, sleeping in the white colonial
> house of the British Embassy, came the growing crescendo of
> rifle and machine-gun fire. Baghdad was given up to the loot-
> ers. All who dared to defend their own belongings were killed;
> while eight miles to the west waited the eager British force
> which could have prevented all this. Ah yes, but the prestige
> of our Regent would have suffered!

Cornwallis's insistence that British troops be kept out of the city, and the decision to withdraw half of Kingcol back to Habbaniya from Kadhimain, were now beginning to raise eyebrows inside the Foreign Office. On June 2, an official, P. M. Crosthwaite, minuted:

> It looks . . . as though the military authorities do not propose
> to station troops in Baghdad West [i.e., around the embassy].
> That seems to me an extraordinary line to take, and one would
> have expected Sir K Cornwallis to press for troops there.

Control of the bridges—possibly by the Kadhimain detachment precipitately dispatched by Cornwallis—could also have changed history. It was on one of them, left open and unguarded, that the spark was struck that ignited the Farhud. On June 2, the second day of rioting, the bridges were "an extraordinary sight," according to Freya Stark in *Dust in the Lion's Paw,* who had a bird's-eye view from the embassy: she saw "streams of people going empty-handed east-ward, coming back laden with spoil." Cornwallis astonished her by saying that he thought the city looked friendly. "I felt it very much to the contrary," she wrote in her diary for that day,

> and think it is a pity we did not bring the Regent in with a
> good show of troops or aeroplanes. Always the choice between
> placating one's enemies or encouraging one's friends. But the

pretence that this is an Iraqi spontaneous restoration is just nonsense, so we might as well get the advantages as well as the disadvantages of being behind it.

Despite growing evidence of the size of the disaster unfolding, the British troops' orders never changed, and they were made to stay well in the background. Stark wrote that there had been

a night of snapping rifles, police posts doubled, Jews murdered (reports vary between a dozen and five hundred) and Abdullah Ezra says he was "wading in blood" up Ghazi Street. The shooting is getting momently stronger. The mayor is telephoning to say he wants to resign: and the new Cabinet is not yet formed.

It is clear from her account that senior aides in the embassy had also become disturbed by Britain's stance and were calling for action. Either acting for himself or on their behalf, Vyvyan Holt, the oriental secretary—Gertrude Bell's old job—twice made impassioned pleas to Cornwallis to call in Kingstone's "resting" force. But the ambassador was closeted with the generals, seemingly impervious to the carnage and mayhem happening across the river. Holt started to make a third attempt but thought better of it, and Stark lamented: "One realises why battles can be lost by a sheer inability to get the data to the people who make the decisions."

How much did the British really know? One Jewish eyewitness, Abraham Twena, reports the testimony of a man who said that a friend at the embassy gave him a gun on the morning of June 1, the day the trouble began, with a warning he would need it. The man allegedly told him that he had given guns to other friends, too. More alarmingly, Freya Stark says that, several hours later that same day, the embassy's intelligence officer told her that he knew the retreating rebels had prepared an uprising. The embassy was aware an attack had been planned and was imminent, but it had gone off prematurely; it had not been expected until the following day. The peculiar aspect of this revelation is that the supposed target of the offensive was the embassy itself—which begs the question, If that were the case, why wasn't Kingcol ordered to cross the river immediately or guard the bridges, or indeed the embassy, at least to protect British lives and property if no one else's?

With nothing to restrain them, the attackers turned on the "internal enemy"—the Jews, who were set upon as British sympathizers—an action that was clearly premeditated and not unpredicted by the British. Since 1938, when the Nazi government in Germany had decided to become active in the Middle East, its propaganda reiterated that the British were the allies of the Jews. Among both the masses and educated Muslims in Iraq, the corollary came to be accepted: because the Nazis were the enemies of the British, the Jews must therefore be the enemies of the Iraqis. It was because of their alleged pro-Britishness that the Iraqi Jews were intimidated and occasionally persecuted by Rashid Ali's regime.

As the Farhud entered its second day, Stark wrote in *East Is West*:

> [The uprising] was to have been directed on the embassy, but the easy temptation of loot and the long-standing influence on Palestine together deflected it to the Jewish streets and houses. The Jews of Baghdad have every reason to deplore the Palestine question, and do so with their hearts. There was plenty of riff-raff about, and the new Cabinet was not yet formed to keep order. All through the day of June 2nd we listened to rifle-fire crackling among the houses like thorns under a pot . . .
>
> How many people were murdered that day will never, I suppose, be known. In the afternoon, the Iraq army were told to use ball cartridges, and killed 60 or 70 of the looters . . . There was a curfew at five, and everyone who showed was shot.

Sitting helpless in the camp eight miles away, de Chair also recalled being asked by his Arab interpreter, who had been so instrumental in creating the bluff of the tanks: "Why do our troops not go into Baghdad? Already there may be looting. I know. There will be many people killed if our troops do not enter."* De Chair

*Although de Chair describes him as Palestinian, the interpreter was, in fact, a Baghdadi Jew, with many members of his distinguished family still living in the city. Shaoul Aboudy Shemtob was born in Baghdad in the same year as Violette, and left Iraq for British mandate Palestine at the height of the Arab Revolt in 1936. There he joined the British Army's Intelligence Corps and changed his name to Reading. Working for an undercover unit similar to MI6, he mingled with senior Arab and Jewish political leaders to gather intelligence, reporting on the movements of Arab terrorist gangs at a time when there were constant murderous attacks against the Jews and the Brit-

agreed, saying the ways of the Foreign Office were beyond his comprehension. However, he was unaware that, from the moment the cease-fire had been declared, it had been Cornwallis's word that had prevailed over the military. "Having fought our way, step by step, to the threshold of the city, we must now cool our heels outside," wrote the disgruntled captain. Bitterly, he added:

> It would, apparently, be lowering to the dignity of our ally, the Regent, if he were seen to be supported on arrival by British bayonets. It was apparently believed in Whitehall to be beyond the imagination of the wily Baghdadis to see that his return was brought about by the victory of British arms. Were there not Iraqi troops enough in the city, now loyal of course to the new Government, to keep order?
>
> It was argued afterwards in the Chancery of Baghdad that the Iraqis would have gone on fighting rather than agree to an armistice on the basis of our immediate entry. Again, it was argued that our arrival would have precipitated street fighting with the brigade which we had pushed back into the town. Yet why, I asked, if they crumpled up on the outskirts, should they have stiffened in the middle?
>
> Diplomacy is the continuation of war by other means, but it should not begin too soon.
>
> Genius is a grasp of the essential; and, after victory, the essential is to keep control of the situation.

One incident from de Chair's book provides a telling insight into the character of Cornwallis, bringing to mind the *Times*'s reference to his ability to "assume the proconsular manner" when he deemed

---

ish. In 1939, a top-secret order came from London to arrest the grand mufti, but Reading's immediate superior declared al-Husseini too valuable a source of information and instructed Reading to tip him off—an order he had to obey. The mufti fled, having donned women's clothes, and made his way eventually to Baghdad.

Captain Alan Shemtob-Reading was made a Member of the British Empire (MBE) for his courage in a daring mission to penetrate Rommel's Afrika Korps headquarters in 1942. He declined to divulge much else of his war work, which was still shrouded in secrecy at his death in 2007 in London, where both he and Violette were members of the Holland Park synagogue.

it necessary, as well as to the indifferent attitude he displayed over Gertrude Bell's dog. De Chair recounts how he was invited to dine at the embassy—a privilege no doubt due to his parliamentary status and proximity to Churchill. It was "an astounding experience after the rigours of desert warfare, to find myself sipping a cool drink in an English drawing room, where oil paintings, gilt furniture and soft carpets carried British diplomacy back to the Garden of Eden (which some believe to have been hereabouts). There were other guests—all men, so far as I can remember, or, if there were women, they made no impression."

The ambassadorial table was of shining mahogany, rosily reflecting the brightly polished silver and the shaded candles that, together, created a glowing, heartwarming scene. After dinner, the ambassador—"a tall man, hard, stringy as a dried bean, with greying hair and a truly imposing nose. His eye was as keen as a vulture's"—asked whether de Chair might care to join a game of bridge, together with one of the embassy's top diplomats and the head of the military mission. He agreed, not realizing that he was in for a surprise.

De Chair continues:

> The library to which we repaired that evening provided me with a shock, for it contained an air-conditioning plant in a walnut cabinet, which lowered the temperature abruptly from the hundreds to the seventies. "It is impossible to keep a cool head and work steadily without it," Sir Kinahan Cornwallis said. He told me that 2,000 people, mostly Jews, were believed to have been killed in the one night's looting, a figure which was subsequently reduced to 700 when more information became available.

De Chair fails to mention the date of this encounter but, as he spent little more than a week in Baghdad, it must have been immediately after the Farhud. About the ambassador, he noted in his favor that "his character, which had the edge and hardness and flexibility of a Toledo sword, may well have saved the lives, while maintaining the dignity, of the British subjects who were for a month at the mercy of an unscrupulous enemy." In the fifteen years since T. E. Lawrence had described Cornwallis (in *Seven Pillars of Wisdom*) as being forged from incredible metal with an extremely high

melting point, nothing had changed. De Chair's observations confirmed Lawrence's opinion that he could "yet look cold and hard"
while remaining hotter than white heat.

The bitterness felt by the British troops was equaled by their
sense of inadequacy. "There was a sense of incompletion about our
conquest so long as we were kept at arm's length outside the city by
diplomatic niceties," wrote de Chair, noting that "the reports from
our embassy immediately preceding the revolt have passed into the
archives of Military Intelligence as classic misreadings of the situation by our accredited representatives." The same can surely be
said of the reaction of the same representatives to the immediate
danger that the people of Baghdad faced after the armistice was
signed on such sweet terms. While the lives and dignity of the British civilians had been Cornwallis's major preoccupation, he seemed
more concerned for the prestige of the Iraqi authorities than for
the lives of people under their protection. With the collapse of
Iraqi resistance on May 30, the embassy was no longer under siege.
How could anyone look on passively while the life and property of
defenseless citizens were at the mercy of the mob?

Diplomacy

The Foreign Office, London, 19.7.41

The following message has been received from the Jewish
Agency, Jerusalem:

Eye witness reports: Fearful picture of anti-Jewish excesses at
Baghdad June 1st, June 2nd, being days of Jewish Pentecost
festival. Massacre began upon return of Jewish delegation from
Regent who had returned that day to Baghdad. Jews removed
from cars and brutally murdered, then mob began attack on
Jewish holiday crowds walking in street. Fearful details received of ghastly tortures and murders occurred.

Dead bodies defiled, children thrown into Euphrates,
wounded poisoned in hospital. Estimated 500 Jews killed and
over 1,000 wounded. Entire streets full of shops ransacked and
burnt. Hospitals overcrowded. Thousands homeless in streets

and synagogues. Armed police, ultimately students, secondary schools and colleges participated. Killing and robbing continued for two days after establishment of new regime, only stopped when British troops took action. Rabbi compelled to sign statement only 70 killed. Official report states Muslim, Christian, Jewish victims. Apparently some non-Jews involved, but mob excesses which resulted in previous fighting clearly directed against Jews, incriminated police not removed. No investigation, no punishment. Air full of poisonous incitement, renewed outbreak feared by community. Implore help and immigrant permits to Palestine.

At four-fifteen in the afternoon of June 2, Cornwallis cabled the Foreign Office from the embassy on the right bank:

Sporadic shooting with murderous assaults on Jews seems to have gone on throughout the night and from early this morning armed mob looted principal shopping streets of the town. Eventually orders were given to the Police and the army to open fire and this afternoon the position is much quieter. Disturbances are at present limited to the left bank of the Tigris. Casualties not yet known.

Back in London, Crosthwaite, the worried civil servant, became increasingly puzzled by the policy that Cornwallis appeared to be pursuing. Supported by Sir Alexander Cadogan, Foreign Secretary Anthony Eden's permanent undersecretary for foreign affairs, he replied to Cornwallis's telegram with a request for clarification. He queried the line that the ambassador had taken and asked what his plans were.

It was a whole day before Cornwallis replied, vaguely referring to the retreating Kingcol troops as "probably ours" (the retreat is clearly recorded in the war diary of Headquarters, Fourth Cavalry Brigade for June 1, 1941; see "Sources"). He offered no further explanation, simply adding that he was trying to arrange for the remainder of Kingstone's men to enjoy a few days' rest at their Washash camp. Desperate to maintain the fiction that British troops had not clashed with the Iraqi army, he was making sure that no British khaki would be seen anywhere near the city center—a position totally at odds with the military's plans, according to the archives. The operations record book of RAF Habbaniya shows that it had been decided as late as May 31 that "a portion of [Kingcol's] main column would enter Baghdad on 2nd June." Someone must have countermanded these orders when the rioting broke out. Cornwallis?

For a fastidious servant of the Crown, it seems strange that the ambassador's telegram of June 2 was the only time he thought it necessary to mention the disorders—and then in such a perfunctory way. Until the Foreign Office received the Jewish Agency's impassioned, highly colored (and deeply flawed) version of events, it had nothing to go on except an RAF situation report of June 2 that spoke of a "slight" disturbance in Baghdad organized by agents of Rashid Ali which had resulted in a "few" Jews and Christians being killed. It took the ambassador almost six weeks to put pen to paper and write about the Farhud, responding to a request from Whitehall only on July 11, and then his dispatch did not reach London until eighteen days later. Why he took so much time has never been explained. The delay was curious, considering that Cornwallis held unique credentials as a rapporteur: during his Arab Bureau years in World War I he had been editor of the *Arab Bulletin,* a confidential review of Middle Eastern military intelligence containing sensitive information that circulated on an "eyes-only" basis among the very top echelons.

The return of the British army just nine years after the country had gained token independence with the ending of the ill-fated mandate placed London in a delicate position. On Friday, May 30, with Habforce poised on the edge of the city, Cornwallis cabled Anthony Eden: "We do not want street fighting in Baghdad or the creation of any further bitterness; with all the chief Axis supporters gone there seems a good chance of restoring the situation." The next day, the eve of Shavuot, the foreign secretary cabled back:

> It is of the utmost importance that, when the Regent forms
> a new Government, it shall be formed on the broadest basis,
> likely to command the widest possible measure of popular
> approval and support. Every effort must be made to avoid

situation arising in which Government is formed by an alleged "pro-British" clique and, if it falls from power, must almost inevitably be replaced by another clique with leanings towards the Axis. I feel sure that from this point of view General Nuri [al-Sa'id] would not be the most suitable choice as Prime Minister of the new Government. I would prefer [Jamil Beg] Madfai but you will know best as to choice of personalities.

And so the diplomatic and political maneuverings began. The massacre of the Jews took place when the regent and the key players of the pro-British regime were already back inside Baghdad and British forces and their erstwhile enemy were practically facing one another on opposite banks of the Tigris, separated by a swathe of fast-flowing water. Indeed, there have been unverified reports that the regent himself was enjoying a candlelit dinner and a game of bridge in Cornwallis's inner sanctum at the embassy on the night of June 1. There existed the Committee for Internal Security led by mayor Arshad 'Umari, comprising the governor of Baghdad, the director general of police, and the commander of the Iraqi army's First Division. But not one of them was willing to accept responsibility for giving orders to shoot at the mob to stop the attacks. All waited for someone in higher authority to give the order—and meanwhile the regent dithered.

In his July 11 report, Cornwallis told Eden:

> The Lord Mayor who, pending the formation of a new Government, was still nominally in control, begged the Director General of Police to use his reserves and to order them to clear the streets and shoot to kill, but the Director General pleaded that he could not accept responsibility for such drastic action unless specific orders were given by the Regent. After some delay the Regent sent the order in writing and also arranged for the despatch of troops to take control. The soldiers did their work well. There was no more aimless firing into the air; their machine-guns swept the streets clear of people and quickly put a stop to looting and rioting. In those few hours however hundreds of families were ruined and brutal outrages were committed which all right minded persons will for long remember with shame and horror. The Jews suffered most, and

there is no doubt that a large number of them would emigrate rather than face the risk of another such pogrom if they could only find a country to take them. Many have made pathetic attempts to obtain visas for India for themselves or their families only to find this way of escape now closed.

His dispatch continued:

There is evidence to show that the riots were instigated by certain officers in the Army and police who took advantage of the temporary absence of responsible authority. Had a Government been formed earlier it is improbable that such a serious situation would have arisen. I had, at my first interview with the Regent the previous day [June 1], urged the extreme importance of forming a Cabinet at once and I again impressed on him the necessity for immediate action when I saw him later that afternoon.

The Regent was in a difficult position. Jamil Beg Madfai was the only apparent candidate [for prime minister]. His name had been put forward by Arshad al-Umari and his temporary Committee, and my enquiries failed to reveal anyone else who had the courage and influence to step into the breach. Jamil Beg, however, seemed to have no zest for the part. The Regent had been dissatisfied with his attitude during the later stages of their stay in Palestine and knew that, though generally sound in his views, he was an ageing man lacking energy and purposefulness and too weak in character to be able to deal firmly with the problems which would face him.

His Highness sought anxiously for alternatives, but found none, and was therefore obliged to call upon Jamil Beg to form a Cabinet. The latter refused and persisted in his refusal all that day.

That night, his friends brought pressure to bear on him and the following morning he sent the Lord Mayor and the present Minister of Finance to me with a message that he would accept if I would promise him my full support. This I promised to give and he assumed office when the rioting was at its height.

Only then did the regent feel able to give the order for his troops to go in.

The depleted Habforce certainly constituted what Churchill would have recognized as quite a small force—*puny* might be a better word—and yet, contrary to his order, it did not break into Baghdad. Apologists have argued that had the troops entered and crossed the river to stop the bloodbath, their small number would have exposed the weakness of the British position and the dangerous game of bluff played over the tanks. But all the same, when the British did finally make a ceremonial entry—not until June 5, joined by the Indian force newly arrived from Basra—it took as long as two hours to file past the astonished citizenry with all their armament and vehicles. These included the six ancient Rolls-Royce armored cars that, even to the nonmilitary eye, could never have passed muster as tanks.

The delay in bringing the rioters to heel has given rise to numerous conspiracy theories, ranging from the questionably plausible to the downright far-fetched. Was there deliberate inaction so that the Iraqi army, the youth squads, and the populace, poisoned by Nazi propaganda and bitter at the fall of Rashid Ali, might vent their wrath on the Jews so that the pro-British regime could be resumed in relative quiet? Could the British have instigated the riots, either to divert attention from the regent's return or to give them an excuse to intercede as peacemakers after a polite interval?

Most cynically, could it even have been a Zionist plot, a ruse to create a wave of refugees and bolster immigration to Palestine? The great majority of Iraqi Jews regarded Zionism as a threat to their harmonious existence as Arabs of the Jewish faith, but after June 2, everything changed. "More than two millennia of historic coexistence abruptly shattered like a fragile knee," wrote Edwin Black in his 2004 book *Banking on Baghdad:*

> Overnight, shocked Iraqi Jews could no longer stand on their ancient history and steadfast loyalty. Zionist visionaries had always been convinced that sooner or later anti-Jewish impulses would drive Jews from their countries, hence the need for a Jewish homeland. Iraqi Jews woke up on June 1 as staunchly anti-Zionist. By the time they fell asleep on June 2, forlorn and traumatized, Zionism and Jewish Palestine had become an option—perhaps the only option.

This was not strictly so, as tortured debate raged for over a decade. But on one point there was no doubt: the British were indisputably in charge and the British Embassy and Whitehall were pulling the strings, with Cornwallis the ringmaster. Everything hinged on the regent's return being perceived as at the behest of the people—just as King Faisal's coronation in 1921 had been manipulated to show that he had been elected as the people's choice, independently of British wishes.

Now, the Foreign Office began receiving urgent supplications from Palestine pleading the case for open-door treatment for Iraq's persecuted Jews to be allowed entry into the Jewish homeland. The cable to the Foreign Office cited earlier was typical, penned in impassioned language and containing those unfortunate factual errors ("Euphrates," "British troops") that did nothing to strengthen the veracity of the case. Others were more compelling.

On July 3, 1941, one month after the Farhud, the president of Vaad Leumi, the Jewish National Council of Palestine, addressed the following considered perspective to the British high commissioner for Palestine. Yitzhak Ben-Zvi, who went on to become president of Israel from 1952 until 1963, wrote:

> I have the honour to submit the following information on the terrible anti-Jewish outrages that broke out on the First Day of the Jewish Feast of Pentecost (June 1st) and were continued until the following day, June 2nd. It is difficult to imagine a more terrible and shocking picture than that which is obtained on the strength of the evidence we collected from eye-witnesses who were on the spot at the time the outrages were perpetrated and who have now arrived in Palestine: Mass-murder of men, women and children, the rape of women, kidnapping and abduction of young men and young girls, pillage and robbery of houses and shops, and above all—all that was done with the full cooperation and guidance of several officers of the Iraqi Army and Police and, as we are informed, some of these officers have been retained in their posts and continue to function to this day. Eye-witnesses also state that students of Iraqi schools took part in and supervised the pillage of June 2nd.
>
> It is difficult to determine the extent of the disaster, and according to the evidence of witnesses, the number of persons

murdered is at least 600, and the victims include women and children. According to the Baghdadians the material damage is valued at One Million Pounds at least. That figure is merely an estimate; but it is a fact that thousands of persons, formerly well to do or who had previously made a comfortable living are now on the streets without bread or shelter, and are in need of immediate relief. According to the information in our possession the Jewish Community in Baghdad is extending to these unfortunate victims what little relief it can afford to give but it is necessary to give adequate help so that they may not starve and may be enabled to return to their homes.

But the primary prerequisite is to insure the maintenance of public security in the future, and that is inconceivable unless the Iraqi Government takes strong measures to inflict upon the criminals the most severe punishment and insure full protection for the Jews of Baghdad.

At the same time it is clear that thousands of Jews who have been completely impoverished or even those who have been left with part of their fortunes have decided to leave Baghdad and migrate to other countries, near and far. Baghdadi Jews have relatives in Palestine and according to the estimate of the Iraqi Community in Palestine the number of Iraqi Jews in Palestine is about 10,000. It is natural that many Baghdadi Jews who long to leave that hell of murder are clamouring for the possibility to immigrate to Palestine and for the issue to them of immigration certificates.

Trustworthy people who have arrived from Baghdad state that posters have been distributed in the town containing threats to the effect that the "Holiday" which they had arranged for the Jews was a minor affair compared to the one that is yet in store for them.

Ben-Zvi asked the British to put pressure on the Iraqi authorities to make them extend full protection to the lives and properties of the Jews as well as make them take immediate steps to locate Jews who had disappeared and severely punish the perpetrators. In addition, the Iraqis should be made to provide support and accommodation for the victims, as well as compensation, and finally, the British should give sympathetic consideration to Jews seeking exit visas.

The letter was written in Jerusalem to an address in Jerusalem. Yet despite its urgent tone, it took a whole month for Sir Harold MacMichael, the high commissioner for Palestine, to forward it to London on August 2. And then came further delay: with the slowness of wartime communications, the diplomatic bag did not arrive until September 17. In a covering note, the high commissioner referred to various further contacts he had had with Vaad Leumi in which the death toll was revised downward to 120, and the number of wounded to 600 or 700. "As regards material losses," he wrote, "the most reliable reports indicate that 890 houses and 587 shops were looted." In these later discussions, Ben-Zvi had underlined the views of the Jews of Baghdad that the Iraqi police could not be relied on; the Jewish community felt insecure and apprehensive of a recurrence of violence.

Ambassador Cornwallis's July 11 report to Anthony Eden had given little comfort in this respect. Special courts had been set up to deal with the worst rebels and rioters, he said, and a large number of Rashid Ali's outstanding supporters had been arrested. A new director general of police had been appointed and many army officers had been pensioned off. "These measures have to some extent improved the situation but they have not been carried out with enough energy to make them fully effective," he added.

> The departure of the Mufti and the Italian Legation has deprived pro-Axis and anti-British propaganda of its motive force but the adherents of Rashid Ali, the many convinced pro-Nazis in the army and the public services and the irrecoverable anti-British elements in all parts of the country are maintaining a widespread opposition to the Government and their endeavours to cultivate a public spirit more friendly towards Great Britain.

Too many prominent supporters of Rashid Ali's regime had been released from prison after only a few days' detention, Cornwallis continued, and the army remained a potential element of danger. He finished with a diplomatic flourish worthy of Lawrence of Arabia: "There the bitterness of defeat still kindles the fires of hatred of the British under the ashes of appeasement."

What happened in Baghdad in the spring of 1941 marked Britain's one single victory against the Third Reich that year, while everywhere else on the battlefronts its armed forces faced nothing but defeat. For a country desperate for good news, and with propaganda machines spinning furiously, this was a heaven-sent opportunity to raise the spirits of a demoralized nation. Yet curiously, silence reigned. The bravery of the RAF at Habbaniya—a forgotten battle that deserves to be ranked in military annals as the Second Battle of Britain—the brilliant Habforce campaign, and the bitter divisions within the British establishment (to say nothing of the Farhud) were never properly reported at the time. Subsequently, they have been lost in the whirlpool of World War II and never accorded their deserved place in history. The opportunity has been lost to celebrate the fact that Britain might have been brought to its knees but for the bravery of a small group of trainee airmen who had no other weapons at hand but rickety aircraft with which they took to the skies to defend their honor and thus alter the course of war.

It is true that there was certainly no shortage of news vying for people's attention, compared with which Baghdad was a sideshow. It was a chaotic period when the world was in turmoil, and the British enjoyed nothing like the communications or the media freedom we are used to today. The events in Iraq merely formed part of a complex Middle Eastern jigsaw that stretched from Cairo to Tehran via Palestine. Britain stood alone, as the United States had yet to enter the war (Pearl Harbor was seven months off). In the Atlantic, German U-boats were exacting a tremendous toll on British shipping, and that May, the Blitz reached a climax with massive Luftwaffe raids on Belfast, Liverpool, and other provincial cities as well as London, leaving a total of more than forty thousand civilians dead over the eight months that the pounding lasted. On the very day that the Farhud began, Crete fell and fifteen thousand British troops had to be evacuated after twelve days of the most furious fighting that the war had seen. Germany claimed that more than ten thousand British and Greek soldiers had been taken prisoner, creating huge sadness and anxiety at home for those waiting for a War Office telegram informing them of the death, disablement, or imprisonment of loved ones.

On May 10, in the aftermath of the Battle of Habbaniya, three thousand people were killed in London on the worst (and last) night of the Blitz—something as apocalyptic as the World Trade Center disaster sixty years later. Exactly then, history took a surreal twist when Rudolf Hess landed in Scotland following his epic solo flight from the Fatherland, causing a sensation that filled the newspapers for weeks on end. It resulted in an almost total eclipse of other war news (though not the loss of the Royal Navy's battleship *Hood* on May 25 and—good news at last—the sinking of the *Bismarck* two days later) and created excited speculation about the deputy führer's motives. The British public was totally distracted by the story of Hess's attempt to contact the Duke of Hamilton, a Nazi sympathizer, in the forlorn hope that he would clear the way for a meeting with King George VI. (Hess believed that he could persuade the king to sack Winston Churchill and make peace with Germany to join forces against the Soviet Union.)

Only many years later was it revealed that one of the major demands Hess brought with him was that Britain should evacuate Iraq, as "Germany could not leave Rashid Ali and the Iraqis in the lurch"—evidence of the prime importance of the Iraqi revolt to Hitler's war aims and that its failure may have cost Germany the war.

The chain of events that led to those two fateful days of the Farhud—the motives and machinations, the mistakes and maneuverings—are not, and perhaps never will be, conclusively clear. Two and a half years earlier, the pogroms of Kristallnacht across Germany and Austria had made headline news and provided the first portent of the scale and horror of what the world was to know as the Holocaust. But here, in a city two thousand miles from Berlin, twice as many Jews (or more) were killed in two days of mayhem that history has forgotten. What a disaster the circumstances foretold for the Jews of Iraq, a people who had lived under the reign of Nebuchadnezzar, Cyrus the Great, and Harun al-Rashid and had witnessed the rise of Islam, the Mongol invasion, and the modernization of Iraq, only to see everything crumble in a flash.

All that Cornwallis would say about the decision to hold back the troops was: "Many years ago I fought, together with King Faisal the lamented who was my friend, for the freeing of the Arabs, and together we built up the Kingdom of Iraq. And do you think that I would willingly see destroyed what I myself have helped to build?"

But the damage was done. The situation deteriorated, and Iraq was placed under British military occupation for the duration of the war. The humiliation this caused lit a fuse that would eventually lead to the revolution of 1958 and the overthrow of the monarchical regime that Cornwallis had done so much to cultivate.

As for Cornwallis's July 11 report on the Farhud, the eminent Jewish-Iraqi historian Professor Elie Kedourie noted: "A few sentences of clipped, business-like prose concluding with a creditable sentiment about brutal outrages 'which all right minded persons will for long remember with shame and horror,' tidily disposed of the incident."

In his *Arab Political Memoirs,* Kedourie wryly added:

> A curious and suspicious reader might perhaps wonder whether—even from a narrowly political point of view—an incident in which, as the dispatch said, "several hundred Jews were brutally murdered" should not have been more fully examined. For, after all, even in the bloodstained history of Iraq a few hundred murders in the capital city still constituted in those days a noteworthy happening. But readers of dispatches, particularly in wartime, no doubt are busy men.

Sir Kinahan Cornwallis remained as ambassador in Baghdad until 1945, narrowly surviving an assassination attempt in October 1942, when a bomb was thrown at him. In 1943, in recognition of the important service he had rendered a foreign nation, he was appointed Knight Grand Cross of the Order of St. Michael and St. George, British chivalry's highest rank. After retirement, he was for a time chair of the Middle East Committee of the Foreign Office and a director of the British Bank of the Middle East. He died in Basingstoke, Hampshire, in 1959, at the age of seventy-six.

Gertrude Bell was buried in Baghdad in 1926. In November 2005, the *Daily Telegraph* reported: "Her tomb, in the British civil cemetery in central Baghdad, has been abandoned to the ravages of time. Her limestone marker is crumbling to dust, as are the cracked gravestones and shattered statues marking the final resting places of her countrymen."

T. E. Lawrence was killed in a motorcycle accident in 1935.

REFERENCES

Archives

Alliance Israélite Universelle, Paris

American Sephardi Federation, New York

Babylonian Jewry Heritage Center, Or-Yehuda, Israel

British Library, London

Imperial War Museum, London

Jewish Museum, London

National Archives, Kew

   Air Ministry Papers (AIR)

   Foreign Office Papers (FO)

   MI5 Papers (KV)

   Prime Minister's Papers (PREM)

   War Office Papers (WO)

New York Public Library, Dorot Jewish Division

Spiro Ark, London

Tel Aviv University

University of Newcastle upon Tyne, England: The Gertrude Bell Project

Military

Air Vice-Marshal B. A. Casey, Report of Operations in Baghdad Area 2 May to 31 May. Royal Air Force archive. http://www.raf.mod.uk/history_old/opsrep.html

Royal Air Force: Campaign Histories, Air Historical Branch Narratives. http://www.raf.mod.uk/history_old/narratives.html

Royal Air Force Habbaniya Association. http://www.habbaniya.org/

Supplement to the *London Gazette,* July 3, 1946: Wavell's Report to Churchill. Issue 37638. Revolt in Iraq, pp. 3437–39

Media

Magazines and Journals

AJEX Journal (Association of Jewish Ex-Servicemen and Women, U.K.), July 2003

Al Ahram Weekly, Cairo, April 23, 2003

Aviation History, May 2004

Nehardea: Journal of the Babylonian Jewry Heritage Center, Autumn 2003

The Scribe: Journal of Babylonian Jewry (multiple refs.)

Newspapers

Daily Telegraph, November 26, 2005

The Guardian, June 22, 2004

New York Times, August 17, 1917; February 13, 1941; June 6, 1959

Oakland Tribune, October 19, 1942

Sunday Times (London), May 21, 2006

The Times (London), May 8, 1945 (Register of Events 1939–45); June 5, 1959

Television and Radio

"A History of Iraq," BBC2, September 17, 2003

Audio recording of broadcast by Salim and Hanina Belboul, New York Public Library, Dorot Jewish Division, American Jewish Committee Oral History Collection

The Farhud

The official investigating committee gave the number killed—"including Jews and Muslims"—at 130. However, one of its members put the true figure at more like six hundred, the new Iraqi government being anxious to play down the death toll (al-Razzaq al-Hasani, *Hidden Secrets of the Events of the Liberatory Year 1941*, Sidon, Al-Irfan Press, 1958). In another confusing reference, Jewish communal authorities evaluated damage that householders and commercial establishments sustained at 650,000 dinars—more than $46 million today (Kedourie, *Arabic Political Memoirs*, London: Frank Cass, 1974).

Details of the pogrom from *The Diary of Abraham Twena,* translated in *The Scribe* 2, no. 11 (May–June 1973): 3–7.

Cornwallis, Wavell, Habforce

Auchinleck disagreement with Wavell: FO 371/27069, 2171, and 2176/1/93; and FO 371/27070, 2314/1/93.

Wavell order to avoid conflict: WO 169/1085; war diary, G Branch Force HQ, May 7–May 31, 1941, appendixes M/8/14 and M/15/C.

Wavell order, "Bold action": WO 169/1085, May 24, 1941, appendix M/24/A.

Wavell's dispatch to Churchill of September 5, 1941: Operations in the Middle East, February 7–July 15, 1941, Supplement to the *London Gazette,* July 3, 1946.

Authority for Cornwallis to be responsible for all policy; directives to be issued only with his approval: WO 169/1039, war diary of Habforce, May 1941, appendix 4A, instructions to Major General J. G. W. Clark, May 11, and appendix JA, operation instruction no. 48 "Task of Habforce," May 12, 1941.

Irgun involvement: KV 5/34, March 1, 2006, release. Also, "Irgun Chief Commanders: David Raziel" (at http://www.etzel.org.il).

Rashid Ali takes flight; right bank–left bank reference: FO 371/27073, Cornwallis dispatch no. 53, May 30, 1941.

Armistice terms: PREM 3/319/5, part 37, May 31, 1941.

Armistice terms accepted: WO 169/1085, appendixes M/31/A and M/31/D, May 31, 1941.

Cornwallis's part in drawing up armistice: FO 371/27077, 3426/1/93; Cornwallis's dispatch no. 148, Baghdad, June 6, 1941.

Cornwallis's plea to delay advancing force from Basra: WO 169/1085, G Branch Force HQ war diary, June 1, 1941.

Withdrawal of Kingcol northern detachment from Baghdad: WO 169/1259, HQ Fourth Cavalry Brigade war diary, June 1, 1941.

Decision for Kingcol to enter Baghdad, June 2: AIR 24/820 operations record book for May 1941, p. 26.

Wavell order to reach embassy and control bridges: WO 169/1039.

Cornwallis telegram to Foreign Office, reporting sporadic shooting: FO 371/27074, 2763/1/93; Cornwallis telegram no. 491, June 2, 1951, 4:15 P.M.

RAF situation report of "slight" disturbance in Baghdad: AIR 24/031, appendix 2/6/41/1, situation report no. 90.

Cornwallis report to Foreign Office: FO 371/27078, dispatch no. 185, Baghdad, July 11, 1941.

Ben-Zvi letter: FO 371/27062.

Early Iraq, Elections, Constitution

Ofra Bengio, senior research fellow at the Moshe Dayan Center and assistant professor of Middle Eastern and African history at Tel Aviv University, cites the following reference works in her essay "Pitfalls of Instant Democracy": Henry A. Foster, *The Making of Modern Iraq* (London: Williams & Norgate, 1936); Abd al-Razzaq al-Hasani (translated by Ofra Bengio), *Ta'rikh al-'Iraq al-Siyasi al-Hadith* (Sidon: Al-Irfan Press, 1957, 3:9); and M. M. al-Adhami, "The Elections for the Constituent Assembly in Iraq, 1922–24," in *The Integration of Modern Iraq,* ed. Abbas Kelidar (New York: St. Martin's Press, 1979, 16–17).

Gertrude Bell

Editors' e-mail correspondence with biographer Georgina Howell, August 29, 2006.

Gertrude Bell Archive, Robinson Library, University of Newcastle upon Tyne: letters: December 11, 1923; October 7, 8, and 15, 1924; November 24 and 26, 1924; February 11, 1925. Bell's letters and diaries are also available online at http://www.gerty.ncl.ac.uk.

Alan Shemtob-Reading

"Behind Enemy Lines," *AJEX Journal,* July 2003: 19–20. Author interviews with Rabbi Abraham Labi, Holland Park synagogue, London. Correspondence with family relatives.

Rudolf Hess

"Rudolph Hess and Rashid Ali," The Scribe: Journal of Babylonian Jewry 68, October 1997: 61.

APPENDIXES

TIME LINE

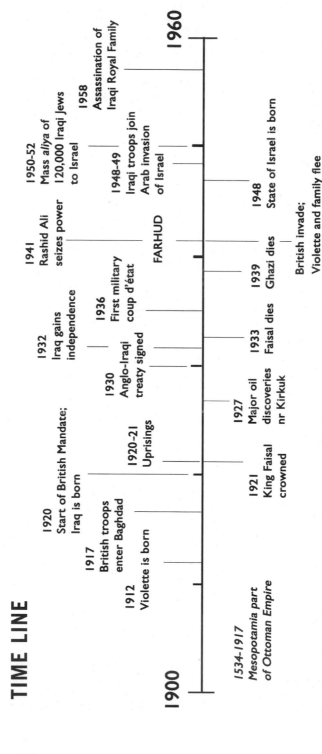

1900

1534-1917
Mesopotamia part
of Ottoman Empire

1912
Violette is born

1917
British troops
enter Baghdad

1920
Start of British Mandate;
Iraq is born

1920-21
Uprisings

1921
King Faisal
crowned

1927
Major oil
discoveries
nr Kirkuk

1930
Anglo-Iraqi
treaty signed

1932
Iraq gains
independence

1933
Faisal dies

1936
First military
coup d'état

1939
Ghazi dies

1941
Rashid Ali
seizes power

FARHUD

British invade;
Violette and family flee

1948
State of Israel is born

1948-49
Iraqi troops join
Arab invasion
of Israel

1950-52
Mass aliya of
120,000 Iraqi Jews
to Israel

1958
Assassination of
Iraqi Royal Family

1960

THE ISHAYEK DYNASTY

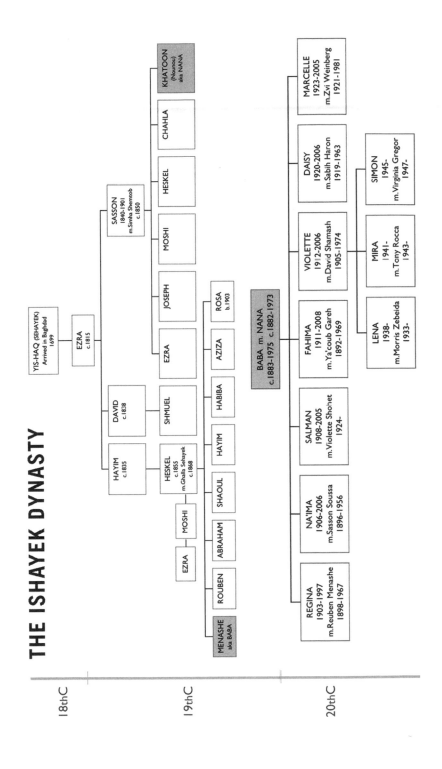

18thC

19thC

20thC

ACKNOWLEDGMENTS

We would like to thank all the many people who gave generously of their time and insights in the course of the book's preparation. Special thanks are owed, in no particular order, to the children of Violette's sister Na'ima: Maurice, Danny, and Frankie Soussa and Doris Sasson; Maurice's wife, Esther, and their children Ronnie and Donna; as well as Doris's husband Meir, son of the community's Hakham Bashi in Baghdad, Sasson Kadoori. Shortly before Na'ima passed away, in April 2006, she was able to recount the story of her escape from Baghdad and aid us in refining many details in the book—amazing for a person of her great age (ninety-nine). The transatlantic phone call lasted for well more than an hour.

We had more help from Regina's children: Yossef Menashe, Aliza, Gladys, and Clara. Many thanks, too, to Mira's brother, Simon; her sister, Lena, and nephew, Robin Zebaida; Violette's late sisters, Fahima Gareh and Daisy Heron; Haron's widow, Violette (Shamash), who now lives in Milan; Saïda Hayim, daughter of Na'ima and Abraham Shashoua; Benny Ammar of the BBC; David Kehela; Lilian Dabby Joury of Bar-Ilan University; Lyn Julius of Harif; Nitza Spiro of the Spiro Ark organization, London; also Anna Dangoor and Eileen Khalastchy. Mira's cousin, David Heron, unearthed the photo of their great-grandparents, and Salman's daughter, Ruthie David, clarified details of some rituals where we were uncertain of our ground.

We had the great fortune to meet the author-historian Sylvia Kedourie, widow of the eminent historian Professor Elie Kedourie, whose perceptions helped us enormously; and their son Georges, a talented Web master whose skills astounded us.

We owe a huge debt of gratitude to our mentor Professor Shmuel Moreh of the Hebrew University, Jerusalem, Israel Prize laureate and chair of the Association of Jewish Academics from Iraq in Israel. His advice and constant encouragement, after devoting generous time to reading the entire manuscript, has been invaluable, both for his scholarly guidance and for correcting our elementary Arabic. Any mistakes that

271

may remain are entirely our responsibility. Dr. Bernhard Fulda, director of studies in history, Sidney Sussex College, Cambridge, also kindly agreed to read the book before publication, and his enthusiastic remarks gave us encouragement. Dr. Daniel Mandel, a fellow in history at Melbourne University, tutored us on the writings of Professor Kedourie, and Professor Avi Shlaim, professorial fellow and professor of international relations at St. Antony's College, Oxford, also gave his valuable time, for which we are extremely grateful.

The author-historian William Shawcross has been our chief, unflagging supporter, and we owe a load of thanks to him, as indeed we do to our other cheerleaders: Avner Muallem, son of Rosa and Abu Nessim, and his wife, Diana (Fattal), who have been tireless in their continuing support. Finding the audiotape of Avner's discussion with Violette in 1987 was a rare piece of good fortune.

Our extreme gratitude also goes to Dr. Naim Dangoor, Order of the British Empire, of the Exilarch's Foundation, a dear friend of Violette and publisher of *The Scribe*, a journal of Babylonian Jewry (www.dangoor .com) who graciously allowed us access to his vast archive of printed material and photographs. We have had great help from the staff of the Jewish Museum of London; the Babylonian Jewry Heritage Center, Or-Yehuda, Israel; and Lynne Winters and Ellen Cohen at the American Sephardi Federation in New York. Thank you, too, to Yvonne Oliver at the Imperial War Museum, London, for permission to raid the Crown Copyright photo archive; to the Prints and Photographs Division of the Library of Congress, Washington, D.C.; to the helpful people at the National Archives at Kew, London; to the British Library; to Debbie Usher at the Middle East Centre Archive, St. Antony's College, Oxford; and to the New York Public Library. Research by Professor Yona Sabar of the University of California, Los Angeles, was especially helpful with regard to the proper names and family names among the Jews of Iraq. Peter Morris aided us greatly with his amazing chronology of the Battle of Habbaniya, and Dr. Christopher Morris and the RAF Habbaniya Association furthered our knowledge of these underreported events.

We have depended heavily on Somerset de Chair's historical account of the desert campaign of 1941, published in his book *The Golden Carpet* (1945). Great thanks go to the author's widow and literary executrix, Lady Juliet Tadgell, for giving us full permission in this respect. The eyewitness accounts of Freya Stark in her various volumes have been particularly revealing. Georgina Howell's insights (in conversation with us) on the relationship between Gertrude Bell and Sir Kinahan Cornwallis were also very helpful, and we thank her publishers, Pan Macmillan, for permission to quote from *Daughter of the Desert: The Remarkable Life of*

Gertrude Bell (copyright Manoir La Roche Ltd. 2006). Extracts from Bell's letters are included by kind permission of the Special Collections Librarian, Robinson Library, University of Newcastle upon Tyne. Thanks are due to Cengage Learning Services for permission to quote from *Arabic Political Memoirs and Other Studies* by Elie Kedourie (1974). Grateful acknowledgment is also made for permission from John Wiley & Sons to reprint an excerpt from *Banking on Baghdad* by Edwin Black (copyright 2004 by Edwin Black). Personal thanks to Mr. Black, whom we met in the course of our research.

Publication of this book, initially in the United Kingdom, was facilitated by Susanne McDadd of Publishing Services; line editors Josephine Bacon and Nancy Duin; Richard Morris our map artist; and Jon Cousins our guardian angel. The others in the team were Nick, Julie, Wendy, Lionel, and Bob. We also thank Doreen Montgomery of Rupert Crew, the London literary agency, for her support and advice.

At Northwestern University Press we are grateful to have received the friendship and help of Anne Gendler, Mike Levine, Jenny Gavacs, and Katherine Faydash, among others.

Other friends in the United States have graciously given us their time and hospitality in the course of this research. They include, in New York: Carole Basri, Nora Iny, Abe Lerner Moallem and his lovely family, Peter Pringle, Ron Rizio, David Shasha, and Dafna Tachover. In Washington, D.C.: Arden Alexander; John and Pat Barry; Lynn David; the extraordinary Monique Daoud and her husband, Edward; Ed and Lynn Dolnick; Ricardo Munster; Ariel Sabar; and the amazing Gail Shirazi. In Los Angeles: Eli Chammou, Joe and Yvette Dabby, Jack and Caroline Fox, Arvik and Elaine Gilboa, Lev Hakak, Edna Shahrabani, Joel Stratte-McClure, and Abigail Yasgur.

We are sure to have forgotten some important contribution received in the years that this work has been in construction; any omissions are entirely unintentional and we thank everyone for their unflinching support. We have sought, but have been unable to identify, all the copyright holders for the material from which we have quoted. If we have infringed any copyright we have done so inadvertently. We ask to be excused, and we respectfully seek permission now.

Judeo-Arabic words and phrases used by the Jews of Iraq. See "A Note About Language" on page xvii.

'abaaya (pron. *'baayi*)   woman's black cloak of silk or wool

abul   father of

abul 'ambah   pickle seller

abul beit   head of the household

abul booz   ice-cream seller

abul fiussah   pressing shop specializing in headgear

abul ooti   man who does the ironing

abul shaadi   man with a performing monkey

agha   magistrate, lord, master

'aghala   the procedure for cleaning saucepans for Passover

Alf Laylah wa Laylah   the tales collectively known as *The Thousand and One Nights*

'alootcha   a sticky sweet

'amaama (pron. *'maama*)   turban

'amida   prayer recited silently while standing

'aqool   thorny desert bush

'arabaana   horse-drawn carriage, gharry

'arabanchi   coach driver

'arak (pron. *'aghaq*)   aniseed-flavored liquor

assoor   forbidden

'atba   doorway, threshold

'awon (pl. *'awonoth*)   a sin

baab   door, gate

baamia   ladies' fingers (okra)

babenjaan   aubergine (eggplant)

baraka   plenty

be'aabe'-ib-dehen   shortbread

beeyoot   a game like hopscotch

beidh 'al-etbeet   Saturday eggs (see *etbeet*)

beit   house

berakha (pl. *berakhot*)   blessing

bezzoona   cat

bghaanii   semiglazed earthenware urns

biirgh tebiila   immersion pool, well (in Hebrew, *mikve*)

b'khaaree   ventilator duct

booma   owl (mild insult)

bournous   gown

brit mila   circumcision, baby-boy party

bustaan   orchard

chaalghi   musical group

char-'ali   woman's garment of white silk and gold thread (see *izaar*)

chitayi   strip of material; also material worn around a fez

daff   tambourine

daghboona   corridor

daroosh   religious sermon

dellaal (pl. *dellaalat*)   matchmaker, go-between

deqqaaqa   female musician

deqqaaqat   troupe of female musicians

deshdaasha   man's gown, white or striped

dhafaayir   hair decorations

dmei Purim   coins given to children at Purim

dossa   a card game played at Purim

dumbuk   hand drum

'eghooq ib-samak   spicy fish cake with onion, tomato, and potato

ekht   blemish, the so-called Jericho rose, caused by an insect

'elba laban   wooden container holding yogurt

el-Majlis el Jismaani   Jewish magistrates' court

etbeet (hammiim)   chicken stuffed with rice and baked with Saturday eggs

ethrog   citron, a knobbly citrus fruit used for blessing during Sukkoth

fanoos   lantern

farhud   violent dispossession, pogrom

fiina   man's red felt hat

fils   currency unit; twenty fils made one *qraan;* a single fils was equal to about one U.S. cent

gargaree   hard candy

gawja   green plums

ghraab   crow (mild insult)

ghuwwasa   whirlpool

goy   a non-Jew

guffa (pron. *quffa*)   a round, black boat (coracle) made of cane and covered with bitumen

hab   salted, roasted seeds (watermelon, pumpkin, or sunflower)

hajji   Muslim pilgrim

hakham (pl. *hakhamim*)   rabbi

hakham bashi   chief rabbi

halaahil   ululations

halba   a type of green bean

halqoon   Turkish delight

hamess   food that is not kosher for Passover

hammaal   porter

hammam   Turkish bath

hammii   see *etbeet*

hawan   pestle and mortar

heffafa   female epilator (body-hair remover)

hejel   anklets with bells

hejra   warehouse (see *khaan*)

hubb   massive earthenware water container

'iid   feast

'Iid el-Ziyaaghah   Feast of Pilgrimages

izaar   long woman's garment in two pieces, made of silk with silver or gold thread

jaadda   road (The Jaadda, Rashid Street)

jaami'   mosque

jeghaadeq   thin, oven-baked discs of unleavened bread

jgheidi   mouse

kaahi   deep-fried puff pastry dusted with icing sugar

kaala   slippers, sandals

kabeshkaan   storage space like a cabin

ka'eeb   game played with sheep's knee bones

kahrab sibha   amber worry beads

kalb   dog

kalla   bed canopy

kamanja   fiddle

kasher lil-Pessah   kosher for Passover

kashiida   big turban

kebba   spicy meatballs with an outer shell of ground rice and meat

kebba baamia   meatballs with okra

kebba shwandagh   meatballs with beets

khaan   warehouse, wholesalers

khash khash   hawthorn fruit

khastawee ya nabeg   lotus berries

khastaweeyah   delicious variety of date

khebz-spania   sponge cake (literally, "Spanish bread")

kheira   advice

khiiliyi   square black veil made of horsehair

khlaal el-tosh   unripened dates

kichree   kedgeree (a dish of lentils, tomatoes, and rice)

kondra   shoe

ktebba   marriage contract

laala   child chaperone

laban   yogurt

laffa 'amba   pitta wrap with mango pickle

lahmi   my skin, my flesh

lailt el-dakhla   wedding night (literally, "night of entry")

lailt el-settee   birth celebration for a baby girl

lailt el-Shebbath   the dinner on Sabbath eve

lebbada   bed jacket

loozina   quince sweetmeat with almonds and cardamom

lsiin el-tyough   bird language (used by adults to confuse children)

lubia   very long string beans

maay qedah   orange-blossom water

maay waghd   rosewater

maderban   garden path

mahallabi   type of rice pudding

mahkama   high court

malezqa   cushion for baking bread in *tannoor* (oven)

mann-essama (also *be'be' Qadrasii*)   nougat, "manna from heaven"

maqaam   type of Iraqi music played by Jewish musicians

marag eb-jiij   chicken soup with chickpeas

mashrabiyah   lattice window

maslak   connecting path

massa (*matzot* in Hebrew)   unleavened bread for Passover

massafaan   a kind of marzipan

massebgha   dye works

mazza (*mezze)*   selection of appetizers

mehila   forgiveness

meidi   special table setting

mekhbooz   baked cookies

melfouf   puff pastry with chopped almonds, sugar, and cardamom

meqaddesh   Jewish registrar of wedding engagements

meswaqchi   market shopper

m-hasha   stuffed vegetables

midraash   boys' elementary school

mikve (Hebrew)   ritual bath or well

minyan   quorum of at least ten men for prayer

Mjalla   Purim, a festival in spring

muallem   teacher

mukhtar   sheriff

mukhutboiya   a game like hide-and-seek

musswa (pl. *musswoth; mitzvah,* in Hebrew)   religious duty, good deed

naadi   social club

nabeg   lotus berries, hackberries

nabqayi   nabeg tree

na'oor   water mill, noria

naqoota   small clay drip water filter

naqqara   double small drums

naqsh-y-hood   a card game like vingt-et-un

nargiila   hubble-bubble pipe, hookah

nebi'im   the prophets

neddaaf   see *teeteepampa*

niim   cool, damp room; cellar, basement

oka, okiye   old Ottoman measures of weight

'oud   string instrument like a lute

paacha   stuffed lamb tripe

Pessah   Passover

pooshi   veil

punkah   ceiling or table fan

qaadi   magistrate, religious judge

qabqaab   wooden clogs

Qaddish   prayers for the dead

qanoon   zither

qasr   palace

qeddoos   blessing (such as on wine for Shabbat evening); also grape juice

qegh'iyyi   a courgette (zucchini) dish

qeimagh   clotted cream made from buffalo milk

qerraayee   bowl of water with sesame oil, used as a candle

qettaala   fly swat (literally, "killer")

qouzi   stuffed baby lamb

qraan   currency unit; four *qraan* made one rupee

rupee   unit of currency during the British mandate

Sabah el khair!   Morning of good fortune!

Sabah el noor!   Morning of light!

saghaaf   money changer, broker, banker

saghaafa   money exchange

salamaat   safe greetings, meaning "Thank God, all is well!"

sandouq el-welayaat   magic lantern (literally, "box of the countries")

santour   zither

saqqa   water seller

sat-h   roof

sat-h-el-'ilee   high roof

sat-h-el-nassee   lower roof

sayyed   dignitary; a descendent of the prophet Muhammad

sbahoth   songs of praise

sembousak   samosas

semmoon   pitta-like bread

semsemiyee   caramelized sesame seeds

sfeenee   dhow, river sailboat

shabboot   large fish found in the Euphrates and Tigris

shadd 'ayoon   a game like blindman's buff

shakarchi   pâtissier

shakarlama   a kind of shortbread

shanaashiil   room with projecting balcony, loge

shashsha   mixture of sweets, nuts, and popcorn

Shebbath   Sabbath

shiva   seven-day period of mourning

shmoura   wheat

shnina   salted yogurt

shofar   ram's horn, blown on Yom Kippur and Rosh Hashanah

shohet   ritual slaughterer (kosher butcher)

sibha   worry beads

sidaara   men's black felt hat that replaced the red Ottoman fez

silaan   date syrup

sirdaab   basement, underground level of house

slah (from Aramaic)   synagogue

souq   bazaar, marketplace, commercial center

souqiyee   market regulars

stikan   small tea glass

sukka   shelter built for Sukkoth

taaza ya fijil   fresh radish

ta'aziil 'iid leftiigh   Passover spring cleaning

takht   bench, benches

takhta   stool, stools

tannoor   clay oven

tantah   canvas awning

taraar   large cloister

tareif   nonkosher food

tarma   balcony

tashrib   broth

tawli   backgammon

Tebq'e essejagh (*Tu bishvat* in Hebrew)   New Year for Trees

tchai   tea

tcheqqal   green apricots

tcheraakh khashab   wood turner

teen-khawa   clay from Khawa, used on hair like conditioner

teeteepampa   mattress fluffer

teigha   low wall separating roofs of adjacent houses

tengaayee   clay jug for cooling water

torshi   pickles

vilayet   province

wabba   plague

wassaf   potion seller, quack

wassfa   prescription

Wudja!   literally, "pain," used as expletive

Ya Salaam!   expression of amazement, wonder

yamanee   special footwear that Muslim men wear

Yammak!   expression meaning "near" or "next to you"

yashmaagh   male head covering

zboon   belted cotton garment with buttons in the front

zdab   a variety of myrtle

zembiil   deep woven palm-leaf basket

zewwada   provisions for a journey

zingoola   deep-fried, honeyed batter

al-Razzaq al-Hasani, Abd. *Hidden Secrets of the Events of the Liberatory Year 1941.* Sidon: Al-Irfan Press, 1958.

Avigdor, Levy, editor. *The Jews of the Ottoman Empire.* Princeton, N.J.: Darwin Press, 1994.

Barr, James. *Setting the Desert on Fire.* London: Bloomsbury, 2006.

Bengio, Ofra. "Pitfalls of Instant Democracy." Pages 15–26 in *U.S. Policy in Post-Saddam Iraq: Lessons from the British Experience,* edited by Michael Eisenstadt and Eric Mathewson. Washington, D.C.: Washington Institute for Near East Policy.

Benjamin, Marina. *Last Days in Babylon.* London: Bloomsbury, 2007.

Black, Edwin. *Banking on Baghdad.* New York: John Wiley, 2004.

Brown, Malcolm. *Lawrence of Arabia: The Life, the Legend.* London: Thames & Hudson, 2005.

Churchill, Winston S. *The Second World War.* Vol. III, *The Grand Alliance,* chapter 14, "The Revolt in Iraq," 224–37. Boston: Houghton Mifflin, 1950.

De Chair, Somerset. *The Golden Carpet.* London: Faber & Faber, 1944.

Douglas-Hamilton, James. *The Truth About Rudolf Hess.* Edinburgh: Mainstream, 1993.

Dudgeon, A. G. *Hidden Victory: The Battle of Habbaniya, May 1941.* Gloucestershire, U.K.: Tempus, 2000.

Fallon, Ivan. *The Brothers: The Rise and Rise of Saatchi and Saatchi.* London: Hutchinson, 1988.

Fathi, Saul Silas. *Full Circle: Escape from Baghdad and the Return.* Central Islip, N.Y.: Saul Silas Fathi, 2005.

Golany, Gideon S. *Vernacular House Design and the Jewish Quarter in Baghdad.* Or-Yehuda, Israel: Babylon Jewry Heritage Center, 1994.

Howell, Georgina. *Daughter of the Desert: The Remarkable Life of Gertrude Bell.* London: Macmillan, 2006.

Kattan, Naim. *Farewell, Babylon.* Vancouver: Raincoast Books, 2005.

Kazzaz, David. *Mother of the Pound.* New York: Sephardic House, 1999.

Kedourie, Elie. *Arabic Political Memoirs and Other Studies.* London: Frank Cass, 1974.

Lawrence, T. E. *Letters.* London: Jonathan Cape,1938.

———. *The Seven Pillars of Wisdom.* London: Jonathan Cape, 1926.

Lyman, Robert. *First Victory.* London: Constable, 2006.

———. *Iraq 1941.* Essex, U.K.: Osprey, 2006.

Mazower, Mark. *Salonica: City of Ghosts.* New York: HarperCollins, 2004.

Oxford Dictionary of National Biography. Oxford: Oxford University Press, 2004–7.

Playfair, Major General I. S. O. *History of the Second World War: The Mediterranean and Middle East.* Vol. 2, *The Germans Come to the Help of Their Ally, 1941.* London: Her Majesty's Stationery Office, 1956.

Polo, Marco. *The Travels of Marco Polo,* translated by William Marsden. Hertfordshire, U.K.: Wordsworth Editions, 1997.

Rejwan, Nissim. *The Last Jews in Baghdad.* Austin: University of Texas Press, 2004.

———. *The Jews of Iraq.* London: Weidenfeld & Nicolson, 1985.

Sassoon, David Solomon. *A History of the Jews in Baghdad.* Letchworth, U.K.: Alcuin Press, 1949.

Simon, Reeva S. *Iraq Between the Two World Wars.* New York: Columbia University Press, 2004.

Simons, Geoff. *Iraq: From Sumer to Sudan.* New York: St. Martin's Press, 1994.

Stark, Freya. *Baghdad Sketches.* Boston: E. P. Dutton, 1938.

———. *Dust in the Lion's Paw.* London: John Murray, 1961.

———. *East Is West.* London: John Murray, 1945.

Warner, Geoffrey. *Iraq and Syria 1941.* London: Davis-Poynter, 1974.

Yehuda, Zvi. *Tombs of Saints and Synagogues in Babylonia.* Or-Yehuda, Israel: Babylon Jewry Heritage Center, 2006.

Page numbers in italics reference illustrations.

Violette Shamash (1912–2006) was born in Baghdad. In 1941, following the Farhud, she and her husband and their two children fled Iraq for India. They subsequently lived in Palestine, Cyprus, and Israel before settling in London in 1964. Violette began writing what would become her memoir in the 1980s.

Mira Rocca, Violette's daughter, worked in the U.S. Embassy in London and in the travel industry before she and her husband, Tony, became hoteliers and winemakers in Tuscany.

Tony Rocca, a journalist, spent much of his career in London writing for the *Daily Mail* and the *Sunday Times,* and in New York as U.S. correspondent for the *Mail.* His freelance work has appeared in a variety of U.K. and U.S. publications, and he is the author of a memoir, *Catching Fireflies.*